A RIDE THROUGH
THE WOOD

A RIDE THROUGH THE WOOD

Essays on Anglo-Welsh Literature

ROLAND MATHIAS

POETRY WALES PRESS
1985

POETRY WALES PRESS
56 PARCAU AVENUE, BRIDGEND, MID GLAMORGAN

British Library Cataloguing in Publication Data
Mathias, Roland
  A ride through the wood: essays on Anglo Welsh
  Literature.
  1. English literature — Welsh authors — History
  and criticism
  I. Title
  820.9'9429   PR8951

  ISBN 0-907476-50-3

Cover Design: Cloud Nine Design

The publisher acknowledges the financial support of the
Welsh Arts Council.

Typeset in Baskerville 11pt. by Afal, Cardiff.
Printed by
Antony Rowe Ltd.

Contents

Preface

This collection of essays, whatever its merits and demerits, is not quite the collection I originally envisaged. But it is only the perfectionist in me that thinks to complain. I had intended to polish and revise each and every one of the constituent pieces, especially those that were written more than three or four years ago. But two things happened to persuade me that such a proposition was folly. The first was that I proved myself incapable of merely tinkering with a study that I had almost forgotten the look of: what I envisaged as the opening essay on Henry Vaughan (not the shorter essay on Vaughan which appears in 'Smaller Clearings'), began to interest me all over again, in the same serious way, and before I realised what was happening I was involved in re-researching and re-writing the piece on a scale that disqualified it as a contribution to a book of this size: it will now, I hope, appear as a small volume in its own right. The second was that the opportunity for the inclusion of essays that I should dearly like to write — on John Dyer, for example, on Gerard Manley Hopkins, on Ivor Gurney — seemed always to recede as the pressure of other work mounted, and some of my friends, notably Glyn Jones and Jeremy Hooker, began, very rightly, to be impatient with me. The number of the critical studies of Anglo-Welsh writers available in print and easily accessible was so small, they argued, that I had a duty to get those of mine that were already written into book form without further delay. My procrastination received its *coup de grace* when Cary Archard intimated that he was waiting for a typescript from me and had been waiting for some time.

Whether the essays in this book will serve the purpose — or even some of it — that my exhorters intend I cannot know at this juncture. There are passages in a few of them, especially those I wrote nearly a decade ago, where I would now wish occasional emphases altered and arguments differently pointed. There are one or two instances,

the most notable of which is provided by John Pikoulis's biography of
Alun Lewis (1984), where additional information may seem to render
my textual inferences and interpretations incomplete and therefore
unsatisfactory. But the general thrust of each of the studies in this
volume still answers my present opinion and, with prohibitions ever
in my ear, I have determined not to add to or subtract from what I first
wrote. *Per contra*, I have omitted from consideration essays I wrote
more than a dozen years ago in accord with the obverse of the same
criterion; I can no longer agree with enough of the view I took in them
to justify prolonging their life. The balance of such decisions is always
delicate. Because, too, there is no Hopkins and no Gurney, it seemed
best to omit from this volume an essay that would otherwise have
qualified, that on John Cowper Powys, so that the collection might
more rationally and containedly devote itself to the work of
unmistakably Anglo-Welsh writers.

In the context of the essays that *are* included, two things are worth
saying. The first is that readers will discern in my criticism an entirely
deliberate intention to write from a point of view that is Welsh — not
Welsh of language but Welsh of feeling. I have been progressively
saddened over the years by the apparently inevitable application of
metropolitan assumptions to the English writing of Wales,
assumptions that have done considerable harm to the attitude of
several generations of readers. It may be discerned, too, that I have
rather less sympathy with Romanticism and its protégés than many
critics have. Not a few shining towers, it seems to me, need sapping at
the base.

The second thing is perhaps no more than a concomitant of the
first. I can imagine that there will be some readers, knowledgeable in a
kind of way, who will assume,from the title of this book and their
memory of other books and poems of mine, that I am besotted with
trees. That may well be true, if in very accidental fashion. But my
purpose, in offering the symbol of the wood, is deliberate rather than
compulsive. I see twentieth-century Anglo-Welsh writing as a wood
of no mean dimensions, only a few corners of which have, as yet, paths
that are recognisably muddy. So far it has been marked by most
influential critics as way out on the periphery of their map of *English*
literature and not worthy even of the kind of attention given by
"Greens" to the disappearing rain-forests of the world. What I have
tried to do within the scope of these essays is to cut a small ride from
the best-known sector of the wood into and across the interior and if I

have done this it has not been cavalierly achieved, as some may punningly have it, but with difficulty and such care as I could muster. One chance has made it easier — the possession of a different map, one on which the wood appears much closer to the centre. In the few steps I take from my house I need to know and understand how the trees I touch first begin to create the shape and shadow of the wood before I can travel farther.

Roland Mathias
April 1985.

I

THE MAIN RIDE

David Jones: Towards the "Holy Diversities"

I am much honoured in being asked to deliver the first Llewelyn Wyn Griffith Memorial Lecture and wish that it were within my power to link the names of Wyn Griffith and David Jones in some literary theme worthy of the occasion. But the link between the two is essentially one of experience, not exactly shared or identical (for they never met in the course of it) but nevertheless formative — ruthlessly so in the case of David Jones — in their development as writers. I refer, of course, to their service on the same battlefields — identically the same battlefields — in the First World War. David Jones, in April 1973, set down for his friend René Hague the exact details of his first period of service (the one relevant in this context) as follows:

> My Division was the 38th (Welsh) Division and I was in the 113th Infantry Brigade of the Div. and the 15th Batt. R.W.F. I was in 'B' Coy of that Batt. in Number 6 Platoon. At least for practically all the time — for a while I was in the Field Survey Company. But only for a few months.[1]

Llewelyn Wyn Griffith, in Civvy Street an Inland Revenue official in London was the officer commanding 'C' Company of the *same* battalion until, as the attack on Mametz Wood was planned and mounted, he became Staff Captain and Brigade Major (Acting). His account of life in the trenches and of the costly and terrible climax of his Brigade's experience was told in *Up to Mametz,* first published in 1931 and reprinted in 1981 by the English-Language Section of Yr Academi Gymreig. It is a personal account, intensely evocative of the sodden and weary realities of trench warfare. Most of the characters intrude only temporarily and are rarely more than lay figures until the action before and in the Wood opens a new dimension. David Jones's *In Parenthesis* (1937), on the other hand, though it covers, literally, the same ground, is a poetic tapestry decorated with characters fictional or disguised (amongst whom the author himself hides) and coloured with a tradition and a meaning that both belongs to the battle and is before it. In terms of troop dispositions and the sequence of events it is as accurate as Wyn Griffith's account and the reality of the experience of both writers has been examined in detail and to most rewarding effect by Colin Hughes in *The Man Who Was On the Field* [2] and in his unpublished work on the action at Mametz [3].

But the plain, if surprising, fact is that David Jones and Wyn Griffith never met until 1940 or later when Wyn called on David at Glebe Place, Chelsea. Thereafter there were occasional letters, two of which, from David, Wyn most kindly allowed me to publish in *The Anglo-Welsh Review* in 1978. It is a sad fact that I was so dilatory in bringing them up to publication that Wyn Griffith died before he saw them in print.

These two letters were dated 1964 and 1967 and, while full of desultory news, offered no theme connecting the two writers. What connects them, of course, apart from their Welshness, is their common initial experience, the harsh and vital experience which, a long time afterwards, made them both writers. It would be possible, no doubt, to embark upon a determined, if somewhat far-fetched, comparison of the content and manner of their subsequent writings, separated as they are circumstantially by a distance which overpowers their beginnings, but I have to confess that it is not within my present compass. In this paper David Jones must take the stand alone.

He was born on 1 November 1895 at Brockley, Kent, then a half-urban, half-rural place soon to be attached wholly to London. His father, a printer's overseer with the company which published *The Christian Herald,* had been born at Treffynnon, Flintshire, in 1860, the son of John Jones, *plastrwr, gynt o* Ysceifiog. "My father", wrote David Jones to Vernon Watkins in 1962, "was a pure Welshman, but a Welshman of that generation . . . whose parents were *determined* that he should be as English as possible. Consequently he had only a rather feeble grasp of the Welsh language, knew virtually nothing of ancient Welsh tradition, but was deeply religious and, I *know,* 'felt' extremely 'Welsh'. From about the age of seven, I, myself, for reasons that I suppose only psychologists could fathom, 'felt' Welsh also". [4] In 1888 James Jones, David's father, had married Alice Ann Bradshaw, daughter of Ebenezer Bradshaw, Thames-side mast-and-block maker, whose wife was of partly Italian descent. David, or Walter David as he was christened, was the third and youngest child of that union. His delicate constitution, all too possibly a repetition of that of his elder brother Harold (who was soon to die), caused his parents to treat him with more than the usual solicitude.

In 1904, when David was eight, he was taken on his first visit to North Wales. "Some rubicon had been passed", he felt then, and when, a few days later, he met his grandfather for the first time, a tall, powerful old man with a stick sitting by the little stone oratory above the wattled sea-weir at Llandrillo, the scene was to etch itself on his memory and in later years associate to itself (over and against a very contrary impression of his grandfather) images of Gwyddno's weir in the Taliesin story and King Maelgwn the Tall, who had his principal seat at Rhos nearby[5]. But that was far ahead in his reading and development. What we have to note here is that David's physical experience of Wales remained very limited. There were doubtless a few other visits to North Wales during childhood, but not many: in the summer of 1913 he went on a three months'[6] painting holiday with a student friend to Tregaron and visited Strata Florida and Pontrhydfendigaid[7]: in 1915 he did squad-drill with the Royal Welsh[8] Fusiliers on the promenade at Llandudno[9]: just before Christmas 1924 he arrived at Capel-y-Ffin in the Llanthony valley to join the Eric Gill Community there and the following March paid his first visit to Caldey Island[10]: he was back at Capel-y-Ffin later in 1925 and spent a good deal of 1926 there[11]: and in 1927 he was once again at Caldey or attempting to get there, as his letter of 27 October from the Coburg Hotel, Tenby, shows[12]. But that was all. In the thirties he itinerated constantly round the circle of his Catholic friends, never going once to Wales, and after 1940 he became increasingly immobile and subject to agorophobia. For the last forty-five years of his life, at the very least, he was a man contemplating Wales from a distance, incessantly reading and writing about it but never so much as moving in its direction. It is also true, however, that islanded in Harrow from about 1947, he became distanced from the old, familiar London too. Much visited and still influenced by friends of earlier days, he was nevertheless in a kind of geographical limbo in which the Wales of his imaginings fought hardily to possess him.

René Hague, in his Introduction to the letters in *Dai Greatcoat,* delivers himself of the opinion[13] that "In spite of all David's attempts to Cambrianize his work, in spite of all he says with such pathos and

eloquence, and in spite of his devotion to a great Welsh myth, it was
the English tradition that was most completely assimilated, and
everything in his work that is most convincing, sincere, and based on
real knowledge and understanding is English". The Wales he was cut
off from, he goes on, was a Wales for which he had no more than 'a
sentimental love': it had come to an end in 1282. He failed, despite
long efforts, to learn Welsh and he used Welsh words, as he used Latin
and German words, ingenuously and with a crudity that he would not
have tolerated in English. This is a verdict astonishing most of all from
an Anglo-Irishman and an old friend, the more astonishing in its use
of the word *sincere*. But then it has to be realised that *Dai Greatcoat* itself
is a portrait based on letters to *English* friends and one from which the
Welsh enthusiasms have been editorially shaded out. David Jones is
on record himself, not once or twice but often, in an attempt to explain
the yearning of the man for whom an English culture and education
are the *data* and for whom Welsh comes as a written language and too
late, but who nevertheless reaches out constantly in learning and
imagination towards his Welsh inheritance and who uses part of the
myth which shapes that to point the direction of his writing[14]. There
can hardly be a sterner test of sincerity than to spend a life largely in
fronting difficulties that an Englishman, in the spiritual sense, need
never have bothered himself with.

Undoubtedly David Jones had to begin with English, in a
suburban, lower-middle-class home that did not differ, except
marginally, from hundreds of thousands of others. But my thesis, in
this paper, is that Wales, after many vicissitudes, won a great battle for
him. It became, so to speak, the shibboleth with which he could put
away fear.

That David's "Welshness", encouraged by that of his father, had
some outlet in early life René Hague does not deny. A programme,
dated 1910, sets out the *fourth* annual entertainment given by the
Dalrymple Concert Party in the Dalrymple Hall, Brockley (which
was really the Jones's front room): David and his sister (his elder
brother Harold was already an invalid, watching from his couch),
with their Bradshaw cousins, comprised the company. "Master W.
Jones", it records, recited 'Griffith's answer to Harold' and passages
from *Henry V:* the "Grand Torchlight Procession" included "Cadwal,
a Briton" (Master W. Jones) and "Britannia" (his sister)[15]. Onsets of
"Welshness", especially when encouraged by the advent of visitors
from North Wales, apparently produced in David's mother a

tendency to leave the front room and bang about noisily in the kitchen[16]. It was an issue which divided the household, if perhaps not deeply. When his Bradshaw cousins teased him by saying that they wanted none of his "Welsh tricks", David was incensed[17].

Amongst his confessions was one that in his boyhood, when visiting Westminster Abbey, he spat on the tomb of Edward I[18]. Much better known is his recollection that, in front of a very English Welsh aunt, he said that *Taid* (his grandfather) "was a bloody old bastard" for forbidding his father to speak Welsh[19]. That these emotional outbursts were occasional and scarcely emanated from the wellsprings of his being is probably true enough, but he was not, in most respects, a difficult boy or one frequently moved to anger. The greatest reason for treating them guardedly is that they were mostly described in age and from a position more designedly Welsh. This father-and-son patriotism, indeed, more surprising in a family that had been brought up 'Church', might well have proved small beer in the end. Even David's desire to serve on the battlefield in a Welsh regiment, touchingly, if a little disproportionately, underlined by his father's letter of September 1914 to Lloyd George asking when the Government proposed to form a London Welsh battalion of the Royal Welsh Fusiliers[20], might have had for residue only the sentiment of which René Hague writes. David, as a Londoner, could hardly, in any case, have ended up as a Welshman of the type of his Private Watcyn in *In Parenthesis,* who sat in the trench-bay "trying to read the scores on the reverse side of Private Thomas's *Western Mail*"[21], "knew everything about the Neath fifteen, and could sing *Sospan Fach* to make the traverse ring"[22]. But that, like Lance-Corporal Aneirin Lewis, he became a man "for whom Troy still burned, and sleeping kings return, and wild men might yet stir from Mawddwy secrecies"[23] is something for which nothing that goes before is adequate explanation.

It must be our concern now to look at the young David Jones more closely. Under examination two things stand out clearly. The first is that David Jones was an extreme example of the creative intelligence that jibs at and refuses all other kinds of order than the one it can and does itself create from its own beginnings and its own ancillary likings. Apparently backward at any kind of lesson except drawing, he was slow to read even in English and his apprehension of French, as later of Welsh, was of the sort to make many a schoolmaster, accustomed to intelligences that are prepared to accept an academic order of thought

outside themselves readily and *in toto,* raise his hands in despair. Yet
the kind of creative intelligence that David had is not uncommon, if
examples of it rarely prove so powerful as his. In later life he was prone
to lament what he thought of as a disability. On 21 January 1959 he
wrote to Aneirin Talfan Davies as follows:

> Alas, I don't make much progress with my Welsh, I fear. I've
> always been such a bloody dolt about learning any language. I
> don't really understand why, seeing that I'm passionately
> interested in words & their forms — but there it is, and at 63
> there is not much hope of any improvement. Still, I do a tiny bit
> more than I did a year ago, but only a *tiny* bit. When one is old
> one *forgets* all one learns almost immediately — That's why it is
> *absolutely vital* that the little children should know Welsh
> properly and as for Yr Arglwydd Raglan in this matter, *Anathema
> sit.*[24]

On 27 April 1964, sending René Hague a closely annotated sketch-
map of Harrow which was intended as a guide to his new abode at
Monksdene, he added:

> Forgive all the confusions of gender, number and case, word-
> order etc of the dog Latin on foregoing sketch-map (but I enjoy
> trying to remember what tiny amount of the words I know. I
> shall never be able to manage the grammar. It's the same with
> Welsh. I think there is something curiously wrong with my type
> of mind).[25]

Here, undoubtedly, is the reason for the only part of René Hague's
criticism of David that may be seen to have some validity, namely his
use — indeed, his over-use in 'The Sleeping Lord' — of non-English
words. It exhibits something of a collector's mania and takes too little
note of the changes created in the associative structure of the work.

The second thing that may be discovered about David Jones is
precisely the associative method just mentioned. He always denied
that he was a scholar, despite the enormous learning which he
acquired. And in the strict sense he was right: he was an
agglomerator, digressive, magpie-like, searching for what *he* wanted:
the needs of a subject, which in terms academic would have required
a completeness of interest in and a confinement of attention to matters
relevant to that subject's own "ground", could not hold him: that kind

of discipline was antipathetic. René Hague explains, perceptively, what David's method of procedure was:

> It was the ability to relate one thing to another that David admired in other writers and thinkers ... Relationships, of shapes, colours, ideas, memories, traditions, were the basis of his poetry and painting. Hence his fondness for lists.[26]

Stanley Honeyman, a younger friend of David's, called what he did "lateral thinking".[27] David himself uses the word *happiness* to describe the moment of lateral perception when it arrives. Writing to Harman Grisewood in 1947 about his painting *Vexilla Regis*, he says:

> .... one is led partly by what evolves as the painting evolves, this form suggesting that form — happiness comes when the forms assume significance with regard to this juxtaposition to each other — even though the original "idea" was somewhat different.[28]

And with writing the practice was not dissimilar, though here philology, geography and history added their perceptual "shapes" to those brought up by the literary memory. Making to "Jim" Ede one of his familiar disclaimers, David writes:

> ....I am not 'learned', I only root about among stuff that scholars write in order to *verify* things I'm *attached to*, to check up on this and that. Actually if it comes to "scholarship" I'm an absolute dud. As you know, I have very few "accomplishments" and practically no "education" in the accepted sense of that word. I try to write by the same process as I paint.[29]

He is here writing about *The Anathemata*, reckoned by most readers to be one of the most difficult works of the modern age! But the phrase "to *verify* things I'm attached to" should be borne carefully in mind. Its implication is that it is the heritage of David Jones that matters, the balance or the bias of it and the directions in which personal emotion and interest had stretched it.

He makes this same point in rather a different way in writing to Harman Grisewood in 1962 about Professor John H. Johnston's analysis of *In Parenthesis*. He was always bored and annoyed by the attempts of critics to identify influences on his writing (not that

Johnston had been especially guilty of that: David was pleased with his article) and was most of all irritated by statements that he owed the "form" of his writing to Ezra Pound, whom he declared repeatedly he had not read before completing *In Parenthesis*. "It's more the whole conditioning civilisational situation into which one was born", he asserts,

> that determines the 'form'. Browning, for example, gave me a bit of a clue of how something *might* be managed, and then the sudden appearance of Hopkins and my reading of Skelton and one's interest at that time in 'negro spirituals' and God knows what all, seemed to 'click' in some way with all kinds of childhood things — nursery rhymes, early readings of Malory and, of all people, Macaulay, and fragmentary bits of Welsh stuff, and the Anglo-Saxon Chronicle and Norse sagas, and Caesar's Gallic Wars, and all kinds of popular cockney songs, and bits of the metaphysical poets, and Lewis Carroll and Lear and God! it's absurd to try to trace the differing and very disparate strands, and behind that being brought up on the Authorised Version and the Book of Common Prayer. And then all this heterogeneous stuff given new point and cohesion by becoming a Catholic in 1921.[30]

Obviously David's *influential* equipment — and here René Hague is quite right — was overwhelmingly *English*. His father's birthday presents of Sir John Rhys's *The Welsh People* and O.M. Edwards's *Wales* (in the Story of the Nations Series)[31] and his constant requests as a much younger child that his sister should read Malory to him could not possibly have outweighed the *English* determinants of his living. But the balance of *In Parenthesis* does not demonstrate his use of that equipment in anything like the proportions that these antecedent influences should have indicated (even granted that the subject called for more Welshness). There were some things that he was *attached to* more than others. It depended, did it not, on what he *wanted* to make of the elements he had been given?

For the moment, however, that is not the point which must be pursued. David's words to Harman Grisewood just quoted were concerned mainly with the "form" of *In Parenthesis*. It was characteristic of David's incessant pragmatism (or his *ad hoc* aesthetic decision-making, as it might be clearer to call it) that he was as individual and radical in the matter of "form" as he was in associating

the bits and pieces of his material. In another letter a year later he
writes as follows:

> I agree about the questions touching 'prosody' are a bore . . . I
> remember having a *charming* letter from Laurie Binyon, in
> appreciation of *In Parenthesis* but which asked *all sorts* of
> questions as to why I changed from dactylic rhythm here to
> something or other else there and then to lines that could be — I
> don't know what, something else, well, I felt almost ashamed to
> say that I didn't know I had! It is, as you say, merely a question of
> making the bloody thing as you want it to be — so that the 'form'
> follows the 'content' and, as you say, you bloody well *know* if it's
> right or wrong, that is you know if it fits with what you intend. *Of
> course*, what you intend may be all balls, but that's another
> matter. But I find it incredibly hard to convince chaps of this.
> They somehow won't believe that that's how it works.[32]

The ex-Army language should not cause surprise. The old sweat's
vocabulary, with its long adherence to the basic qualities of *thing*ness,
*stuff*ness and *bloody*ness, in which many of David's letters and some of
his conversations were conducted, may be a sign that, like Sassoon
and Blunden, he "could never get that 1st War business out of his
system"[33]: it may, on the other hand, signal his determination to
tackle an incredibly difficult task of creation without either the usual
academic or professional props or the jargon and pretentiousness that
too often accompany the poetic experience when it earns the public's
attention.

However that may be, there was a price to be paid for trying to
undertake such an enormous task in this way. David had several
serious breakdowns in the course of his life, two of them lasting for
periods of years. This neurosis, personalised in his letters as 'Rosy',
was *not* the result of his war experience. René Hague says so[34] and
David himself confirms it[35]. His service in the trenches was a period
during which, although he was once wounded, he felt secure and in
1919 he even talked of joining the British Army in Russia[36]. What the
war did for him was to offer him the comradeship of ordinary men
which he would not otherwise have had and, since, by his own wish,
he was never more than a Private, to allow him to organise himself
according to the decisions *of others*. In other words (though those were
not the days of creation for him) he was free of the weight of decision-
making which so afflicted him later. He was not a bad soldier despite a

comparatively weak physique: it is he, in the person of John Ball, who is hard on the heels of old Dawes and Private Watcyn when the latter takes the wire "with blameless technique, and even remembers to halloo the official blasphemies"[37]: all three make it to the shelter of the edge of the wood that is beyond "First Objective". He was not, in fact, as in the Preface to *In Parenthesis*[38], "grotesquely incompetent, a knocker-over of piles, a parade's despair". Nor was he as Pick-em-up Shenkin, the pseudo-Aneirin of 'The Book of Balaam's Ass', "the least sure-footed of men, and the most ungainly and the most easily confused of any man of the island of Britain, and the most slow to make his extremities do what his stomach or brain desired, and the most forgetful of men, and when he slept no one knew at what hour he would waken"[39]. His John Ball is conventional self-depreciation: Pick-em-up Shenkin is a self-portrait mainly in the sense that it is an amusing cartoon of the accidentally surviving poet.

All his life, it seems, he needed to have as much decision-making as possible taken away from him. Writing to Harman Grisewood in 1935, during the first of his long periods of neurosis, he is remarkably revealing about this:

> I've always always as long as I can *ever* remember felt my business (however blindly) to be my work, and always knew that everything had got to go for that. I've always felt 'agnostic' about every other matter — though other people 'knew' about the legislature, the command of men, marriage, council, the whole realm of prudence and affairs, I've always known that I must be and am essentially a private soldier, in and out of the war, who with fear and trembling might *just* manage to learn to slope arms, and *sometimes* remember to turn left on the command 'Left' and *just* have the physical stength to *not* fall out on the line of route perhaps: but that my *own* real life was that of judgement of the work to be made — line by line — to be unfettered when about that work, and that that was the *only* sphere I *knew* about, that my only contribution was that. Not indeed that it *was* a contribution, but that anyway perhaps it *might be* — or anyway that I was a fool *indeed* at all else.[40]

There could hardly be a clearer declaration of his awareness that decision-making in the context of his work was, even in his good times, all that he could ever handle. The reference to his having known this as far back as he could "*ever* remember" must, however, take us back, if momentarily, to his childhood in Brockley.

David was "the baby" of the family. He was also the slowest to develop, the longest immature. There is no positive information on this, but it seems extemely likely that his parents, already worried by the poor health of his elder brother Harold, avoided pressing him personally or academically. René Hague, describing David as an adult, discards the words "lazy and spoilt" in favour of the more judicious phrases "constructively inactive" and "joyfully served"[41], force of which will appear as his later life is described. Pressure always had to be very light. It was very unusual for a boy of fourteen to be sent, without a secondary education, direct to a School of Art and it is reasonable to see in this decision by his parents not merely a gesture towards the only thing that David could do (with his mother's long-ago prowess in drawing softening her attitude) but also the inevitable response to his refusal to bother with anything else. It was certainly not prompted by a recognition of their son's genius, for none of it was then visible. After the War David, then at the Westminster School of Art, refused to take any examinations that would qualify him for a teaching post or a career in commerce. Knowing that his parents could never support him wholly and on the thinnest external evidence of supreme talent, he had already acquired an obstinate determination to be an artist. What he felt in himself, how he thought of the practicalities of existence, we can only conjecture. But that ultimately formidable intelligence must have been formulating the necessary self-knowledge. Devotion to the idea of *his work* and the belief that he was likely to prove "a fool at all else" evidently warned him that he must seek the help of another discipline to remove from him those decisions that the intended work, conceived then as painting, would not intrinsically require. This sort of self-knowledge amongst those who have been "spoiled" in youth is by no means uncommon[42]. In this sense it is less of a surprise to find David Jones, not so long demobbed from an Army in which his mind and imagination had begun to flourish untrammelled by day-to-day moralities, joining the Catholic Church in 1921. It is, of course, perfectly true that Fr. Daniel Hughes S.J. (the Fr. Martin Larkin of *In Parenthesis*) talked to him when they were on the Ypres front and lent him a book on Francis de Sales[43] — David adds characteristically that all the other Welsh officers were Nonconformists — and that at some time he was afterwards unsure of he squinted through a crack in a derelict farm-building not far behind the front line and caught his first sight of the Mass being celebrated, with "Old Sweat Mulligan, a somewhat fearsome figure, a real pugilistic, hard-drinking Goidelic Celt, kneeling there in the smoky candlelight"[44]. It is also true that at the Westminster School of Art he began to develop aesthetic reasons for moving towards Catholicism, telling his Catholic friends there that post-Impressionist theory in the arts fitted his own view of the Mass as the making of a real thing[45]. But it is difficult to avoid the conclusion that the most deep-seated reason of all was an instinctive need for a *universum*, for as absolute a moral discipline as the Christian Church could offer and a ritual whose Latin provided both a magnetic pole and a field of verbal reference for those thousands of as yet unattached and unmeaningful words which haunted his brain. After the Army the Catholic Church. It was a way of lightening the load, making the work possible. And so, at Ditchling, at Pigotts, at Capel-y-Ffin, under the eye of Eric Gill, he learned the artistic equivalent of sloping arms and turning left. He learned with amazing patience, if at first with little practical ability and sense of order — not to be the decisive, opinionated master-craftsman that Gill was, but to fit himself for the difficult, flexible body of work he was to undertake within the outer shell of the firm opinions he had embraced[46].

It was at Capel-y-Ffin and on Caldey that he first found out what his "direction" should be and began to make possible the things that he was attached to. Malory still haunted him and in Wales "the Matter of Britain" was never far from his mind. In 1929 he found Jessie Weston's *From Ritual to Romance* all the more interesting because of "this Arthur business in my head"[47]. Once facing the way he meant to go, indeed, he went at first with comparative speed. He records that in 1932, in the summer before he became ill, he completed no fewer than sixty paintings[48].

Yet this period, if in some ways halcyon, was not truly representative of the way his mind worked. His juxtaposition of words, fragments, images, apparent inconsequences was intrinsically a task of the utmost difficulty and David's procedures were often very slow. This is more than a simple inference from the fact that it took him from 1928 to 1932 approximately to complete the main body of *In Parenthesis*: more importantly, it was 1928 before he began to want to write it. Whatever experiences he had, even such ineradicable ones as the trenches of the First World War had provided, had to sink in, at their own unhastenable pace, and become a part of his creative consciousness. He was the very opposite of the fluent, lyrical poet with many poems of "occasion" to his name. Everything he wrote was part of himself, of his innate loves, his indissoluble problems. He hated "doing the sights" or going anywhere because other people did. What he took from life had to be assimilable on his own terms. The most striking and demonstrable example of this comes from the year 1934 when David, still "not up to much" and unable to work, was taken out by friends first to Egypt and then to Jerusalem. Eric Gill, who was already there at work on some sculptures for the Hebrew Library, was much annoyed that David remained persistently indoors in the heat reading *Barchester Towers*[49], and when he ventured out would do no more than meander about the Suq and the crowded, narrow streets of the Holy City. Occasionally, by his own account, he looked out from his south-facing window, with the Mosque of Omar in the middle distance and the Mount of Olives to the left, watching the crowded scene below[50]. Once or twice a British soldier off-duty made him think of "a rain-soaked Givenchy duck-board trackway". But, much more significantly, marching squads of such soldiers "placed" themselves in Jerusalem images already in his mind. In "their full parade rig, the light khaki drill shorts, the bronzed arms bare from above the elbow to the wrist & pale khaki shorts leaving the equally bronzed legs bare from above the knee to the brief ankle socks, the feet in heavy field-service hob-nailed boots, but above all the riot-shields aligned to cover the left side and in each right fist the half-grip of a stout baton, evoked not the familiar things of less than two decades back, but rather of two millenia close on, and the ring of the hob-nailed boots on the stone sets and the sharp commands, — so they were a section from the Antonia, up for duties in Hierosolyma after all!"[51] Years later, in the period 1947-52, when he was writing *The Anathemata*, he also wrote several "fragments" about Roman soldiers in Jerusalem which, although rejected for use in his work then current, were published later as 'The Wall', 'The Fatigue' and 'The Tribune's Visitation'. Striking as this slowness and this rejection of other people's significances may be, there is an addendum to it. One of the few visits David made outside Jerusalem in 1934 was to a Franciscan monastery, where he was shown a stone whose inscription commemorated the Tenth Legion, the "Fretensis, the Legion whose Aquilifer was first to leap ashore through the Kentish shoal in 58 B.C."[52] There the heart made the connection: David was back in Britain, with the Celts meeting the first Roman attack, and ultimately, as his "order" asserted itself, with Celtic legionaries serving abroad in the wider Empire. Hence, besides the "fragments" already referred to, we have Lugo the Celt in 'The Dream of Private Clitus', seen through the eyes and understanding of his bivvy-mate.

David's experiences worked on a very slow fuse, took time to find their place in his thinking. What was their appropriate juxtaposition? It might be years before he found out. But this was only one aspect of the difficulty his method encountered. Decision-making took its toll, even within the Catholic fold. But in some ways the weakness he showed from 1932 onwards may be attributed to the terms on which he had enrolled himself. He never embraced the moral teaching of his Church with the same enthusiasm as steeped him in its ritual. There are clear signs — in a letter to Tom Burns, for example, in which he urges that "*you ought to do whatever you bloody well feel inclined to do*" and that the question (whether Burns should stay in Madrid near a girl friend or to return to Britain to become more involved in the war effort) is not "a moral one (I mean, except that everything is!)"[53], an afterthought which, within the tone of the letter, does not convince — that in downgrading moral decisions he was no part of the Puritan wing of Catholic opinion. In a way the "easiness" seen here exemplified the broad road that led David to near-destruction. He was to be guilty, in the essay entitled 'Art in Relation to War', of arguing (possibly on the basis that war had been a good thing for him) that "conceptually, at all events, the end of war is peace (a good)"[54] and that it was perfectly justifiable to discuss the *beauty* of the strategy and tactic of *blitzkrieg* in modern warfare and those of delay in the campaign leading to Cannae in the same terms as one might compare the beauty of the Cathedral at Chartres with that of the Parthenon. "All art . . . has beauty for its end, without qualification", he asserts[55]. An aesthetic which could equate beauty with good without noticing a loss of moral content and which could by-pass entirely the Christian refusal to justify bad means even in the cause of a good end was thus flowering dangerously in David's mind as late as 1946, concurrently with a continuing demand for discipline which had long since extended itself beyond the spiritual dominion of the Catholic Church to an additional and not positively identified secular power. In David's poetry that secular power is provided by the Roman Empire and its army, from a distance the perfect example of the "original" Christian Church sufficiently armed at all points. In terms contemporary, what was he saying? It is much less certain. In 'The Roland Epic and Ourselves' he writes obscurely of a "baptised

Fuhrership"[56]. It is no surprise to discover that he had been reading not only Spengler's *Decline of the West*, with its call for a "new" ruling class which should be strong and confident, but also Hitler's *Mein Kampf*. There is no evidence that impressions of western decadence played any part in his becoming a Catholic and for the fact that they affected him later we must presently attempt to offer reasons. Meanwhile, in the years immediately before the outbreak of war, he was preferring Dictatorship to Democracy, a conflict which he regarded as "largely an affair of the *sword* against *money*"[57]. Although he found some aspects of *Mein Kampf* antipathetic, he declared that he would back Hitler "still against this currish, leftish money thing" — an identification barely understandable today but related, obviously, to the anti-semitism then current which saw the Jews as the international financiers of revolution. His criticism of Spengler was of the manner rather than the matter of the thesis: he did not doubt the "necessity" for a new and ruthless leadership but objected to cant about the nobility of beasts of prey and resented the "cheapness and brutality and inhumanity" apparently intrinsic to the concept[59]. In the last resort he could not take expressions like "Who cares if they do go under?"

David's natural sensibility was offering rearguard resistance to this feeling of "necessity". What had gone wrong? He was writing, as late as 1962, of "a changed world" and that in his father's time there had been "a much more *unified culture* . . . . for all this bloody stuff about democracy"[60]. How could the man who in the period 1928-32 had written with such marvellous retrospective delight in ordinary humanity (in *In Parenthesis*) refer so desperately in 1940 to "the lower orders (of whom I have *great fear* and whose reactions I *hate,* but for whom I feel a deep *understanding* at the same time)"[61]? René Hague records that in the winter of 1924-25 in the Llanthony valley David found the local countrymen strange and frightening: in contrast with his non-Welsh companions, he spoke to scarcely any of them.[62]

What we have to understand, I think, is that the Catholic Church had not been able to do for David Jones the whole of what the Army had done for him. In the Army, by his dexterous continuance as a Private, his professional and social roles were as close as intermittent warfare allowed: he essayed so little as an artist that it separated him not at all. Within the Catholic context, however, the artist had no role which provided a central connection between the intentions of the hierarchy and the feelings of ordinary worshippers: Church patronage was largely a thing of the past: if becoming a Catholic had removed some spiritual and moral burdens from David, it did not cloak his decisions as an artist within a firm and certain personal role. He was confined (or confined himself) first to small like-minded communities such as that of Eric Gill and later to the society of upper-class Catholic friends, in one or other of whose houses he was a frequent guest. The peripatetic nature of his existence, especially in the decade up to 1940, is matter for surprise to those who recollect only the immobility of his later years. He was unmistakably a hanger-on who did not earn enough to keep himself but was supported partly from home and partly by the hospitality and financial generosity of his friends. I set this down not to invoke the old Puritan work ethic to chastise him with and certainly not to ignore his belief in private patronage. I mention it because his neurosis, as he himself acknowledged, was not unconnected with his own social insecurity. "I feel it", he was writing in 1940, "in *my own self*— being neither flesh, fowl, or red herring, socially — but by having become by one accident or another 'supernumerary, attached, pending allocation to unit' (as the military jargon goes) to the upper classes — yet with my roots among the lower orders . . ."[63]. The "excellent anonymity of the army" was not to be recaptured (and we may recollect that that anonymity had been so important that David had, with some deliberateness, not lasted long in the Field Survey Company). It was perhaps the supernumerariness of the artist he had not bargained for, he for whom *Homo Faber*, Man the Maker, was humanity's central and justifying figure.

Neurosis battened on this lack of centrality, but not on this alone. The difficulty of the method of work was more constant. "Painting", David Jones wrote to Jim Ede in 1939, ". . . . is so 'totalitarian' [surely a significant word] and you DO have to be strong to do it, once you know the snags"[63a]. If this was the tap root of neurosis, the cry for strength was nevertheless one and the same with the demand for centrality: the apparently disconnected aesthetically could only be connected by a mind satisfied of its own place within an agreed unity. By becoming a Catholic David had sought, not merely to avoid decisions that were not work-connected, but to provide himself with a field of reference for those that were, so that in searching for the "lost" or the apparently insignificant he had the shape of a certainty, of an agreed and comfortful certainty, on which to fall back when difficulty occurred. But he had found himself still not strong enough. The need for *strength* obsessed him: that was the *necessity* he argued in his poems. That, and not the Decline of the West or "bloody Democracy" (except insofar as they affected his view of the spiritual strength of his required Unity) moved him to demand that the secular arm should protect the central core of belief. His world had to be secure and complete before he could put fear aside and devote himself to the decisions and juxtapositions that are his work.

The evidence for this demand can be seen more explicitly in his letters than in his poetry. In the latter it is the presence of the Roman Army, the completion and warrant of that strong unified world, which speaks of that *necessity* he had. Not just the Church, but Empire. This combination is, of course, as much personal as abstract in its psychology, for its security harks back to Flanders trenches and is projected onwards to the Caesarea of the "Italian band" by the Jerusalem insight of 1934. It is that projection, in which the figure of Christ and the mundane "duty" of secular force intersect at a *crux* that is both Biblical and personal to David Jones's thinking, which begins to undo his security and makes powerful again the image of lesser sacrifices such as those of Celts stripped and enveloped by the demands of Empire.

The necessity he felt to re-construct Empire, however, must not be underestimated. His responses to the contemporary world are very limited. 'A, a, a, Domine Deus' expresses, in the context of the immanence of God, bewilderment at and distrust of the Machine. The fragment from 'The Book of Balaam's Ass' opens with an uneasy look at Cicily and Pamela-born-between-the-sirens and Bertie and "poor Clayton" which almost immediately leaves them for a glimpse of the Otadini north of the Wall and rummages about in *Romanitas* before settling to the central episode from Passchendaele. Both this and the Mametz Wood of *In Parenthesis,* of course, set down the matter of *real* experience within the knowledge of many still alive. The message of *In Parenthesis,* if it be insisted that it has one, is about the need to recall to the present certain elements forgotten but, by implication, powerful and valid, elements which, accepted and understood, could recreate the desired *universum.* But its application loses force, as we shall see, because of the temporary association on which it is based and its location outside the Britain to which it should apply. *The Anathemata,* again, though shaped in the present by the office of the Mass, is composed largely of elements which are pre-Reformation in date. In the 'Redriff' section, it is true, there is an extra-temporal approach to Eb Bradshaw and the dignity of the craftsman (this, so to speak, the writer as artist-craftsman making his professional, if also theological, point to the present) and in 'The Lady of the Pool' section the multi-personalised Britannia is allowed to appear first as a lavender-seller, the maker of one of those "Cries of London" that might have been heard at any time from the sixteenth century or earlier to a late point some four or five generations ago. Much use is made in this section, too, of John Stow's 1598 *Survey of London,* in which its churches, with their evocative Catholic-sainted names, are set out. But for the rest David Jones moves, with a confidence seen perfected only in *The Anathemata,* inside a pre-Reformation world. He is concerned in and involved with pre- and proto-history, the Classical, Roman and post-Roman eras and Arthurian and post-Arthurian Britain. Whatever he may be saying to the contemporary world, it is patterned in the ages through which alone he roves freely.

It is not unreasonable, of course, to attribute this all-but-exclusive predilection, in part, to a particular cast of mind. David records that at Camberwell Art School before 1914 his "attempts at figure composition [were] nearly always of some mediaeval subject introducing a vested priest" and instances even then his "interest in Morris's poetry and Rossetti & Co"[64]. His was a philological and an onomastic, as well as a ritualistic, mind and the amazing Ancient and Mediaeval world of reference which he built up is unquestionably a product of his love as well as of his tireless endeavour and formidable memory. It is no less fair to add that his lack of confidence in the contemporary world is characteristic of a conservative and anti-revolutionary mind schooled in the beliefs of a minority group in English society with a well-rehearsed history of persecution and discrimination suffered into times not a century from his. Even in David's most confident periods, such as that which saw the completion and publication of *The Anathemata* in 1952, he could envisage himself as doing no more than speaking to a contemporary public of what they had forgotten, of the talismanic past that could make *their* present whole. What he was about then, he wanted to make clear, was "the Catholic thing which has determined so much of our history and conditioned the thought of us all"[65]. But in such present as *The Anathemata* has (that is, in the context of the contemporary Mass within which the poem's wholeness is displayed) he is nevertheless conscious

that dead symbols litter to the base of the cult-stone, that the
stem by the palled stone is thirsty, that the stream is very low.[66]

The priest, indeed, "stands alone in Pellam's land", Malory's Waste
Land as it stretches NOW.

There is, plainly, no unified world of belief and reference which
David Jones can invoke in the present. And it is in his blacker, more
neurotic moments that the metaphor of *Empire* seems attractive, the
idea of the preservation of once-paramount values by force. The
Roman army "fragments", afterwards published in *The Sleeping Lord*,
were not unnaturally excluded from the relative confidence of *The
Anathemata*, but the threat of The Ram — the original Medo-Persian
Ram whom Daniel saw "pushing westward, and northward, and
southward; so that no beasts might stand before him, neither was
there any that could deliver out of his hand; but he did according to
his will and became great"[67] — had its spiritual connotation too. If
The Ram was the image of Empire moving ever outward in a military
aggression which it justifed by the watchword of *necessity*, it could
serve too as the shadow of a spiritual tyranny even more terrible. In
the 'Keel, Ram and Stauros' section of *The Anathemata* the stout
timber from which the keel of the ship of Christ and His Church is to
be built can be set also to evil: "horizontal'd", it suggests to the poet's
mind another version of The Ram, the military siege-engine which
flattens the walls of heresy. And he catches a glimpse of the horror of
the priest blessing the act of aggression:

> He can gloss text and context
> for a park of ordnance.[68]

This is the utmost darkness, the Church involved in inhumanity.
Christopher Dawson and David had talked about this in 1942.
Dawson had said that

> he found that Catholics, in his experience, since he became a
> Catholic, were getting far more, not less, 'institutional' (in the
> bad sense) and mechanical, so to say . . . a belief in effecting
> things by organisation and formulas . . . growing rather than
> lessening.[69]

Mild as this diagnosis may seem in the poetic context of a supposedly

Christian war, it nevertheless pinpoints David's fears of a simplistic carelessness about persons, about divergences of belief, and of a demand for uniformity which may invoke Anti-Christ. It is not far, as we shall see, to "the grids of the Ram's survey when he squares the world-circle"[70].

But brotherhood of race — that is, perhaps, a too great reliance on a unity that history suggests — could be a betrayer too. It was David's horror of the "fratricide" that began in 1939 that, still deeply felt, emerges in the conclusion of the Angle-Land section of *The Anathemata,* where he sees "all our easting waters" from Spey to Thames as "confluent with the fathering river" Rhine and "oned with him / in Cronos-*meer*". His disclaimer that he is writing of a time *before* "the fratricides of the latter day" is cancelled at once by a bracketed exclamation:

> (O Balin O Balan!
>   how blood you both
> the *Brudersee*
>   toward the last pháse
> of our dear West).[71]

Try as he might, he could not keep his doubts entirely excluded from the world-circle, the "Alpha es et O" of *The Anathemata,* which at its most joyous he could make only of the spiritual heritage of "The Matter of Britain". One is bound to ask, therefore, without further ado, what it was that warred with the *necessity* David undoubtedly felt in himself and represented it from time to time not merely as a blade that cut two ways but even as a spiritual wickedness in him. My contention is that it was the love of Wales. What, Wales?! Left-dominated, "bloody democratic" Wales, the pitiable remnant of a tradition going back to Troy, the Wales of David's present?! Yes, it was *family,* after all, and not to be put away. And there was still the Welsh language, which had produced, after the Greek and Roman, the oldest literature in Europe. He could not learn it properly, but he loved it and used words and phrases from it even to excess. When English denigration of it got under his skin more than usual, he was moved to write letters to the papers, as he did to *The Manchester Guardian* in 1957 and *The Times* in 1956 and 1958[72]. Despite their learning they were guarded and probably ineffectual letters. But, as David put it to Vernon Watkins:

> I *hate* writing to the press & very seldom fall to the temptation or compulsion, but I was *so* annoyed by the way the politicians talk & think of what is left of 'Wales' & I hoped someone better qualified to speak would do so, but, as they didn't, I at last sent my mild comment.[73]

Beneath the skin the *Taid*-basher still breathed. To Harman Grisewood David wrote in 1964: "They prove by statistics that the Welsh language is dying, and that it has no practical value anyhow. Damn such bloody arguments"[74].

But was it really "what is left of 'Wales'" that moved him and fought one side of his inner battle? Wales after 1282 appears in his work scarcely at all. Was it not Britain, the *unity,* that he loved? Well, yes: he loved it as he thought it had been, but not as it was. No, his weakness was a weakness of the latter days and could only be countered by a contemporary strength, or at least by another weakness that had the power to convict the first. Did he really *know* much about "what is left of 'Wales'"? Yes, he did. He may never have had the wish to keep up with "the Neath fifteen" but his interest in theology, even the theology of Protestantism and Dissent from the Church late Established, had acquainted him with Methodist hymns[75] and equipped him to allege the religion of "Bryn Calfaria" as the origin of Wilfred Owen's images of death[76]. His knowledge of the geology and geography of Wales, so apparent in both the 'Rite and Foretime' sequence of *The Anathemata* and in 'The Sleeping Lord', more than entitled him to write the Introduction to a new edition of *Wild Wales*[77] in its centenary year of 1954, with whatever difficulty he stomached George Borrow's virulent anti-Romanism. It must be sufficient here, without further recourse to detail, to uncover a small corner of David's extensive knowledge of Welsh history after 1282. In 'The Book of Balaam's Ass' Pick-em-up-Shenkin overhears Dai Meyrick in his death-throes before the Aachen Haus, making

> his dolorous anaphora, like the cry of a wounded hare, on Magons and Maponus, because his mother was of the line of Caw of North Britain and her love was beyond the Wall with the Men of the North (albeit she sat under her husband in his Moravian bethel, at Drws-y-Coed Uchaf in Arfon in the apostasy of the latter days).[78]

In this single Gododdin-like meed of praise can be seen not only David's fluid treatment of centuries but the obstinacy with which he makes claims for his older world. How many Welshmen can lay hand on heart and say that they know of David Mathias's Moravian mission base with the Griffiths family in Dyffryn Nantlle during the years 1771-72? And how many can add that the fictive Meyrick was, like Mathias, a Pembrokeshireman by name and that his family had arrived there from Anglesey, itself perhaps only the end of an earlier journey with Cunedda from Manaw Gododdin close to, if not in, the Pictlands of the far North? But the time-stretched Dai has to call not on his Hussite or Zinzendorfian God but on Magons and Maponos, pagan Celtic gods who were *before,* not after, the apostacy. It is, so to speak, required. Nothing significant must escape the walled world, not in the time of uncertainty. But this closing of the gates cannot entirely obscure a knowledge and affection that have made forays outside and have survived.

I must attempt now to show how Wales and the idea of Wales plays a part in David Jones's work, how it first joys and balances the oneness of Britain, and then how, as the fears and disillusions mount, it cries out constantly against the alleged *necessities* of the Ram. It may even appear that in the poems last-published the Ram has deserted his titular centre in Rome and stepped toward this Island.

David's first work, *In Parenthesis,* is clearly an attempt to re-establish "the Matter of Britain" in the English mind. That its circumstances are fact and that the events it describes actually happened does not alter this. The elements of the poem were right to hand. His "companions in the war were mostly Londoners with an admixture of Welshmen . . . Nothing could be more representative. These came from London. Those from Wales. Together they bore in their bodies the genuine tradition of the Island of Britain, from Bendigaid Vran to Jingle and Marie Lloyd. These were the children of Doll Tearsheet. Those are before Caractacus was . . . ."[79] Cockney influences, he tells us, determined the form of the poem because they are somehow intrinsic to the *sound* of the Army (a thought we may reflect upon in the later context of homogenising the diversities) but it is the Welsh who, outnumbered on the ground, provide almost all of the spirit and the regenerative myth of the unit. (This again may be no more than fact: Robert Graves, Siegfried Sassoon and other non-Welshmen who wrote about the War found their service with Welsh units memorable above all others). David Jones's purpose, however, is to re-establish the "corporate inheritance"[80], though, sadly, it re-appears outside the Island to which it belongs and for a temporary period only. There are no doubts here about Empire or attempts to justify it by asserting the heterogeneity of participation. For one thing, only two sets of people participate. For another, the unity recalled is not so much Roman as British: Dai Greatcoat remembers his service with the "Dandy Xth" at Golgotha[81] but only in the context of his presence throughout history, at every change and crisis-point, up to the time at which disregard of the Celt as the originator of the central, constantly regenerative myth begins. The essential *worth* of "The Matter of Britain" is not in doubt and the Welsh part in it, denigrated and forgotten, is there to be re-established in its original and greater glory.

Two points must be made here. First, David was well aware how unfashionable the stance of *In Parenthesis* was. Not since the middle of the seventeenth century and the *Familiar Letters* of James Howell (or, more correctly, his *Parly of Beasts* of 1656, when the Orosian goat made his "beastly" answer to the jokiness of the Ram) had the heritage of Wales been seen as the more ancient and honourable part of the Union. Maurice Kyffin, Thomas Churchyard, John Davies of Hereford, Arthur Kelton and others, with their poems in praise of the Tudors and their heritage from Wales or in praise of Wales itself had been buried under more than two centuries of near-contempt, and the preoccupations of Tennyson and the pre-Raphaelites, Frenchified in origin and then acceptably "English" as they were, had provided no counterbalance at all. *In Parenthesis* was a mark of David's great love for Wales as well as a record of events whose memory he found ineradicable. At the same time, it is, both as fact and interpretation, the work of a London Welshman: the Union is no more in doubt than it was for the Welsh *advenae* of Elizabeth's day, for whom reality of an economic sort, expressed most eloquently in the grant of *English* lands and their own success at Court, justified and made necessary an *English* metropolis. Nevertheless, time has brought some disillusion: Victorian and Edwardian England had long forgotten gratitude and spoken only of itself. That the Welsh tradition, if not solely "before Caractacus was", never comes within half a millenium of Doll Tearsheet, is of course essential to David Jones's particular kind of rehabilitation.

In any case there could be no doubt about *necessity*. Britain was at war. But in 'The Book of Balaam's Ass', which was written next[82], there is a heavily implied doubt about *necessity* even within the military situation. In this "fragment" of a much longer but discarded writing the observation is no longer at first hand: the scene, probably Passchendaele,[83] belongs to a much later period of the War than Mametz Wood: the telling-time, moreover, is October 1937 or later, with bored Cicily and Pamela-born-between-the-sirens having to listen to a narrator who begins by slipping a millenium and a half and taking on the character of Emeritus Nodens (the Latinised form of the Celtic god Nudd or Nith) going on about the cat-eyed Otadini coming over the Wall in the mist or dilating thrills from Pontus in Asia. There is a tale to tell but not without preliminary didactics:

> Lime-wash over the tar-brush?
> No, but rather, cistern the waters of Camelot to lave your lousy
>   linen[84]

— which I interpret as, "Send in your Celts instead of your darker 'colonials'? Well, they'll do your rotten job and make a legend out of it afterwards". And David Jones then comes to the point: he offers the tale of the Irish Mill (or the Aachen Haus) Gododdinised. Briefly, it is the story of a renowned German strong-point and the terrible, coverless plain before it. What is called at first "the G.O.C. in C.'s diversion before the Mill" becomes at the end "the tomfoolery of the G.O.C. in C."[85]. This sort of comment would have been a polite one from Tommy Atkins and a commonplace amongst war historians later, but in David Jones's work it constitutes a departure. Nothing of this sort occurs in *In Parenthesis* about the not dissimilar brass-hat follies before Mametz Wood. Moreover, one should note, with the dryness that phrases it, that "it was urged by some" that the intercession of the Holy Mother "conditioned and made acceptable" that tomfoolery — a long, wry mile from the poet's own ultimate cry, like that of the dying on the field, to "God the Father of Heaven . . . because by Him even the G.O.C.'s diversion before the Mill can shine with the splendour of order"[86].

More significant than this, for the present purpose, is the narrator's insistence on the unequal nature of the sacrifices made. In the early Spring of 1915 "the men of Lower Britain" — that is, the Jocks — had been sent forward to occupy a drain from which they were afterwards blasted. Only three of them got back and the "chequered cloth" of the dead could still be seen on the wire through field glasses. Later, once in Spring and once in Autumn, an Irish battalion had been despatched to storm the Mill and

> from the tangled spread of the iron hedge hung the garments
> peculiar to the men of Ireland and their accoutrements, and
> carcases of the Irish were stretched on some of the iron bushes
> . . . . . [87]

Now, as the central narrative begins, it is the turn of the men of Upper
Britain, and though this time the command is English and the
attacking force is far more English than ever the "London Welsh" had
been in the 15th Battalion R.W.F., it nevertheless contains Colour
Sgt. Michael Mary Gabriel Olav Aumerle from Sord Colum Cille of
the dark tribes of the Féni, "signaller Balin and his incompatible
mess-mate linesman Balan"[88], Isaac Prosser and "Punic Trelawny,
his Cornwealas confidant"[89], Dai Meyrick and Madoc Sey "searching
for a mountain" on the open plain[90], and, of course, Pick-em-up-
Shenkin, who exercises the privilege of awkwardness by falling in a
crater and staying there. It is he, of all this carefully assembled Celtic
brotherhood, who, with Squib Lucifer and Ducky Austin,
representing the Force of Evil and the Church respectively, completes
the twice-repeated Gododdin motif and comes back to tell the tale.
Whether we are to infer that the concept of "Britain" is invoked only
when the "High Command" has been sufficiently frustrated in its
"tomfoolery" to realise that sacrifice is required from elements other
than the expendable ones on its fringe is not altogether clear: the
"representative" Celts, as distinct from Celts in the mass, seem to
suggest that. But the story's Gododdin shape (even if it does imply the
Celtic ability to make a glorious myth even out of disaster — a sense in
which Celts are occasionally necessary) does not sit easily with this,
the less because Shenkin / Aneirin is an elongation of the John Ball
caricature. The story, in any case, besides being a "fragment", is an
episode in a serial: Good and Evil live to fight again another day,
though Good is slightly tarnished by false suggestion and the narrator
for the time being is...well, Pick-em-up Shenkin, whose "baptism" is
"by cowardice".[91]

There can, nevertheless, be little doubt of the presence of
disillusion, affecting as it does both the *necessity* of the occasion and the
spirit in which *necessity* is treated. Only the play of laughter over the
dreadful scene clouds and disguises it. Only the earnest display of the
"origins" of the sacrificed participants mitigates it, suggesting that the

core of the "Matter of Britain" remains a "unified culture", a homogeneity of choice.

In *The Anathemata,* a construct of much greater dimensions, disillusion has a smaller place. Much of the Welsh material in it appears in the section entitled 'Mabinog's Liturgy', really the liturgy of the Infant Jesus and the celebration of Mass at a Romano-British court and in various other parts of the Roman Empire. The Rome here is untroubled, religious. In the section called 'Middle-Sea and Lear-Sea', however, there is a two-page-long passage in which Clio, the Muse of History, tells how Mars, "m'lord / the square-pushing Strider . . . . the squat Georgie" (that is, the one-time farmer, *georgios)* — David Jones is perhaps making a point here not merely about the violence of Cain to Abel but about the Norman-English who seized Welsh land and afterwards called Taffy a thief for rustling to live — enlarged the territories of the Roman people.

> Though he was of the Clarissimi his aquila over me was robbery.
> 'T's a great robbery
>   — is empire,[92]

she concludes, lifting a phrase from St. Augustine. But her account, though it takes the form of personalised hostility, is concerned mainly with the initial aggression, with the War-god visualised in rape, encumbered with all his accoutrements, and goes on to suggest the half-attraction felt afterwards to the nature of "his glory"[93]. Fuller justification follows: Roman law and civilisation could not have flourished without the victory of Roman arms:

> The Urbs without edged iron
>   can you credit it?[94]

By the first century A.D. there is general admiration for the Roman constitution: "all the world-nurseries" are prepared to admit that "Roma knows great"[95]. But as time passes, Rome falls and the Dark Ages supervene. Clio's indictment is seen in the dimension of history: "the acute coarsening of the forms"[96] of the later Empire is an inevitable concomitant of the natural cycle of human endeavour: if the "Good Time Coming" appears abruptly cancelled, there *was* a Good Time nevertheless: the end, even in short, has justified the means. What this section says, in effect, is historical, not polemical:

Clio's portrait of Empire does not threaten the praise-structure of the whole poem.

That conclusion is important for the significance of another section, that of 'The Lady of the Pool', which *in primis* is concerned with the more diffuse glory of Britannia and of London as the epitome of "the corporate inheritance". London is the "Troy Novaunt" of Geoffrey of Monmouth: it inherits the ancient tradition of Brutus the Trojan and the kings of Wales. But it is also Rome revived and it is "the boatswain, from Milford"[97] who makes the connection. I take it that this bo'sun is of Milford in order to make the Tudor link apparent: he is later called "this Welshook Milford bo's'n"[98]. Henry Tudor landed in 1485, it may be noted, at Dale, not far from the *South* Hook. This Milford seaman is a trimmed-down Dai Greatcoat, the shorter and the less bombastic largely because he is *reported* by the shape-changing lavender-girl who is Britannia and his stories muddled and generalised by her (David's view, no doubt, of the effects of Union). Even so, not all significance is lost: "for each circumstance" the bo'sun finds "antique comparison". Like Dai he has been present in every age, though apparently ignorant of any person or happening in Wales since 1282 except for the image of Derfel Gadarn. He affirms not merely Madoc in the New World but the truth of the much-maligned Geoffrey. It is, however, his last assertion that is important in the present context. In the days of Gruffydd, the father of Llywelyn Olaf, he says, the sailors of Gwynedd, standing "to brimward / of Ongulsey Sound / the out-mere to wander" flew from the stern-post "a red rampin' griffin", just as Caesar did[99]. Unhistorical as this may be (for the dragon standard of the Roman army, filched originally from the Scythians — very possibly the "princely tribes" of the continental Celtic Confederation — was never *red* before the ninth century writing of Nennius and, despite Geoffrey's attribution of it to Cadwallader the Blessed, cannot be verified in its redness before it was carried by Edmund and Jasper Tudor), it serves to make David Jones's point: his London of the end of the fifteenth century, with its "British sea-thing"[100], inherited both Troy (through Wales) and (again through Wales) the stable Catholic world that came down from Rome. However obliquely, he succeeds in bringing home from the trenches of *In Parenthesis* the "corporate inheritance" of the men of Britain, even if (that quick look at Eb Bradshaw apart) he can advance it no further than 1500.

Yet he is not satisfied. In strict history he should have been, for there was never a time like 1500 to satisfy a London Welshman. St. David's Day celebrated at Court, the red dragon standard flying, the King's guard in their old Welsh colours of green and white, another Arthur heir to the throne — it was still the semblance of the Welsh "victory" that Bosworth had brought. But 'The Lady of the Pool' is not strict history: its imaginative strands cannot be tied by time or held long in place. Moreover, it is the twentieth century that speaks to David Jones and makes him dissatisfied. So when he has his London maid say

> What's under works up.
> You never know, captain:
> I will not say it shall be so
> but, captain, rather would I say:
> You never know![101]

he is indicating the need for an alteration of the existing balance of the "corporate inheritance" in the Welsh or old Romano-British favour. His maid speaks of slumberers in the marls and gravels of London, slumberers who

> was great captains, cap'n:
> tyrannoi come in keels from Old Troy
> *requiescant.*
> For, these fabliaux say, of one other such quondam king
> *rexque futurus.*

If these should stir, she says,

> then would our Engle-raum in this
> Brut's Albion be like to come to some confusion![102]

The word *Engle-raum* is far more than a reminder of the Germanic origins of the English: it is a bitter, even violent, recall of twentieth-century German imperial ambitions, from designs on Africa in the first decade to Nazi aggrandisement in the third. "Brut's Albion" is the Britain which Angles and Saxons engrossed long after it was formed and which they now insist on calling *England*. It may be that David Jones means only that prophecies *will* be fulfilled, that in his book Arthur is the once and *future* King. But I think not: *Engle-raum* reads sharply in the context and the "What's under works up" theme recurs in other poems.

The apparently praiseworthy conjunction of so much tradition in the London of 1500, then, is disturbed by imbalance and a vision of "some confusion" to come. But this does not change the tone more than momentarily. "You never know" four times repeated and "let's say *requiescant*" do much to mute the outrage of *Engle-raum*. *The Anathemata* remains David Jones's celebration, taken as far as he can make it go, of "the Catholic thing which has determined so much of our history and conditioned the thought of us *all*"[103].

The Anathemata, of course, was the product of the years 1947- 52, when David was whole again after long neurosis. But much that had been written earlier had not found a place in it. Instead of the fluid, seafarer's world, this discarded material is concerned with the walled world: its image is Rome itself and its Empire: its tone is one of continuous philosophical, even theological, conflict. Let us look now at the "fragments" which have emerged from the discard-pile, all of them dramatically conceived and in some instances marked by compelling irrelevancies (like the portrait of Brasso in 'The Dream of Private Clitus'). The field they cover is plainly one of obsessive interest to their author.

There is, first of all, the theme of the *necessity* of Empire. Established, with all the virtues of its legally-ruled peace and its flowers of culture, can it not relax? Must it continue its aggressions? This is as well seen as anywhere in 'The Narrows', David Jones's last published poem that has claims to be complete[104]. Two legionaries, the speaker and his comrade Porrex, stand on the Gaulish shore of the Channel, looking across at "the White Island . . . . riding a mooring / just off Europa's main". All the Hercynian and Teutoburgan tribes are conquered. Must the army now go on?

No end to these wars, no end, no end
at all. No end to the world-enrolments
that extend the war-shape, to police the
extending *limes*, that's a certainty.[105]

Britain belongs to Europe, would be easy to cross to. The two legionaries count the cost in lives already, but to question, or even to talk too much, leads to ruin: it is indeed to "tell together / the beads of Comrade Spartacus", the rebel slave leader, and suffer the fate meted out to revolutionaries. Would things be any easier "far side the Styx"?

'The Wall' uses as commentators two similar soldiers on duty on the walls of Rome, which here are characterised as "the robber walls of the world city"[106]. Their duty, they suppose, is to march everlastingly "round and round the cornucopia", seeing little of "the swag and spolia / o' the universal world". But they are aware, vaguely, of changed purposes in the practice of Empire.

> ... they used to say we marched for the Strider, the common father of the Roman people . . . . . but now they say the Quirinal Mars turns out to be no god of war but of armed peace. Now they say we march for kind Irene, who crooks her rounded elbow for little Plutus, the gold-getter . . . .[107]

It is the shopkeepers who now add their voices to the cry of triumph (we may here recall David's version of a more modern conflict as "largely an affair of the *sword* against *money*"[108], the latter much less acceptable). And what is it all for? Is this what the careful auguries of the original *patria* foretold? If it contained "a world / from the beginning", was "the *civitas* of God" first parcelled out

> that we should sprawl
> > from Septimontium
> a megalopolis that wills death?[109]

These are fundamental questions that it is not for the ordinary man to answer. But the two legionaries do not like the attitude of the crowds at a triumph:

> They crane their civvy necks half out of their civvy suits to bait the maimed king in his tinctured vesture, the dying *tegernos* of the wasted *landa* well webbed in our marbled parlour, bitched and bewildered and far from his dappled patria far side the misted Fretum[110]

In 'The Narrows' Celtic Britain was still untouched. Here, in 'The Wall', it is already despoiled. The prisoner is the Fisher-King, the Grail-Keeper, inheritor of Christian myth, however untrue to historical sequence this may be. The implication is that the cry of "Io Triumphe, Io, Io" is the cry of *barbaritas*, not *Civitas Dei*, so much so that *all* can now face

> the dying god

the dying Gaul
without regret.[111]

Where the tradition of the sword, the mark of the Strider, honoured an enemy, alive or dead, the followers of "that sacred brat" Plutus trample without thought the Celt and his mythology. *The Dying Gaul*, while plainly here Dai Greatcoat as victim, was, under that title, the commanded creation of Attalos of Pergamum in Asia Minor and its only real connection with Rome lies in the sculpture's surviving copy in the Museo Capitolino. It is, I think, plain from the historical spread of these references and their lack of application to the *Roman* Empire at any single period in history that David Jones is not merely generalising about Celtdom but pointing at a more modern target than appears. Empire has become something much more (and worse) than a military necessity and its opponents, forever unsuccessful, are the poet's own people.

In 'The Fatigue' there is an examination of the reasons for attendance at (if not necessarily responsibility for) a similar *triumph*, the crucifixion of Jesus by the leaders of the Jews. The target here is the excuse of heterogeneity, the inclusion in the world-order (that is, in visible terms, the Roman army) of people from every land and culture. What takes place at Golgotha, it may be argued, is the result of the widest possible will. If 'The Wall' confronts David's fears with his own origins, 'The Fatigue' goes further: it casts a sidelong look at his own method of working, whether as artist or writer. The idiosyncrasy of his own juxtapositions and the apparent heterogeneity of his sources might give some countenance to the idea of a will and an order other than his own, even if the deliberate exclusion of much from the walled world militates strongly against that. The heterogeneities, though not the same, were possibly analogous: their limitations had the same root, in his own fears. In choosing the Crucifixion David Jones demonstrates Empire collaborating in the removal of the Love which casts out Fear and the less timorous part of his thinking again perceives that it is from the Celts, strangers within the Imperial pattern, that the criticism of "common will" has to come.

Two legionaries, Gauls or island Celts, are drafted to the fatigue-party for Calvary Hill as a penalty for reporting, identically, a shadowy movement in the Virgin Post area of Jerusalem's walls. The Virgin Post area is not their responsibility and they are getting above themselves, in the sergeant's eyes, in seeing, not merely the *same* thing but something which the roster has not allowed for. After further elaboration, we are given a glimpse of the central administration dealing with "world-routine"[112] and are led to realise the long line of accidents which determine the acts in which a soldier may be involved. Even at the last, in the immediate vicinity of decision

> By your place on a sergeant's roster
> by where you stand in y'r section
> by *when* you fall in
> by if they check you from left or right
> by a chance numbering-off
>   by a corporal's whim
> you will furnish
>   that Fatigue.[113]

There is nothing in the procedure that can be defined as Will, either for the individual or the Machine that begins it all, once the ruling fear of *Barbaritas* is assumed. Indeed, the act itself is so routine that it has no name. But it is "little Ginger the Mountain / the Pretanic fatigue-wallah / (shipped in a slaver to Corbilo-on-Liger / marketed at Massilia)" who knows that the place of it is called *Lle'r Benglog*, the Place of a Skull[114]. It is the two Gauls, who together see what is not laid down, and the little slave-Welshman who knows the *name* of the place they have all reached, who deny the phoney heterogeneity, which is also, in its result, the anonymity and mindlessness of official vision.

That heterogeneity is, in any case, a travesty of St. Paul's message to the Corinthians[115], that "there are diversities of gifts, but the same spirit". The Tribune in 'The Tribune's Visitation' travesties it again. "All", he says, "are members / of the Strider's body. / And if not of one hope / then of one necessity. / For we are all attested to one calling / not any more several, but one". Necessity? What necessity? *Idem in me.* We live to Caesar. That is all there is.[116].

But the kind of diversity the Tribune, in his startling frankness, is concerned to do away with is not that of gifts but of "dear pieties", "sweet remembered demarcations", the things of "our own small beginnings" that make us whole men, individuals, and therefore, according to some thinkers, better able to serve Caesar. Those pretty notions, he says, must go. "Only the neurotic look to their beginnings"[117]. "The cultural obsequies must be already sung before empire can masquerade a kind of life"[118]. Why? Surely,

> ... lest, thinking of our own, our bowels turn when we are
> commanded to storm the palisades of others and the world-plan
> be undone by plebeian pity.[119]

What then, he goes on, what then? Are we supervising "the world-death / being dead ourselves long since?" There is no answer to that but the *necessity* which *is* Caesar. In other words, the Tribune recognises that it is intrinsic to the nature of Empire to show hostility to any of its cultural ingredients which might encourage a man to think or believe anything other than the centralising necessity commands.

The Tribune's address to "the Italian band" at Caesarea about 40 A.D., which this poem purports to convey, does indeed pay more attention to differences of locality and custom *within* Italy than do its predecessors, but even here there is a Celtic dimension — in fact, a Welsh dimension rather even than a British:

> Bucinator Taranus, swilling his quarter's pay with his
> Combrogean listing-mates, tough Lugobelinus and the radiant
> Maponus (an outlandish triad to wear the Roman lorica)
> maudlin in their barrack cups habitually remember some high
> hill-cymanfa; thus our canteens echo with:
>> *'No more in dear Orddwy*
>> *We drink the dear meddlyn'*
> or some such dolorous anamnesis.[120]

True, the Welshness of this is more generally Celticised by the use of the names of three Celtic gods (Taranus is a mistake for Tanarus), but the lines adapted from the eighteenth century ballad 'Of Noble Race was Shenkin' and, more specifically, the Tribune's remark following, that "their Ordovician hills are yet outside the world (but shortly to be levelled to the world-plain)" — a prophecy of Claudius's invasion of Britain in 43 A.D. — indicate clearly that we are intended to see the "dear *pagus*"[121] of these three legionaries as differing in *kind* from "the variant sweets of Mother Italy", already partly *conditioned* to "the world".

The emphasis on Wales, though nowhere allied to name, is much stronger in 'The Tutelar of the Place', that poem which most extols the "known-sites" and the "differentiated cults" and which appears to face the Ram at very close quarters. There is no claim here for the necessity of the world-plan: the Ram has decreed against "the utility of the hidden things" and must be resisted. The whole poem is a cry to "Tellus of the myriad names", the Earth-Mother, to protect her "little children" from the determination of the Ram "to square the world-floor and number the tribes and write down the secret things and take away the diversities . . ."[122]

> Queen of the differentiated sites, administrix of the
> demarcations, let our cry come unto you.
>> In all times of imperium save us when the
> *mercatores* come . . . .
> When they proscribe the diverse uses and impose the rootless
> uniformities, pray for us.
>> When they sit in *Consilium*
> to liquidate the holy diversities
>> mother of particular perfections
>> queen of otherness
>> mistress of asymmetry
> patroness of things counter, parti, pied, several
> protectress of things known and handled
> help of things familiar and small
>> wardress of the secret crevices
>> of things wrapped and hidden
> mediatrix of all the deposits
>> margravine of the troia
> empress of the labyrinth
>> receive our prayers.[123]

Unquestionably the poet invokes the female principle to confound the male. Less obviously, he appears to invoke the language of an older Rome against later imperial exactions: the advent of the *mercatores* and the *negotiatores* (a reprise of the theme of 'The Wall') is reinforced by the introduction of the German word *Gleichschaltung*; the threat from the centre becomes more and more pressing. Though the poem is a *general* prayer against the imagined necessity of *imperium*, it is hard to avoid the conclusion that the lines following refer specifically to the hardships in and the emigration from Wales in the thirties:

> Remember the mound-kin, the kith of the *tarren* gone from this
> mountain because of the exorbitance of the Ram . . . . remember
> them in the rectangled tenements, in the houses of the engines
> that fabricate the ingenuities of the Ram . . . . Mother of Flowers

save them then where no flower blows.

   Though they shall not come again because of the
requirements of the Ram with respect to the world plan,
remember them where the dead forms multiply, where no
stamen leans, where the carried pollen falls to the adamant
surfaces, where is no crevice. In all times of *Gleichschaltung*, in the
days of the central economies, set up the hedges of illusion round
some remnant of us, twine the wattles of mist, white-web a
Gwydion-hedge
             like fog on the *bryniau*
             against the commissioners
and assessors bearing the writs of the Ram . . . . . [124]

Whatever of balance there was in the poems previously discussed, it
has decisively tipped in one direction here. The *universum* has become
an unmistakeably imperial aggression, an aggression against that
part of living which alone has particularity and savour.

'The Hunt' is a poem which, while limning the distress of Wales,
points also to the continuance of spirit, to the possibility of
regeneration which exists in it. The Arthur of this "fragment" is
strictly the Welsh Arthur of the Cilhwch and Olwen story in pursuit of
Twrch Trwyth, but he is also the lord "of wounds" . . . "who directs
the toil", a kind of tendrilled Green Man who has some of the aspects
of Christ himself. Like 'The Sleeping Lord', which sees Wales very
specifically as the resting-place of Arthur, the concerns of 'The Hunt'
no longer make any pretence of being *British*. The leadership of
Arthur is a leadership of example and personal sacrifice; his forehead

                    is corrugated
          like the defences of the hill
                         because of his care for the land
          and for the men of the land.[125]

His garments are torn, his body bloodied with hog-wounds and his
face with hog-spittle. He is wounded *for* his people, willing and
unwilling, as well as *with* them. In 'The Sleeping Lord' there are
further clues to the interpretation of 'The Hunt'. It is the hog Trwyth,
we learn,

                    that has pierced through
          the stout-fibred living wood

that bears the sacral bough of gold.
It is the hog that has ravaged the fair *onnen* and the hornbeam
and the Queen of the Woods . . . . . .
It is the great *ysgithrau* of the *porcus Troit* that have stove in the
wattled walls of the white dwellings, it is he who has stamped out
the seed of fire, shattered the *pentan*-stone within the dwellings;
strewn the green leaf-bright limbs with the broken white limbs of
the folk of the dwellings, so that the life-sap of the flowers of the
forest mingles the dark life-sap of the fair bodies of the men who
stood in the trackway of the long tusked great hog, *y twrch dirfawr
ysgithrog hir.*[126]

This hog is destructive without apparent or necessarial excuse, but he
is plainly related, if rurally, to the Ram.

It is, however, the identification of the Arthur of the hog-wounds
with the land of Wales, its sharp contours, deep streams and striated
hills that, in 'The Sleeping Lord', makes the point more significantly.
Though enormously digressive and concerned in detail with those
rivers and mountains which in *The Anathemata* were no more than a
geological study, 'The Sleeping Lord', within a time-scheme which is
post-Arthurian and at the end of the poem apparently Norman,
attempts, it seems to me, to do two things: it stresses the *Christianity* of
Arthur and marks out the priest or candle-bearer as the
remembrancer of the fallen and dead of the Island: and it asks
repeatedly whether individual rivers, springs or hills represent
aspects of the Sleeping Lord.

Is the Usk a drain for his gleaming tears
who weeps for the land
                              who dreams his bitter dream
for the folk of the land . . . .?[127]

It is still Arthur who sleeps "on the cold, open *moelion*"[128] until the very
end. But the end is surprising:

Is the configuration of the land
                              the furrowed body of the lord
are the scarred ridges
                              his dented greaves
do the trickling gullies
                              yet drain his hog-wounds?

> Does the land wait the sleeping lord
> > or is the wasted land
> that very lord who sleeps?[129]

This last question has been read by many without any heightened interest. It has seemed no more than a clever twist to the theme, a new poetic chord with which to conclude. But how if it means what it says? Is it the "wasted land" of Wales — wasted by what Hog from the pages of history rather than myth — for which the Candle-bearer and the Priest of the Household have so long kept faith? Does the Sleeping Lord indeed

> ...... cock his weather-ear, enquiringly
> lest what's on the west wind
> > from over the rising contours
> may signify that in the broken
> > *tir y blaenau*
> these broken dregs of Troea
> > yet again muster?[130]

There is no forcing to this interpretation. There is the Geoffrey-echo again, long after the Milford bo'sun, and an infinitely stronger urge to remedy what was formerly seen as an imbalance. It is particularly interesting to observe David Jones using the "whoreson March-lands / of this Welshry"[131], the country round Hay and Capel-y-Ffin that he knew, the land where "the small black horses" (which he painted so effectively) "grass on the hunch"[132] of Arthur's shoulders, to ask his dangerous question. Can it be interpreted as a harmless literary démarche? I think not. Earlier in the poem he refers to

> > the long, long
> > and continuing power-struggle
> for the fair lands of Britain
> > and the ebb & flow of the devastation-
> waves of the war-bands
> > for no provinces of the West
> were longer contested than these provinces
> > nor is the end yet
> > for that tide rises higher
> nor can it now be stayed.[133]

Even here, it seems, he had in mind those Silures who defeated a

Roman legion in open battle and compelled the Normans to build a small copse of castles along the banks of the Usk and the Wye.

It is useful to relate the reverberating question of 'The Sleeping Lord' to a passage in a poem that I have so far omitted, 'The Dream of Private Clitus'. In this poem Clitus, a Roman soldier serving on the Limes Germanicus of the Empire, dreams that an enormous statue of the Tellus Mater (in reality a marble relief on the north road out of Rome which was dedicated in 9 B.C. after what was thought of as "the pacification of the world" by the Emperor Augustus) leans towards him and all but touches "the bivvy-sheets with her strong marble fingers"[134]. Clitus's mate, Lugo the Celt, though asleep in Clitus's dream, is, like him, caught up on the marble lap, "into that peace". The two of them, "ageless emeriti . . . a perpetual signification of Roma and her sons"[135], are high up on the wall outside the city's north gate. But Lugo wakes up and cries first "Modron . . . and then — but very low-voiced though: Porth Annwfyn", which latter phrase Clitus makes out as "Gate of Elysium"[136]. Later, outside the dream and back in the realities of warfare, Lugo is killed. He cries "loud the same cult-name, but not the last bit, for he was done before he could utter it"[137]. Clitus's optimistic understanding, reflecting the way in which the Romans paired the identities of Celtic and Roman gods in Gaul and Britain, is that "his Modron and our Matrona are one"[138]. Now *Annwn* or *Annwfn* has many translations, but *Elysium*, with its connotations of bliss, is not one of them: *Annwn* may be the other world, a bottomless gulf, an abyss, the deep, hell, the state or receptacle of the dead. Lugo, then, on first awakening, mistook his *Modron*, but opening his eyes more fully and seeing the marble hands, *sotto voce* recognised himself as consigned to hell, or at best to death. And Lugo *was* killed, crying on his real Mother. This is not the conclusion of the poem: the dream and its possible message are obscured by the portrait of the old sweat Brasso, a convincing irrelevancy which brings the reader's thought back to the supposed integration of the Roman army, its heterogeneity, and Clitus's fond belief that "Lugo fancied his weight as an inmate of our Asylum and reckoned himself as Ilian and as Urban as the Twins"[139].

But what Lugo mutters can hardly be mistaken. This poem is farther back in the movement of David Jones's sympathy: its point of reference is old-style Celtic rather than Welsh. But what it is saying seems to me more than the Milford bo'sun's discontent: it is a potential *break* with the whole idea of Empire, as 'The Sleeping Lord' is with that of Union. What, it may be asked, is David Jones trying to say?

Aneirin Talfan Davies asked him this outright in 1956 when he had read 'The Tutelar of the Place'. Did he intend a message for the present? David's reply was splendidly obfuscatory:

> ... *The Wall* and *The Tutelar*... have as their theme two aspects of much the same thing, viz. the abiding situation of the good and bad things of an *imperium* face to face with the local & diverse and loved things — which also have goodness and badness. You say, most rightly, that it applies to our present situation; but it was not written with that intention — far from it — yet I incline to think that *probably most* of the stuff I write is round and about this dilemma, *in differing ways*, because it is something which seems to me insoluble .... I mean, to our human understanding, it presents, throughout history, and in innumerable ways, problems which don't seem patient of being resolved.[140]

But Aneirin's query had plainly frightened him a little: he went back to it again in a letter of three days later:

> *The Tutelar of the Place* must *not* be thought of as a pleading for anything on my part. It is merely an expression of a state of mind which must have belonged to countless communities of people in various situations in history & that it corresponds with certain of *our feelings today* is accidental.[141]

It is difficult to accept these denials in full. That David did not intend a direct political message may well be agreed: despite his friendship with Saunders Lewis he was politically timid and quite unfitted to leave or aggravate his many long-term friends who were not Welsh: in his letters to the papers, as in the message he sent to support the Nationalist candidature of Valerie Wynne-Williams for Parliament, he had concentrated on the need to preserve the Welsh language: not one word aspired to Independence. Moreover, the poems that go far enough to make it seem possible that a message was intended are still too guarded for general understanding. What then may be said? The movement towards Wales in the later poems in *The Sleeping Lord* is unmistakable (though this may reflect a decision to publish rather than a change in the sentiment of what had perhaps long been written). Does it not, at the very least, suggest that the walls of *imperium* had been breached?

The best separate evidence for this comes from David's constant reference, in letters and in conversation[142] to the year 1282 and the end of what he thought of as Welsh independence. Amongst three unsolicited references to it in his letters to Aneirin Talfan is this of 16 December 1971:

> It is always a sad time of the year anyway & last Saturday [was] *unfed dydd ar ddeg o fis Rhagfyr* [11th December] near *Llanfair ym Muallt* [Builth] — the historians can say what they like — but I believe the *marwnadau* [elegies] of *Gruffydd ab yr Ynad Coch & Blyddyn Fardd* express the truth. Blyddyn Fardd's noble resignation (which comes through even in translation) would take some beating.[143]

There is, too, a long, involved footnote emphasising the significance of 1282 in his article entitled 'Wales and Visual Form'[144]. "The historians can say what they like", he says. And indeed they do doubt whether the independence that ended in 1282 was any sort of independence of *Wales*. But that is not the point here. What is David Jones doing with *independence* amongst his valued things? How does it sort with *imperium*?

It doesn't, of course, and it is a waste of time to seek to establish a political or constitutional balance. David, like many of us, was at odds within himself and the only resolution of opposites we can reasonably look for is that of victory and defeat, which may change in degree with the passage of time. The *dilemma* that he writes of in his letter to Aneirin Talfan[145] as being that of many people in different ages was nearer than that: it was *his* dilemma, and an obsessive one. The arguments of the poems are directed, often enough, by one part of himself against another. There is even an element of self-caricature. The frequent references to heterogeneity nag not merely at his fears but at the justification he had offered for his working methods. The rather ridiculous *Tellus Mater* figure, so unlikely for a dream, and the various references to marble in other poems, may satirise his own love of inscriptions (in themselves a better resolution of his dilemma — flexibility of shape within a fixed frame — than he managed in any of his writing after *In Parenthesis*). The *imperium* had been the emblem of his own need for strength and reassurance: Wales spoke to him constantly of freedom and a separate tradition. In the later years of his better health Wales came, of the two, to seem the more desirable and he moved towards it as far as he was able. The move was, after all, as much back to his beginnings as anywhere else.

NOTES

1.   *Dai Greatcoat: A self-portrait of David Jones in his letters*, ed. René Hague (London, 1980), p.241.
2.   Published by the David Jones Society in 1979, its sub-title is '*In Parenthesis* as Straight Reporting'.
3.   Colin Hughes, having taken many photographs of the terrain of battle around and in Mametz Wood, was encouraged by both David Jones and Wyn Griffith to undertake the full research which ultimately emerged in the form of an M. Phil. thesis for the Open University in 1975 entitled 'The Capture of Mametz Wood'.
4.   *David Jones: Letters to Vernon Watkins*, ed. Ruth Pryor (Cardiff, 1976), pp.56-57. The 14-page letter from which this quotation is taken is dated April 11th, 1962.
5.   *Epoch and Artist* by David Jones (London, 1959), p.27. Hereafter referred to as *E & A*.
6.   *The Long Conversation: A Memoir of David Jones* by William Blissett (London, 1981) p.118.
7.   *Mabon*, eds. Alun R. Jones & Gwyn Thomas, Vol.1 No. 5, Spring 1972, p.18. The information comes from a letter from David Jones to Saunders Lewis dated 'After Christmas 1971'.
8.   Colin Hughes has pointed out that the spelling "Welch", though the original spelling and now long since restored to use, was not in force during the First World War.
9.   *E & A*, p.28.
10.   *Dai Greatcoat*, pp.32-33.
11.   *Ibid.*, p.40.
12.   *Ibid.*, pp.42-43.
13.   p.24.
14.   *Vide* Thomas Dilworth, 'Wales and the Imagination of David Jones' in *The Anglo-Welsh Review*, No. 69, 1981, especially p.45.
15.   *Dai Greatcoat*, pp.47-48.
16.   *Ibid.*, p.23.
17.   Dilworth, *op. cit.*, p.42.
18.   Blissett, *op. cit.*, p.57.
19.   Dilworth, *op. cit.*, p.42.

20. *Dai Greatcoat*, p.26.
21. *Op. cit.*, p.95.
22. *Ibid.*, p.89.
23. *Ibid.*
24. *David Jones: Letters to a Friend*, ed. Aneirin Talfan Davies (Swansea, 1980), p.40.
25. *Dai Greatcoat*, p.204.
26. *Ibid.*, p.147.
27. *Ibid.*
28. *Ibid.*, p.137. Letter of 24 August.
29. *Ibid.*, p. 155. Letter of 17 December 1952.
30. *Ibid.*, p. 190. Letter of 22 May.
31. *Mabon* V, p.21.
32. *Dai Greatcoat*, p.194. Letter of 27 September 1963 to René Hague.
33. *Ibid.*, p.210.
34. *Ibid.*, p.58.
35. *Ibid.*, p.111.
36. *Ibid.*, p.28.
37. *IP*, Part 7, p.167.
38. *Ibid.*, xv.
39. *The Sleeping Lord*, p.106.
40. *Dai Greatcoat*, pp.75-76.
41. *Ibid.*, p.178.
42. A surprisingly high proportion of secondary schoolboys seen voluntarily square-bashing in the C.C.F. after school hours used to belong (if they do so no longer) to the category of those who, as a result of serious "spoiling" at home, were incapable of hard or consistent work at their academic studies.
43. *Dai Greatcoat*, pp.217-18.
44. *Ibid.*, p.249.
45. *Ibid.*, p.28.
46. The paradox of his spiritual condition is perhaps best exemplified by his many inscriptions, the fact that he should deliberately choose an art form which is, almost by definition, rigidly enclosed and shaped, and make of it something irregular, wayward and yet satisfying as a balance for that rigidity.
47. *Dai Greatcoat*, p.46.
48. *Ibid.*, p.123.
49. *Ibid.*, p.56.
50. *Mabon* V, p.20.
51. *Ibid.*
52. *Ibid.*
53. *Dai Greatcoat*, pp.102-03. Letter of 28 August 1940.
54. *The Dying Gaul*, p.146.
55. *Ibid.*
56. *Ibid.*, pp.99-100.
57. *Dai Greatcoat*, p.90. Letter of 11 April 1939.
58. *Ibid.*, p.93. Letter of 23 June 1939.
59. *Ibid.*, pp.115-17.
60. *Ibid.*, p.186.

61.   *Ibid.*, p.107.
62.   *Ibid.*, p.33.
63.   *Ibid.*, p.107.
63a.   *Ibid.*, p.92.
64.   *Ibid.*, p.246.
65.   *Ibid.*, p.156. Letter to Jim Ede, 17 December 1952.
66.   *The Anathemata* (London, 1952), p.50.
67.   The Book of Daniel, c.8, v.4.
68.   *The Anathemata*, p.176.
69.   *Dai Greatcoat*, p.120. Letter to Harman Grisewood.
70.   'The Tutelar of the Place': *The Sleeping Lord*, p.64.
71.   *The Anathemata*, p.115.
72.   The 1957 and 1958 letters are printed in *E. & A.*, pp.51-55. The 1956 one is referred to in the letter to Vernon Watkins following.
73.   *Letters to VW*, p.30.
74.   *Dai Greatcoat*, p.209.
75.   *Ibid.*, p.122.
76.   *Ibid.*, pp.245-46.
77.   *E. & A.*, pp.66-82. The publishers, however, did not make use of this Introduction until their 1958 edition of *Wild Wales*. *Dai Greatcoat*, p.164.
78.   *The Sleeping Lord*, p.110.
79.   *IP*, Preface, x.
80.   *Ibid.*, General Notes, note 4, pp. 191-92.
81.   *Ibid.*, p.83. *Vide* p.21 *supra* for the discovery of the Fretensis at Jerusalem.
82.   *Ibid.*, p.250.
83.   *Ibid.*, p.90.
84.   *The Sleeping Lord*, p.100.
85.   *Ibid.*, pp. 106 and 111.
86.   *Ibid.*, pp.111 and 107.
87.   *Ibid.*, p.104.
88.   *Ibid.*, p.101.
89.   *Ibid.*, p.103.
90.   *Ibid.*, p.104.
91.   *Ibid.*, p.110.
92.   *The Anathemata*, p.88.
93.   *Ibid.*, p.87.
94.   *Ibid.*, p.88.
95.   *Ibid.*, p.89.
96.   *Ibid.*, p.90.
97.   *Ibid.*, p.149.
98.   *Ibid.*, p.153.
99.   *Ibid.*, p.154.
100.   *David Jones* by René Hague (Cardiff, 1975), p.61. Undated letter from David Jones to the author about the Lady of the Pool.
101.   *The Anathemata*, p.164.
102.   *Ibid.*
103.   *Dai Greatcoat*, p.156.
104.   First published in *The Anglo-Welsh Review* No. 50 (Autumn 1973), pp.8-12

and subsequently in *Agenda*. In 1981 the Interim Press brought out the poem in an edition of its own but because the pages in it are not numbered reference hereunder is to its publication in *AWR*.

105.   *AWR*, p.8.
106.   *The Sleeping Lord*, p.14.
107.   *Ibid.*
108.   *Dai Greatcoat*, p.90.
109.   *The Sleeping Lord*, pp.12 and 13.
110.   *Ibid.*, p.11.
111.   *Ibid.*, p.14.
112.   *Ibid.*, p.39.
113.   *Ibid.*, p.41.
114.   *Ibid.*, p.37.
115.   c.12, v.4, I Corinthians.
116.   *The Sleeping Lord*, p.58.
117.   *Ibid.*, p.51.
118.   *Ibid.*, p.56.
119.   *Ibid.*, p.55.
120.   *Ibid.*
121.   *Ibid.*
122.   *Ibid.*, p.63.
123.   *Ibid.*, p.62.
124.   *Ibid.*, p.63.
125.   *Ibid.*, p.67.
126.   *Ibid.*, pp.89-90.
127.   *Ibid.*, p.91.
128.   *Ibid.*, p.87.
129.   *Ibid.*, p.96.
130.   *Ibid.*, p.95.
131.   *Ibid.*, p.96.
132.   *Ibid.*
133.   *Ibid.*, p.80.
134.   *Ibid.*, p.19.
135.   *Ibid.*, p.20.
136.   *Ibid.*
137.   *Ibid.*
138.   *Ibid.*
139.   *Ibid.*, p.16.
140.   *Letters to a Friend*, p.34.
141.   *Ibid.*, p.37.
142.   *The Long Conversation*, p.32.
143.   *Letters to a Friend*. p.113. The translations in brackets are presumably not part of David Jones' original letter but editorial insertions by Aneirin Talfan.
144.   *The Dying Gaul*, p.84.
145.   *Letters to a Friend*, p.34.

Lord Cutglass, Twenty Years After

"It sometimes seems", wrote John Ackerman in number 49 of *The Anglo-Welsh Review,* "as though there are two ways of disliking [Dylan] Thomas: one is to dislike him, the other to disparage the later poems." And that is, I believe, a fairly accurate summing up of the position of such detractors as dare to show their heads in 1973. I shall not, in this article, be concerned directly with the "disliking", except in so far as this may be seen as arising out of a conflict between the poet and his natural environment — more specifically, as having to do with the degree of his Welshness — and it is no part of my intention to go into the frequent excesses and the chronic wretchedness of the poet's life. My purpose is twofold: first, to look at certain aspects of Dylan Thomas's childhood and upbringing which appear to determine the degree of his Welshness and, not at all incidentally, his attitude to poetry, and second, to ascertain whether these aspects reflect, in the end, on the later poems — which have, in the last decade, become the King Charles's Head of any critical operation.

Perhaps we are now far enough away in time to treat the facts of Dylan's youth and upbringing with the "distancing" objectivity which the academic approach expects. And perhaps not. I remember, if still with some astonishment, how taken aback I was when, in attempting to raise a collection for Caitlin, on the news of Dylan's death in New York, I had to deal with a deputation which, with some hostility, urged me to drop the idea. The deputation did not, as it happens, represent what might be called the prim or the Nonconformist element in the community. It did, indeed, object to the "life" of the poet, but even more to what was felt to be the anti-Welshness, the general disservice to Wales which Dylan's attitude had appeared to represent. I was surprised then, and readers accustomed to years of an assessment which is, ostensibly, purely literary will be surprised now. But the two responses which Dylan

evoked in Wales cannot simply be divided into the suspicion and the
hostility of Welsh-speakers on the one hand and the pride and
amusement of English-speakers on the other. The original
equivocation which provoked them was there in the nature of the poet
himself. His own attitude to Wales was based first on deprivation and
the clever hostility that sometimes comes from it, then on a gradual
realization of loss and a disillusionment with the ambitions that had
created that loss (in his parents and himself). My thesis is not merely
that these factors reveal themselves in the letters and ultimately, if less
clearly, in the poetry, but that the first phase, even after its personal
effects had appeared to fade, remained definitive, even limiting, in the
poetry — particularly perhaps in the later poems by which many
critics assume that Dylan Thomas stands or falls.

Outside Wales people experienced, and experience, some
difficulty in understanding the duality of response from readers and
hearers which was characteristic of Dylan's reputation in his lifetime,
because they tend to believe that his life was typical of that of the
uninhibited Celt, that he wrote as he did *because* he was Welsh (in
terms of his subject-preoccupations and of the grandness of the
manner) and that as a poet he was a Welsh type, that is, he rose
naturally from a Welsh background. Some of these assumptions are,
if not absolutely wrong, much more dubiously based than is
commonly realized. They take their colour from the superficialities of
the poet's names — Dylan, the golden-haired boy of the *Mabinogion*
story, *Dylan Eil Ton,* Sea Son of the Wave who became at once "a part
of the sea", and Marlais, the bardic name of his nineteenth century
great-uncle, who earned a reputation both as a radical preacher and
as a poet. These names, which fit his father's attitude to the Welsh
heritage so little, can be explained only as a momentary atavism
created by the fact of a son's birth. Nothing else about Dylan (a name
which he was quite content to have pronounced *Dillen* or *Dillun* by his
cronies) was anywhere near as Welsh as this involuntary prefix. Let
me explain this view more fully.

In the first place he was born in Swansea, which in the eighteenth
century was well-known as an *English* watering-place, a resort of the
upper classes and minor literary figures like Walter Savage Landor.
Number 5 Cwmdonkin Drive is a house in a very steep street in the
Uplands area, which, with Mumbles and Sketty and the places
between, best exemplified the Little Englander complex. Dylan
Thomas knew almost no Welsh himself and would have heard none

amongst his playmates, most of them the sons of shopkeepers or aspiring professional men. When he was a boy, two-thirds of the people of Swansea spoke English only, and scarcely any were monoglot Welsh. Yet north-west of the town, away from the English-speaking playground of Gower, the old, agricultural Wales of "the good, bad boys from the lonely farms" rubbed shoulders with the Welshness of the miners of Pontardulais and Ammanford, and north-eastwards the Swansea Valley itself, as it climbed only one degree to Morriston and Clydach, echoed with voices more unashamedly Welsh. The real Wales indeed, from its forward points at copper-poisoned Landore, Llangyfelach and Gorseinon, was still watching the privileged, commercial enclave of Swansea, but its representatives were allowed in only to market, to inhabit some of the ramshackle houses in the dock area and to beachcomb in times of holiday. When Dylan Thomas wrote that

> outside, a *strange* Wales, coal-pitted, mountained, river run, full,
> so far as I knew, of choirs and sheep and story-book tall hats,
> moved about its business which was none of mine

he was antithesising merrily, writing up what his childhood only part comprehended. But there was an important truth there just the same. He knew *about* Wales right enough; he didn't really imagine the women wore tall hats. But he hadn't been inside the tradition of Wales. He had been to Sunday School when staying with his aunt "Dosie" at English-speaking Newton, where his uncle, David Rees, was minister of Paraclete, but this was as a small child. He had no real notion of what it was like, either morally or spiritually, to have been brought up in the Welsh Nonconformist tradition. What he saw of it he saw from the dissident window of No. 5 Cwmdonkin Drive, from the refuge provided by a lapsed father. Out of that window he was what he calls in 'Do you not father me' *the wanton starer:*

> Sunday in Wales. The Sunday-walkers have slunk out of the
> warrens in which they sleep and breed all the unholy week, have
> put on their black suits, reddest eyes, and meanest expressions,
> and are now marching up the hill past my window . . . I see the
> rehearsed gestures, the correct smiles, the grey cells revolving
> around nothing under the godly bowlers. I see the unborn
> children struggling up the hill in their mothers, beating on the
> jailing slab of the womb, little realizing what a smugger prison

they wish to leap into.

He was writing here to Pamela Hansford Johnson (15 April 1934) and
what he was describing was a rapidly declining sabbatarianism in a
Swansea where Puritan influnces had always been weaker than in
Welsh-speaking Wales. What we really hear, of course, is the voice of
the young satirist identifying himself as made for better things by
separating himself from the bourgeois and philistine and provincial
environment (*his* probable words, not mine).

> Am I not all of you by the directed sea
> Where bird and shell are babbling in my tower?
> > ('Do you not father me')

No, indeed not. Most certainly not. Not in that clever adolescence of
his.

But the point I have tried to make thus far is the smaller of two. If
Dylan Thomas was separated, through no fault of his own, from the
older Welshness of Wales, that was a separation shared by hundreds
of thousands of others, not a few of them poets and writers. If he added
his own personal will to this separation, he was not alone in this either,
and the root cause lies in a deprivation that was the more serious
because deliberate.

If Swansea was relatively weak in Welsh tradition, it was a lack that
his home could have satisfied. But although his parents both spoke
Welsh (or had at one time spoken Welsh) they never used the
language at No. 5 Cwmdonkin Drive "(the young Dylan's *Glamorgan
villa*) with its neo-Georgian respectability, its middle-class decorative
gestures in knitted texts and reproduction Greek Statues, and its
resident maid" (Walford Davies, *Dylan Thomas,* p.4). Dylan's father,
David John Thomas, who was intellectually and personally the
dominant partner, had forsworn his Welshness in a way
unfortunately characteristic of many ambitious Welshmen sixty
years ago. This particular brand of Dic-Shon-Dafyddism is
uncommon now amongst the professional classes of Wales, who may
find it hard to appreciate that ethic which insisted that to *get on in the
world,* socially, professionally or commercially, it was essential to
discard Welsh and embrace English. In the case of David John
Thomas the discarding was determined and comprehensive: he had
his son and daughter given elocution lessons, at which there was born

Lord Cutglass: he cut himself off absolutely from his Welsh-speaking relatives to the west — never going to see them and never letting his children deputise for him: and he had long since severed all connection with the Unitarian practice and tradition of his great-uncle Gwilym Marles, from whose radicalism he had distanced himself even further. The son of a railwayman from Carmarthen, David John Thomas had taken first-class honours in English at the University College of Wales, Aberystwyth: he was a poet manqué, with a fine reading voice but no sufficient poems: he was a good, though severe, teacher with the sort of histrionic talent that possession of such a voice would suggest: and he regarded his position as Senior English Master at Swansea Grammar School as status less than worthy of his academic record. (It may be mentioned, in parenthesis, that he was perhaps not quite unjustified in that opinion. When, in 1922, the post of Professor of English at the new University College was advertised, he applied for it but was passed over. The man ultimately appointed had academic qualifications inferior to his). His library was the library of a particularly alert and well-read teacher of English who was alive to contemporary developments in poetry and drama, but his attitude to life was negative. Indeed, he had chosen literature instead of life, having decided long since to maltreat and sever the lifeline that came down to him.

For the young Dylan, then, this deprivation was decisive. That his mother was still in contact with her relations in Welsh-speaking Wales and sent her son on visits to them was ultimately important but not immediately so, because Dylan, in his cleverly superior adolescence, despised his mother's garrulity and lack of intellect, taking his father's stance in this as in most matters. His Aunt Annie at Llangain and her family, kind as they were to the superior young man who sometimes came and stayed, partook in his mind of his mother's folly and chattering concern. Welsh-speaking Wales, as we shall see, was full of similar mindless dolts.

What was left of the Welsh umbilical cord, what few frayings remained? First, there was the Bible, which D.J. Thomas, though an agnostic, read regularly to his son from his earliest years — the Bible as literature and with it the sonority of D.J.'s voice. That this was of the utmost importance I hope to show later. Of tradition little remained beyond a few oft-told tales of great-uncle Gwilym Marles: as a cub reporter on *The Swansea Evening Post* and as young-man-about-the-pubs he heard plenty of gossip about the "primitives" higher up the

Valley and was regaled in The Mermaid at Newton or elsewhere upon his friend Wynford Vaughan Thomas's epics of his mythical preacher Jones Goppa. But friends from a more genuinely Welsh background like Wynford were a rarity: Dylan's Wales was what Swansea knew of it, and the most "emancipated" part of Swansea at that. In brief, he never had first-hand knowledge of what it felt like to belong to a *Welsh* community — in this respect he was totally unlike, say, Glyn Jones or Idris Davies and perhaps Alun Lewis, wholly or partially bereft of the Welsh language as they too were. He had more in common with Vernon Watkins, who lived first in Swansea and then in Gower and was sent away to school at Repton, but with Vernon the deprivation was circumstantial and gradual, involving none of the initial contempt and the ultimate need for redress that Dylan felt. In the case of Alun Lewis, although he too was sent to boarding school, his roots in the basic radicalism and democratic feeling of Welsh community life were so strong that his poetic sensitivity was unable, in the end, to withstand the weight of the pity and the alienation he felt in India. He died, it may be said, for reasons precisely the opposite of those which hampered Dylan Thomas who, so far from being a product of a Welsh community, had much more in common with boys of the sixties and seventies in not being a product of a community at all. When Dylan made a political or social gesture it was almost always at second-hand. The only letter he ever wrote to the press, dated January 14 1934, was intended to attack the restrictive attitudes of Nonconformity. In this he urged the editor to give his readers

> some little consciousness of the immoral restrictions placed upon them, of the humbug and smug respectability that works behind them all their handcuffed days, and to do this, not from any political bias, but from the undeniable conviction that the God is not the lukewarm soup and starch of the chapels, but the red hot grains of love and life distributed equally and impartially among us all.

He had been listening, of course, to his left-wing Socialist friend Bert Trick (whom he called, wrongly, his "Communist grocer" and who gave him a severe dressing-down for breaking into print in this way). His own freedom from community pressures of any kind will appear presently and one may well wonder in whom, in the end, the greater smugness lay. His inability to write politically-motivated or socially conscious poems is well-known (the only serious attempt he made here emerged as the virtually abstract 'The hand that signed the paper'), though it must be admitted that there is more to this than a self-centred, romantic attitude and plain ignorance about the nature of the public good.

It may be well at this point to document a little Dylan's early hatred of the Wales which circumscribed Swansea. It was a country of "miles of desolate fields and scattered farmhouses", in which it was impossible to speak to anyone except about "the prospect of rain and the quickest way to snare rabbits" (Letter to Pamela Hansford Johnson, late October 1933). At Llangain (his Uncle Tom's house) he could hear "the beastly little brook that goes gingle-gingle past this room" and had to converse, if only for a few moments, with a man with close-set eyes like those of "the terrible thing he held in his hand", Billy Fach the ferret. One night "the long road to Llanstephan" (which he had to walk from his Aunt Ann's farm because he was out of cigarettes) was "bounded by trees and farmers' boys pressed amorously upon the udders of their dairy-maids", and in the end there was no cigarette machine in Llanstephan (ditto, early November 1933). It was a crude world of "farmers . . . sitting at their fires, looking into the blazing wood and thinking of God knows what littlenesses", of stuffed foxes and china dogs, stale ferns, Fauntleroy photographs of himself, insanitary buildings and stupid relatives who spoiled and petted him beyond endurance. On the way to this perpetually rained-upon backwater he had passed through little mining townships where he had seen "little colliers, diseased in mind and body as only the Welsh can be, standing in groups outside the Welfare Hall". It was a horrible world, that Wales, and even in London some years later he did not wish to consort with Welshmen unless they had been friends of his in Swansea. To Pamela Hansford Johnson, the penfriend with whom he was already prepared to be in love, he wrote in October 1933:

> It's impossible for me to tell you how much I want to get out of it all, out of the narrowness and dirtiness, out of the eternal ugliness of the Welsh people and all that belongs to them, out of the pettiness of a mother I don't care for and the giggling batch of relatives . . . I shall have to get out soon or there will be no need. I'm sick and this bloody country's killing me.

As he said on a later occasion,

Land of my fathers, my fathers can keep it.

Much of this self-conscious arrogance soon disappeared. It was, in any case, part of the *âme damnée* pose which he dropped when he found that it did not impress Pamela. But it had another root in his great desire to get to London. "The fact that I am unemployed helps . . . to add to my natural hatred of Wales" he wrote in March 1934 to Stephen Spender, one of the well-known poets who had already picked out his work as startlingly different. But that unemployment had been deliberately willed, and the mere fact that, irrespective of economics, he saw his *métier* as being in London tells us something important about what his notion of being a poet was.

Perhaps I ought to make plain at this point why I emphasise Dylan's background so strongly. It is because I see in it the key to his poetic development or, rather, the keys, because there was a closing and an opening, not of the same door. Let me indicate first how closely Swansea and the major part of his poetic output are intertwined. Between the ages of fifteen and a half and nineteen and a half Dylan Thomas wrote over 250 poems which he considered successful enough to be transcribed into his four cheap red notebooks (threepenny ones with Danger Don'ts on the back cover) and of these fifty-four, most of them considerably revised, he published in his lifetime. That means that more than half of all the poems he chose to publish (as distinct from those that have been published since by Daniel Jones) were given their basic or original form before he left Swansea. That basic form is, of course, more important in terms of the subject-matter, the poetic preoccupation, it contained, than in its precise connection with the more polished version that appeared in *18 Poems, 25 Poems* or any later book. It is not my purpose here to examine this subject-matter closely: it must be sufficient to say that whether, using John Donne and others, he attempted a metaphysic of the bodily functions, whether his work was a genuine reflection of a loss of identity in the womb (as David Holbrook would seem to be suggesting in *The Code of Night*) or whether, as Raymond L. Hogler has recently indicated (in *The Anglo-Welsh Review* Nos. 47 & 48), he deliberately played the poetry market until he found a subject-matter and a mode that would make his mark for him in the shortest possible time, one thing is obvious enough: his poetry was inchoate, suffocatingly romantic and obscure, reflecting very little of what might be called objective life and background experience in the community to which he nominally belonged. His revisions, of course, often tend towards clarification and in one or two notable instances they alter the whole tone of what little he had written about that objective life and experience.

His friend Vernon Watkins gave it as his opinion that Dylan had at the age of twenty-four what might be called a religious experience. But then Vernon, who thought the best of everyone, was convinced that Dylan afterwards became "a Blakean Christian". This postulated experience affected Dylan's prose immediately and his poetry more slowly, precisely because here he was not writing afresh but revising and modifying older material. The change, Vernon asserted, is most succinctly expressed in 'Once it was the colour of saying', where two pairs of lines indicate the turning point:

> The gentle seaslides of saying I must undo
> That all the charmingly drowned arise to cockcrow and kill.
>
> Now my saying shall be my undoing,
> And every stone I wind off like a reel.

Thereafter the *Roget's Thesaurus* formula-writing came to an end and alterations made in the drafts of poems were "all away from ironical statement and in the direction of religious truth".

Whether we accept this diagnosis or whether we prefer to talk about the process of growing up and unwinding, about the disillusion with the metropolis that had once gleamed golden like the towers of Samarkand, or about the natural revival of feeling for Wales which almost every Welshman experiences when he's away from it and can see it in balance against other societies and other values, in 1938 (when Dylan was twenty-four) we have a notable example of re-writing which gave us one of his best-known poems. Let us go back to the original version.

In January 1933 Dylan wrote to his friend Trevor Hughes saying that his Aunt Ann was in Carmarthen Infirmary dying of cancer of the womb. Her prospective death lent "a little welcome melodrama to the drawing-room tragi-comedy of my most uneventful life". He analysed at length his total unmovedness at the expected disappearance of one who loved him. "Many summer weeks I spent happily with the cancered aunt on her insanitary farm. She loved me quite inordinately, gave me sweets and money, though she could little

afford it, petted, and spoiled me. She writes — is it, I wonder, a past
tense yet — regularly. Her postscripts are endearing. She still loves —
or loved — me, though I don't know why". It was, for him, a theatrical
occasion upon which he could analyse his own selfishness. On the day
of the funeral he wrote a poem into his red notebook which Professor
Ralph Maud's book, *Poet in the Making,* makes available for us. This is
the final stanza of that poem;

> Another gossips' toy has lost its use,
> Broken lies buried amid broken toys,
> Of flesh and bone lies hungry for the flies,
> Waits for the natron and the mummy paint
> With dead lips pursed and dry bright eyes,
> Another well of rumours and cold lies
> Has dried and one more joke has lost its point.

Even for "the cancered aunt on her insanitary farm" this was a
ruthlessly cold conclusion.

But in 1938, when he re-wrote it into that well-known poem, 'After
the Funeral', he became not merely "Ann's bard on a raised hearth"
but "a desolate boy who slits his throat / In the dark of the coffin". The
first line, with its satiric intention, remains —

> After the funeral, mule praises, brays,

but the conclusion has become a triumphant paean of remembrance:

> Her flesh was meek as milk, but this skyward statue
> With the wild breast and blessed and giant skull
> Is carved from her in a room with a wet window
> In a fiercely mourning house in a crooked year.
> I know her scrubbed and sour humble hands
> Lie with religion in their cramp, her threadbare
> Whisper in a damp word, her wits drilled hollow,
> Her fist of a face died clenched on a round pain;
> And sculptured Ann is seventy years of stone.
> These cloud-sopped, marble hands, this monumental
> Argument of the hewn voice, gesture and psalm,
> Storm me forever over her grave until
> The stuffed lung of the fox twitch and cry Love
> And the strutting fern lay seeds on the black sill.

Here the old disenchantment is exorcised by the deliberate use of those cold front-parlour ornaments, the stuffed fox and the stale fern: their "activity" activates all that was previously trivial and stagnant and stale-smelling: the poem is not merely the vindication of that Welsh rural atmosphere which the stories were to complete — it accepts the validity of the religious convention that was central to that atmosphere, the *scrubbed and sour humble hands,* the fierceness of the mourning, the idea that somehow this mourning can and will ultimately be contained in the graveyard statue, so that the *scrubbed and sour humble hands* become *cloud-sopped, marble* and are fixed forever in a speaking gesture which points heavenward, is psalmic. This *monumental argument,* the poet is telling us, *storms* him *forever* now.

It is a complete reversal of the arrogance of those letters to Pamela, but it uses the same vision, turning it inside out. It's not a new, matured vision which has a different slant, which is mediated through developing and thoughtful ideas based on other experience. This is partly because it is *remembered* — *re-remembered,* if you like — but it is basic to my argument that this new, developing thought is missing from Dylan Thomas's later work in any case. Indeed, another look is needed here at his childhood and youth if we are to reach a conclusion both about the degree of his *Anglo-Welshness* and about the relation of that childhood and youth to the nature and quality of the later poems.

Spoiling of children in a Welsh community used to be the rule rather than the exception (though I hasten to comment that that spoiling had nothing in common with the modern "buying" or bribing of the child by the provision of *things* — toys, machines and so on — as a substitute for personal attention). But such spoiling almost always stopped short of going soft on academic effort. The Welsh boy had to work hard at school and college. Education was deemed by almost everybody of the first importance. But Dylan's mother was so soft with him that a sickly child with weak lungs and what his wife Caitlin afterwards called "those chicken bones of his" was allowed to stay away from school altogether until he was seven and to retire to bed whenever life became too much for him (which was frequently). In the result he did exactly what he wanted, misbehaving badly outside and retiring to the safe haven of home whenever the going got rough. Undoubtedly the personal incompetence and indiscipline of his later life begin here: the self-centredness too. He wrote poems, tens and hundreds of them, from the beginning, but he would do nothing else, not even when he went to Swansea Grammar School.

He was top in English and bottom in every other subject and not even his father's presence as a member of staff could prevent it. Moreover, having long ago routed his mother, he resisted his father's wish that he should go to university by a cunning insistence that he wanted nothing except to be a poet — a ploy which he knew, or guessed, touched his father's deepest ambition for him. These facts are important only in so far as they reveal, first, that the concept of duty, however lightly phrased, and wherever directed — to his parents, his school or the community of which he was ostensibly part — had never had great meaning for him and that *involvement* (except in an exercise like the school magazine which was closely related to his real apprenticeship) was almost entirely absent from his experience: second, that his education, except in English literature, was remarkably limited and his sense of any wider academic discipline small: and third, that his conception of being a poet was single-minded, professional, individualistic, exclusive of all else. The second and third factors impelled me to state elsewhere that Dylan Thomas was not so much an Anglo-Welsh poet as a poet *á l'anglaise,* and although I can now see factors possibly no less weighty which would point to the opposite conclusion the matter is so essentially arguable that it is worth examining it in more detail.

It was in his father's brown study (those words are to be taken literally) that he read voluminously and "wrote imitations of whatever I happened, moon-and-print struck, to be goggling at and gorging at the time". His father read Shakespeare to him at the age of four, sweeping his mother's protests aside. The same resonant voice read the Bible to him frequently. In later recollection he wrote:

> I bulldozed through print, tore through the babbling dead like a tank with a memory. On the very green fields of my youth I stomped pun-shod and neigh-nonnied in a nosebag of adjectives. I *had* to imitate and parody, consciously and unconsciously: I had to try to learn what made words tick, beat, blaze, because I wanted to write what I wanted to write before I knew how to write or what I wanted to.

He is admitting there to the precedence both of the desire to write and the preoccupation with words over the emergence of a subject-matter which of itself might compel him to write. But certainly the breadth of his preparatory reading was all but incredible for one of his age. What we need to understand clearly is that this reading was done, all of it, so that the poet might learn his trade, vocationally, not for any high and general academic ideal. Indeed, the whole academic approach became more and more hateful to Dylan because, in the first place, he had chosen to ignore it, because, in the second place and consequentially, he had failed academically, and because, in the third place and again consequentially, he began to develop an inferiority complex about it. His deficiencies began to show in his twenties: he was still sharp, he picked up a lot at second-hand — but the young man who had commented so precociously on Pamela Hansford-Johnson's poems, whose knowledge of the "scene" made his reviews of published poetry so masterly, whose perceptions of the literariness of some of Vernon Watkins's cadences were near-infallible, the young man, in brief, who had so spectacularly chosen literature instead of life, never really added much to his poetic material, after he left Swansea, from the reservoir of an educated and thoughtful mind. That he could write brilliant film-scripts is not in doubt: technically he remained second to none. But his reading fell away and he had never, since he went into the cloud of his poetry-packed adolescence, been either a thinker or more than an intensely subjective observer of a wider life. It was this lack of development, I believe, that made him so often refuse to answer questions on the occasion of his many readings and recitals. He would read in that organ voice of his and refuse to speak thereafter. He was sure that the academics were getting at him or would want to get at him and he was equally sure that if he began to argue he would be found out. It is not surprising that he retreated, for his subject-matter, into the one region where criticism could not follow him, the one region where subjective memory had a validity equal to or even superior to that of fact — the world of childhood. Old insanitary Fern Hill became the perfect refuge.

That extraordinary early fertility, I suspect, had exhausted itself. Once it was all words, "Once it was the colour of saying", and when he began to feel that a development of thought from the original crux was required, he found it increasingly difficult to provide. Was he played out as a poet? Was his legend incommoded by his living as long as he did? What kind of a poet did he consider himself to be?

Early in November 1933 he referred in a letter to Pamela Hansford Johnson to a "damned diabetic doctor" who had told him he had only four years to live. This statement he made several times, always to people who did not know him well or were not in a position to check his health. All his life he had been dying every time he took a knock and undoubtedly the image of the damned, doomed and dissolute poet he was creating required the suggestion that he had TB. Rayner Heppenstall recalled that in February 1936 he and Dylan went to a pub in the morning.

> As we went out into the cold Dylan began to cough and spit.
> He looked down at his spittle in the roadway and said: 'Blood, boy! That's the stuff'.

There was nothing seriously wrong with his lungs. Had he not indeed won the cross-country at school several times? But the image he required was one of early death. His father had cancer of the tongue in 1933: Dylan was already, as Professor Maud has noted, "a veteran graveyard poet". But in whose image was he making himself? I haven't the smallest doubt. It was that of John Keats. The name of Keats comes up in his letters more often, far more often, than that of any other poet. *He* was a lyric poet and he died at the age of twenty-six of tuberculosis. Very significantly, at the end of his life Dylan said to John Davenport: "I can't go on. I've already had twice as much of it as Keats had." If it was turning out to be a distance-race after all, he had employed the wrong tactics at the beginning.

These points, then, are all connected. Dylan wasn't going to educate himself in full because there wasn't time. As Constantine Fitzgibbon remarked of him, "A man who is to be hanged next week will not start to learn Chinese . . . All his life the clocks ticked away his death for him as they did for his Lord Cutglass in *Under Milk Wood*." Lord Cutglass, you will remember, was his nickname amongst friends in Swansea. It was quite plain *whose* metaphorical house was full of clocks.

This needs to be related ultimately to what I said earlier about possible effects upon his later work. But for the moment I am concerned to "place" Dylan, to set him in his true relationship with Wales and the poets whom we call Anglo-Welsh. Was he recognisably a Welshman in his poetry? When Fitzgibbon said that "no major English poet has ever been as Welsh as was Dylan" he was begging too many questions for his statement to have any value. Let me assemble first those points which suggest that he saw himself as an *English* poet who happened, by accident of birth, to belong to the geographical area of Wales.

Amongst these I do not, of course, count his use of the English language and the priority he gave to that. Any Anglo-Welsh poet, compelled by his linguistic inheritance, must necessarily do the same. But we have seen — and this is the true first point — that his literary ① field of reference was entirely English, by his father's decision. He was deliberately cut off from such Welsh traditions and influences as might reasonably have affected the subject-matter of his writing. This point is underlined by his own endorsement of his father's attitude, by his self-regard, by his non-involvement in a Welshness of life which was available, if in diluted form, even in Swansea. Secondly, this ② Englishness of his field of reference is given active form in his desire to go to London. This was where, he believed, English poetry was born and made. Thirdly, his intent to be a poet and nothing else was ③ intensely romantic and integral to the English romantic tradition. Poets in Welsh were almost always part of the community, writing for it: they were part-time poets, farmers, shop-keepers, shepherds, preachers, teachers: they did not see themselves primarily as individualists and romantics because they had another position from which to see the community and contribute to it. Anglo-Welsh poets of the first generation tended to inherit this attitude. Dylan, in insisting that he was never to be anything other than a poet, was accepting an alien model. Although he was for a time a reporter, he equivocated even about this brief experience in his first letter to Glyn Jones when he said: "I am not unemployed for the reason that I have never been employed." It was an untruth fashioned for his image.

Fourthly, his precocity, inseparable in practice from his notion of ④ the full-time romantic poet who had not long to live, was no part of Welsh practice. It was generally believed in Wales that the poet spoke to his fellows from *experience,* and it was therefore advisable to be old enough to have some. Fifthly and sixthly, his dismissal of education, ⑤–⑥ so dear to the Welsh heart, and the absence in him of any noticeable social commitment — again alien to the socialism or radicalsim of genuinely Welsh communities — all mark him as non-Welsh, like his accent. It was certainly an oddity that England in the thirties produced, in Auden, Spender, Day Lewis and MacNeice, a dominant group of poets whose philosophy of poetry was in these last respects close to the Welsh practice, while Wales sent to London a sonorous romantic for whom the matter of society seemed to have little interest.

The fact remains, however, that Dylan was recognized as a

Welshman by more than the "instant Dylan" he could turn on for his
cronies. The Welsh-ness was there, it was asserted, in the poetry.
What does this mean?

The first answer I would give is perhaps superficial when it is
isolated, but as part of a complex of answers it is true enough. Many
readers recognized a biblical tone about much of his work, partly a
matter of vocabulary — an Authorized Version atmosphere,
generated by words that are short, basic and old-fashioned rather
than fashionable. Here is the first stanza of 'Before I knocked', one of
the best of his earlier poems:

> Before I knocked and flesh let enter,
> With liquid hands tapped on the womb,
> I who was shapeless as the water
> That shaped the Jordan near my home
> Was brother to Mnetha's daughter
> And sister to the fathering worm.

Even more the last two lines of a later stanza:

> My heart knew love, my belly hunger;
> I smelt the maggot in my stool.

The Old Testament is perhaps the most obvious provider, but we
cannot ignore Donne (the *Devotions* as well as the *Poems*), Blake, whose
Prophetic Books gave Dylan the obscure Mnetha he mentions, and
Milton. The Welsh, of course, have no exclusive rights to the Bible
and the effect of the vocabulary on its own is, as Dylan's reading would
suggest it ought to be, Anglo-Saxon. It is the language shaped during
and after Elizabethan times by the Puritan tradition — even if that
language is used for strange and seemingly unPuritanical purposes.

Why do I suggest, then, that a Biblical tone is a Welsh quality?
Well, the word *tone* is the key. It is tone, not vocabulary, that suggests
Welshness in Dylan. And the tone is a preaching tone, a sonorousness
of delivery, very occasionally rising to *hwyl*, but never falling to the
conversational. It has been suggested that this tone is a manifestation
of *bardic impersonality*, but I see little contact with the bardic in Dylan's
story. Instead I hear the cadences of the voice of David John Thomas
as he read the Bible to his young son, the cadences of a man who
thought he had cut off his Welsh heritage for good but nevertheless
carried ineradicably in his voice-habit the remembrance of the old

Welsh preachers of West Wales. The Bible was literature, the
language often poetry. Could the young Dylan have failed to associate
his father's tone with it? Doubtless Wynford Vaughan Thomas on
many occasions subsequently simulated the *hwyl* of the Rev. Jones
Goppa. Wales was full of action stories of preachers in those days.

Then, closely associated with it — and another function of the
preaching zeal which was part of Dylan's being without his knowing it
— was the habit of *affirmation*. Very often one may feel that the ②
affirmation is based on nothing or next to nothing — what can be
offered, for instance, as a logical lead-up to the repeated declaration
that "Death shall have no dominion"? Undoubtedly the reader,
especially when reading or listening to the early poems, assumes that
he is dealing with a profound and complicated metaphysic and that
the affirmation appears to him isolated only because he has not
understood what went before. But as the poems became more
"open", this affirmatory style, enormously successful as it is, can be
seen to be standing up on its own. If we take the "argument" of 'A
Refusal to Mourn the Death, by Fire, of a Child in London' (to my
mind one of the most enduringly attractive of all Dylan's poems) we
may ask, cynically, what kind of *other* death the reader was foolishly
expecting. And what kind of assurance is it that prompts the poet so
dramatically to refuse to mourn? Is it sufficient, as the poem does, to
suggest that the child goes to join the "first dead" and becomes one
with the Earth-Mother in corruption and — corruption and what?
Rebirth? Is it because the child's body enters the vegetable cycle that
it will never afterwards suffer death? It is not my purpose here to
pursue the meaning of this poem or others. I merely want to suggest
that the strength of the affirmation is disproportionate to the strength
of the supposed reasons for it. This, again, is an aspect of the
preacher's manner — and I intend no cynicism: in a brief sermon
there usually isn't time for all the run-up arguments, only for the
asseverative conclusion.

Is this Welsh? No, not specifically. Zeal is a characteristic of poor
and unprivileged societies everywhere. But Dylan was in Wales and of
Wales and there can be no question where he got it from.

Perhaps I may touch on another point which emerges from the
same poem. It *sounds* intensely religious. No, that is inexact, there are
present in it religious or sacramental terms which seem integral to its
argument: *the round / Zion of the water bead, the synagogue of the ear of corn,
salt seed, valley of sackcloth, stations of the breath*. All this is there to

strengthen and validate the affirmation, though the affirmation itself
is not Christian at all. It would not be difficult to point to instances of
the use of Christian terminology which are blasphemous — "my Jack
of Christ" will serve for one — and one is compelled to the conclusion
that this terminology, this particular imagery, *comes in a package with*
the affirmation — not perhaps out of deliberate intention to mislead
or deceive so much as out of an inability to separate one element of the
inheritance from the other. Dylan was unusually dependent on that
earliest period of his life for the poetic images he developed. That
Biblical terminology was there, part of him, inextricably, even though
he often wished to use it for different and, as we should think, strange
purposes.

There is the Welshness, then. The Nonconformist preaching
tradition with all its outward trappings but deprived of the faith that
fired it. The tone of voice not entirely typical, but constant — *part* of
poetry for him. He was like a Puritan version of the lapsed priest (see
Joyce: *Ulysses*, Pt.II, sect.12 as a source for *Under Milk Wood*).

I must, however, mention briefly one other consideration.
Although Dylan Thomas began by experimenting with free verse the
main body of his poetry is characterized by a determination to achieve
and impose on the thought the most demanding form. It is, I believe,
useless to talk about an inheritance from Welsh poetry, in which the
requirements of *cynghanedd* had for centuries appeared to place
intricacy of form above poetic content — useless because Dylan could
not have read such poems and never displayed (unlike Gerard
Manley Hopkins) any interest in them. How, then, do we explain this
special passion? Vernon Watkins, saying of himself that he didn't care
for tennis without a net, added that Dylan Thomas would have liked
two nets. To explain this passion for poetic form as in some way native
to a Welshman I feel to be highly dangerous and in the end
unsupportable by argument. Nor am I very much happier with the
idea that Dylan saw the poet as *maker* — in the sense of craftsman —
which was part of the bardic tradition, for the reason that I have
already mentioned, that he knew little or nothing of that tradition. We
must simply accept two similarities that cannot be adequately
connected by argument — the tradition of formal intricacy in Welsh
poetry and the kind of demanding versification to which Dylan
Thomas felt impelled, a form in which at first he packed his images so
tightly that the narrative or thought line was obscured and later the
individual line was so decorated verbally that the effect is sometimes

as cloying as the earlier works were difficult. Where, one asks oneself helplessly, where in all his reading of Keats, Milton, Donne and others, did he find anything like his plan for the Prologue to the *Collected Poems*, in which 102 lines rhyme 1 with 102, 2 with 101 and so on? One can see the derivation of the 'Vision and Prayer' poems, shaped on the page, from George Herbert, whom we know he had read and studied. But what of the others? Hopkins might be a link with Welsh poetry, and Dylan was perhaps disingenuous in denying his influence. What we have to accept is that Dylan was a word-man, a punster who was sonorous rather than cross-word-puzzlish, and that the individual word or the grouping of words was, until very late in his poetic life, as important, more important, than the total content of what he had to say. And this was certainly true of a good deal of poetry in Welsh.

Without attempting a balance to this complicated equation, I must now turn quickly and finally to my other problem. Dylan returned to Wales, living during the war for a time at New Quay, and later, more permanently, at Laugharne, where much of his later work was written in the shed at the top of the Boat House garden. There is one curious and important thing about his location at Laugharne. The English-Welsh linguistic line is strangely broken there: Laugharne is English-speaking, but across the Taf estuary lies the Welsh-speaking countryside of his youthful experience, some of its features visible from the Boat House window. Is it not apparent that this was the perfect way of keeping that memory — that re-remembering, if we recall 'After the Funeral' — unblurred, the physical features in sight and visitable if need be, but the personal and speech impressions unaltered by the overlay of more mature impressions?

However that may be, I must proceed by telescoping my argument. When Dylan came to write the later poems by which most readers now know him, he appeared to have no subject matter except childhood and its memories, the countryside and its "holy" or sacramental qualities, and death. There is almost nothing about the matter of living as an adult. I would reiterate here Dylan's non-involvement as a child, his failure to become a developing thinker, and his failure to solve his own personal problems, other than poetry, in any meaningful way. What we have in 'In Country Sleep', for instance, is the poet preparing the child — the *child*, mark you — for death:

Never, my girl, until tolled to sleep by the stern

Bell believe or fear that the rustic shade or spell
Shall harrow and snow the blood while you ride wide and
                                                                         near,
For who unmanningly haunts the mountain ravened eaves
Or skulks in the dell moon but moonshine echoing clear
                                                         From the starred well?
A hill touches an angel.

What he is saying is that the countryside is clear and sacred. Its tales
come from man's imagination: there is no need to be frightened by
them. *A hill touches an angel.* Not vice versa. Man is the maker, and he
has no need to fear anyone except the Thief, "meek as the dew" — the
stealer-up night by night, Death.

Dylan returned to Wales, then, and did justice, chiefly in his stories,
to his childish and youthful memories. But he appeared to have no
adult approach to his surroundings. Except, of course — and it's an
important *except* — that he sought to come to grips with mortality,
which is the most adult problem of all. Nevertheless, the absence of an
understanding of other adults, of the community and its rules and
intentions, is apparent. Ah! you will say, but what about *Under Milk
Wood?* Well, what about *Under Milk Wood?* Let us dismiss
immediately any argument as to whether it is a portrait of Laugharne
or New Quay. Let us dismiss it as any kind of portrait of a Welsh
community. For the first thing to realize, as Walford Davies puts it in
his book, *Dylan Thomas,* is that its *ambitions* are *essentially low-key.* It is
"unashamedly a trivializing work in that it reduces a view of life to
immediately entertaining details" (pp 68-9). This is not to deny that it
is probably the best radio play yet written. But it is meant to be funny
and extravagant and poetic, not objective, and the medium lends
itself to all these qualities. Raymond Williams gets closer to what I
mean when he says (in *Dylan Thomas,* ed. C.B. Cox, p.97):

> It is not a mature work, but the retained extravagance of an
> adolescent's imaginings.

I have read arguments (in the work of David Holbrook and Martin
Gingerich — the latter in *The Anglo-Welsh Review* No. 49) of the kind of
frustrated love the characters exhibit — all very serious and high-
minded. Surely the one thing that is obvious about the love, from

Polly Garter to Mr Waldo to Mrs Dai Bread One and Two, is that it is cynical-adolescent, with its sole pathos reserved for Polly Garter's Little Willy Wee. Mog Edwards, the strictly economic lover residing in Manchester House, is the cub reporter's joke. The Rev. Eli Jenkins, more maturely because restrainedly observed, appears as *eisteddfodwr*, not as minister. Nowhere is there a word to show how the community ticks, what conventions, what aspirations it shows, by what rules it lives. The community is a group of very diverse entertainers who don't live together at all.

What of it, you may argue. That's what Dylan Thomas wanted to write. But in his later poems "what he wanted to write" was curiously limited. And my contention about *Under Milk Wood* is that he couldn't have written the mature, more objective play that a portrait of Laugharne or any other observed community might demand. One piece of evidence at least supports this contention. Dylan originally intended that the play should be called *The Town that was Mad*, with Captain Cat being called upon to defend his fellows in court. As the plot unfolded, the prosecuting counsel was to set out the norms of human behaviour, on hearing which the Town would be moved to vote not to defend itself any longer but to accept the label of *Mad*. Dylan abandoned the plot he projected for what seems to me the obvious reason that the presentation of those norms was beyond him. His entry to responsible adult preoccupations was far from certain enough: it was easier to retire upon "the boy's eye view".

One of the noticeable features of the text of *Under Milk Wood* is the use of nursery rhymes and children's games, a fact I discovered consciously only when I was called upon to explain parts of it to foreign teachers. Christopher Page, in *The Anglo-Welsh Review* No.52, shows that the "clacking scissor-man" from *Struwwelpeter*, the children's story-book that Dylan had read at dame school, appears on many occasions in his earlier poems as the image of castration, unmanning and death. Brian John, in *The Anglo-Welsh Review* No.51, shows that the "dilly, dilly . . . Come and be killed" of the loft hawk in 'Over Sir John's Hill', comes straight out of the Victorian nursery rhyme 'Mrs Bond'.

> Oh, what have you got for dinner, Mrs Bond?
> There's beef in the larder and ducks in the pond;
> Dilly, dilly, dilly, dilly, come to be killed,
> For you must be stuffed and my customers filled.

'In Country Sleep' is built upon the nursery tales of Red Riding Hood and Beauty and the Beast. Walford Davies calls 'Poem on his birthday' an "assertion of innocence in the face of ideological blankness" (*ibid.*, p.81). The direction of my arguments is, I trust, becoming clearer. I am seeking to suggest that in his last poems Dylan Thomas faced death certain only of the equipment of a child and that the pastoral scene of Laugharne was the sacramental covert in which he waited for it. Or, to put it another way, that, life having given him as an adult neither satisfaction nor mastery, he had retired upon the imagination — not in the still-determined, shaping manner of Wallace Stevens, but recessively, into what could still be recaptured of the child's wonder at the natural world and his innocent population of the mind.

Much of what I have written here has, I am aware, been put crudely and sketchily, and not solely for lack of space. It is an argument that needs deeper consideration and a great deal more textual flesh. But I have been moved to write it not by an erudite psychological perception so much as an instinct more literary in genesis, if not yet precise and fully knowledgeable. The issue, for me, is not whether 'Over Sir John's Hill' is the finest poem in English of its decade — there is no dispute over the continuance, even the perfection, of Dylan Thomas's technical gifts — but whether this poem, together with 'Fern Hill', 'Holy Spring', 'In Country Sleep', 'A Winter's Tale' and 'Poem on his birthday', do not demonstrate such a narrowing and closing of poetic interest that the end is clearly foreshadowed. And that that end has a closer connection than is commonly appreciated with much of what happened at his beginning — this I believe too. His Laugharne was the only morsel of Wales he had really made his own.

"Any Minute or Dark Day Now"
The Writing of Under Milk Wood

Under Milk Wood (or 'Llareggub' as it was known by its author until no more than a few months before its first performance) was the last but one of Dylan Thomas's writings to be completed. One might reasonably expect it, therefore, to be a work of maturity. That it was not so, for all its many virtues, is matter for comment. The history of its writing tells us a great deal about the inevitability of its turning out to be the kind of play it was. But there are other, deeper reasons which can be no more than touched on here. *Under Milk Wood* is brilliantly balanced upon the contracted core of being over which Dylan still had control.

It is worth noting, by way of preface, that the name "Llareggub" appears first in Dylan's short story 'The Orchards', published in *A Prospect of the Sea*. It is seen here in company with Aberbabel, LlanAsia and other more innocent confections. Daniel Jones, in *My Friend Dylan Thomas,* writes of the mad and imaginative play-sessions he and Dylan had as boys at his own house 'Warmley', and refers to what he calls "palingrams" — that is, reversals of letter-order — in a programme put out by the Dylan/Daniel favourite front man, the Reverend Percy (whose musical pieces for four hands were a feature of their scene). Item 4 of this programme —

Zoilreb Pogoho will read his poem Ffeifokorp

— conceals the names of the composers Berlioz and Prokofieff. Daniel Jones goes on to declare that such reversals were a habit of *his:*

It occurred in my speech so often that my parents became worried. 'No, Dan', they would cry, 'not ananab, navarac — caravan, banana!'

Since Dylan and Daniel were ready to do "a Percy" even within a year or two of the former's death, it is not surprising that palingrams rose readily enough to Dylan's mind — he noted with glee, for example, that T.S. Eliot was very nearly "toilets" backwards — and that "Llareggub" should have pleased him enough to earn a repeat. The publishers, who had not noticed it in 'The Orchards', were alerted by the time they came to publish *Under Milk Wood*, and Richard Church, who edited for Dent, insisted on changing the word to Llaregyb. But by then Dylan was dead.

The all-serving palingram, however, offers as little real clue to authorial intention as *Milk Wood* itself, a title which John Malcolm Brinnin alleges Dylan suggested to him in a taxi when they met in London in the autumn of 1952. The *wood* plays no significant part in the play's narrative, and the suggestion of "milkwood trees" (which produce latex), if not inconsistent with Dylan's often sniggery sense of humour, leads nowhere in particular. But then it may be that the play had as little direction six months before it was finished as it had had in more distant conception, as the account of its writing will show.

The first inkling of a play of the kind *Under Milk Wood* became may be traced back to 1943, when Dylan was writing film-scripts with J. Maclaren-Ross. One of the ideas he put up was for a script about the Home Guard and a village "stuffed full of eccentrics". The modern *Dad's Army* series adequately conveys the essential unseriousness of the intention, never implemented because the Ministry of Information cancelled the script early on. In 1945, his documentary film work over, Dylan became a freelance writer for radio. One of his scripts, entitled 'The Londoner', which begins

It is summer night now in Montrose Street. And the street is sleeping . . . . .

in part anticipates the opening of *Under Milk Wood*, but to notice this is to realise little more than that an atmospheric opening is intrinsic to the unplotted language-centred style he favoured. It was in 1949 that a radio play called 'Llareggub', though largely unwritten, first appeared in the list of work in hand which Dylan's agent optimistically drew up. Dylan, where he refers to this at all in letters to friends, calls it an "awful" or a "wretched" script, with which he was pretty obviously making little progress. In 1950 either he or his agent sold an idea for the script to the B.B.C. The title was to be 'The Town

that was Mad' and Douglas Cleverdon wrote from the B.B.C. in
October to say that the Third Programme would take it under that
title or any other that Dylan might prefer. Implicit in the title
proffered was an attempt to make progress by the provision of a more
developed plot than Dylan was accustomed to. He had, after all,
already written an extravaganza — it was afterwards published in
Quite Early One Morning — based on a small seaside town (in that case,
New Quay: it was written while he was living at 'Majoda') and he
probably felt (or his agent did) that the loose association of fanciful
portraits and atmospheric airs would not do for a more considerable
work of the sort envisaged. Plot, indeed, had been a weakness with
Dylan. As a word-man he resented it. But for a while he went along
with the new idea.

Late in 1950 he sent thirty-nine pages of script to Cleverdon with
the comment that he was "very enthusiastic to finish the thing. And
quickly." What happened ultimately to these thirty-nine pages is
matter for conjecture. Daniel Jones remembers Dylan describing to
him at a cricket-match one of the sequences from it: a citizen from
Mad Town confessed to lusts of the flesh and a male voice choir (the
jury) chanted "Ach y fi" after each revelation. But this recollection
only takes on meaning in the light of the plot intended — which was,
broadly, that a small seaside town full of eccentrics would be declared
insane by the representatives of the world outside and that, resenting
this, the independent-minded citizens would demand a hearing in
court at which Captain Cat, their spokesman, would put their case.
The prosecution, however, in speaking first, was to advance what
might be called the norms of the sane world for comparison and the
seasiders, on hearing them, would decide to withdraw their plea,
preferring to live cut off and unapproved beyond some *cordon sanitaire.*
That this design was never really proceeded with, beyond the thirty-
nine pages, is usually set down to Dylan's uneasiness with plot, to the
restriction of free imagination which it entailed. I should like to
suggest, however, that there may be another reason. Dylan's state as a
citizen was relatively immature. He had no real convictions about
either moral or social revolution. And those norms, those
conformities of the outside world, had they not legal, historical, moral
and psychological bases which required understanding? Did Dylan
understand them? Did he, indeed, even know enough about them (in
the sense that they had been part of his life)? I have a profound feeling
that he could not go far along this road, and certainly not with the

assurance needed to decorate the picture with wit and laughter.
When 'Llareggub' took a very different final form, one in which the
eccentrics have it all their own way and are organised only in the sense
that they are "contained" within an imagined locale and the dawn to
dusk of a spring day, that was a development inevitable because
Dylan was the man he was and no other. Further explication of this
must wait till the final version of *Under Milk Wood* is looked at more
closely.

Let us for the time being continue to look at the progress of the
typescript. Or rather the lack of progress. For Dylan went off to Persia
and 'Llaraggub' slipped down the priority list. While he was waiting
for his *Collected Poems* to appear, however, he began to work on it again
and by the autumn of 1951, the 'Mad' script now entirely discarded,
he had written about half of a new one, much more loosely knit, with
the space needed for an inventive comicality. This apparent dawn,
nevertheless, was still false. Eight months later, back from America,
he had made no further progress and Douglas Cleverdon, fearful that
he had bought an idea that would prove only sterile, persuaded the
B.B.C. to pay Dylan five guineas every time a thousand words of the
script reached his hands. (This was the same Cleverdon who in the
summer of 1952, by his own account, locked Dylan in the B.B.C.
reference library all night to get out of him an Introduction to Edgar
Lee Masters's Spoon River Anthology). But the financial ploy was
ineffective, basically because the instalments were too small and the
total sum offered, ninety guineas, was rather less than munificent.
The Americans, as it turned out, were to pay much better.

Cleverdon, nevertheless, had one more shot in his locker. He went
down to Laugharne to talk to Dylan about the script. The pep talk
worked, if only for a while. In Dylan's engagement-book after this
particular week-end in October appears a declaration of intent:
"Solid week on Llareggub, to finish it." But the reality of experience
amended this: the word "week" is scratched out, "sixteen days"
written in. And even then the script was not finished. Dylan was off on
poetry readings again, glad to be relieved of this and other
responsibilities. The truth was that writing and the need to write had
by this time reduced him, by his own confession, to "a state of terror".
He felt drained. He had nothing to say. Increasingly he was convinced
that he would never again successfully complete anything, not even a
poem.

Early in 1953, still thinking mainly of escape, he arranged with

John Malcolm Brinnin to do another tour in the United States, this time to last only six weeks. Brinnin had been given to understand that he would bring *Under Milk Wood* complete and ready for a performance at the New York Poetry Centre on May 14. But when Dylan landed on April 21 the manuscript he brought was still incomplete. Nevertheless, defended from interruptions by Brinnin's assistant, Liz Reitell, he did work seriously at the play between his readings at universities and on May 3 he gave a solo reading of as much of it as he had written at the Poets' Theatre at Cambridge, Massachusetts. Eleven days remained, and hectic days they were, before the performance promised. Less than an hour before the curtain went up, Dylan was still scribbling bits into the typescripts prepared for the cast of three men and two women, and Brinnin and Liz Reitell and two typists were standing by for re-types until the last moment.

Conceived as a radio play, *Under Milk Wood* had a cast of fifty characters, some of them with no more than a few lines to say. Dylan read *First Voice* and three other parts: the cast of six sat on stools at reading desks and the recording made by the Poetry Centre on this occasion remains the only one in existence of Dylan performing in his own play. The audience, perhaps expecting the sonorities of the Thomas manner in reading his own poetry or perhaps merely convinced that poetry was bound to be a serious matter, sat silent until the Mog Edwards speech of love for Myfanwy Price persuaded them that it was comedy of a sort that they were hearing. Then the laughter began. At the end there was a long ovation. The cast took fourteen curtain calls together before Dylan, "squat and boyish in his happily flustered modesty", as Brinnin puts it, came out onto the stage alone.

On May 23 he wrote to Caitlin that he had finished his "infernally, eternally unfinished 'Play'" and that he would be home on June 2, a week later than intended. Back at Laugharne once more, he talked deprecatingly to Mimi Josephson about *Under Milk Wood*, describing it as "prose with blood pressure". Revisions were made to it from time to time during the summer: the original undertaker, Thomas the Death, was cut out and replaced by a rather less fearsome Evans ditto. But it was all very slow: Dylan was in a daze most of the time, unable to get on. In August he made his first appearance on television, reading a tale of a charabanc outing which was afterwards published simply as 'A Story'. Even here the chronic seriousness of Dylan's plight opens up to hindsight: the script was not completed until after he had arrived for the broadcast and he had not memorised the text fully, as he had apparently been expected to do. The Controller of TV programmes in London thought "the programme was appalling", but the reviewers and the public enjoyed it hugely. This was Dylan's last completed work. What followed were only attempts at poems, either despairing or maudlin.

Meanwhile, the magazine *Mademoiselle* had bought the publishing rights of *Under Milk Wood* and Douglas Cleverdon of the B.B.C. had at last (by October 15) got his hands on a complete script of it. Copies were duplicated and the original returned to Dylan, who lost it over the week-end, apparently in a Soho pub, whence Cleverdon later got it back. Bound for America again, on what was to be his ultimate escape, Dylan took with him some of the B.B.C.'s duplicated copies and there were four more successful performances of the play at the New York Centre late in October. But Dylan himself was in a serious physical and mental condition, drunk, quarrelsome and ill. In the early hours of November 5 he was admitted to hospital in a coma and by November 9 he was dead.

Under Milk Wood was as near the end, then, as that. What may we say of it in retrospect? One aspect of it is still, I think, so widely misunderstood that a word or two of explanation is called for. Many readers and hearers of the play think of it as a portrait of Laugharne (or, alternatively, of New Quay — for this, too, has been argued) and some inhabitants of the little town, like many throughout Wales, were offended (and perhaps still are) by the bawdy of the writing and by an apparently derogatory view of a Welsh community. Such responses are mistaken — not because one cannot make a case for the appearance in it of some of the physical aspects of Laugharne and not a few place and personal names under very thin disguise — but because the town of Llareggub is plainly, if one reads the text at all carefully, not presented as a realistic entity. It is, indeed, that town of eccentrics that Dylan first thought of. It is not a community in which people work and get on together, in which there could be said to be a way of life. Each of the eccentrics goes through his or her performance either in fact, dream or recollection, a performance held in relationship to that of the others only by a stated locale, a very limited quantity of dialogue and the passing hours of the single day that *Milk Wood* is. There is no "norm", no organisation of society sufficient to justify the seeing of it as a portrait. Jobs or functions are noted, if at all, only to set the laughter going. Sometimes it is simply the name, often expendable in a line or two: like Mae Rose Cottage, Organ Morgan, Mrs. Dai Bread One (or Two). Willy-Nilly Postman delivers letters but only to show that he has read them before delivery: Ocky Milkman dreams that he is emptying his churns into the Dewi River (rather than vice-versa): Mr. Beynon Butcher is professional only so that he may appear in his teasing role as cat and dog killer. Here and there a few individuals comment on life by speaking their dreams: Gossamer Beynon high-heeling it to and from school (but never teaching), her elegant exterior concealing a desire to be taken roughly rather than otherwise: Mog Edwards fitting love into the economic register: and the Reverend Eli Jenkins, the "straightest" of them all, voicing to the sky, no more than a little comically, the nearest thing to a generalisation about the town and its people. "We are not wholly bad or good", he recites, and a thin aura of morality (or religion) scents the day. But the Reverend Eli is there, it is important to note, as the maker of "the White Book of Llareggub" and *eisteddfodwr*— for the play's purpose, the poet as *bardd gwlad,* in totally understandable vein - and as morning and evening marker, not as minister: for to appear as minister might have meant a serious intrusion of moral, or even social ideas. There is no denying that the *bardd gwlad* is the natural functionary of a *community,* and Dylan has undoubtedly gone some way here to suggest that Llareggub is an entity with a way of life. But the Reverend Eli is one of the deliberately Welsh markers of the scene, much more a part of a remembered Swansea than of an observed Laugharne. When it comes to it, what he has to offer to the others in the town is "jelly and poems". And the first of those words is as accurate as may be.

The nearest we get to a social idea or comment is the sight of Polly Garter scrubbing the floor of the Welfare Hall for the Mothers' Union Social Dance, a Polly Garter snubbed and hissed at by the respectable wives of the town. But what we are conscious of, at these few points where real life seems to be adjacent to the scene of the play, if not actually to touch it, is a sense of pity for "all poor creatures born to die". And that may be linked with one or two other revelations of Dylan's life-view which will be detailed presently.

Reality breaks in (or rather, accurate recollection breaks in) most of all in the soliloquies of Lily Smalls and in the voices and games of the children. Llareggub is a map of childhood echoes, decorated with verbally exuberant descriptions of objects. And it is all wrapped up in the bawdy and poetry of a singular imagination. The jokes are mostly the jokes of adolescence, rarely developed beyond their first statement. A few of them are not very good, but most have the basic appeal not of folklore but of universal memory. They are the jokes that every Welsh boy of Dylan's age had made or heard, but how jewelled with words! It is in the pathos, already hinted at, that one may not unreasonably detect the vision of the Dylan who was not far from death. At the revision stage he seems to have thought that there was too much heart on the author's sleeve: Thomas the Death (where else in the play is there a happy, counterbalancing Thomas?), for whom "the eyes of all the inhabitants are full of fear" — "Not me, not me", eyes scream at him — was cut out in favour of an Evans who dreams he sees his mother making Welsh cakes in the snow. Lord Cut-Glass, however, who "lives in a house and a life at siege" — and Lord Cut-Glass, we must remember, was Dylan's nickname amongst his friends in Swansea in the early days — survived the revisions, however discrepant he may have seemed from the mood of Llareggub as a whole. "Any minute or dark day now the unknown enemy will loot and savage downhill", intones First Voice on his behalf. But the virtuosity of the clock-descriptions conceals the full impact of this. Whatever other inhabitants of Laugharne imagined they were caricatured in *Under Milk Wood*, there was one real face in it that the author knew only too well.

It may be, too, though this is much more arguable, that the "Little Willy Wee who is dead, dead, dead", Polly Garter's unshakeable favourite, was conceived not merely as a popular counter to the rampagings of Mr. Waldo but as a piece of sentiment wished upon the whole shape of life. It was perhaps the vindication of a "little" Dylan, so wretchedly unsuccessful in extracting happiness from living, who nevertheless cherished the belief that death would do for him (in a personal rather than an authorial sense) what life could not.

The reasons for the ultimate form of the play go back into Dylan Thomas's life. This is not the place to attempt to develop a thesis demonstrating the way in which his upbringing and his conception of what being a poet was had hampered the growth of a mature appreciation of life and the powers that were necessary to bring it under some sort of control. It would need room for exegesis not available here. All I can do is to assert that Dylan had reached the year 1952, in which *Under Milk Wood* was largely written, facing directly only one human problem and that the greatest — mortality —, equipped with no wisdom or confidence or happiness or belief that had come to him in adult life but certain only of the memories of childhood and adolescence, the one region of the mind that no criticism or later unhappiness could vitiate. *Under Milk Wood* is what it is because Dylan wrote it out of that memory-bank of which he had sole and perfect control, discarding those aspects of living that he had never been able to manage or understand fully and hinting, once or twice but no more, at the terrible fate that awaited the world of his comic, inventive, poetic and imaginative youth. If a *plot* for a work of genius is required, this is, if accidentally, as good an any.

Grief and The Circus Horse:
A Study of Mythic and Christian Themes in the Early Poetry of Vernon Watkins

That Vernon Watkins was a Christian both by upbringing and by personal conviction needs no arguing. Any one who knew him as more than a passing acquaintance can confirm some aspect of his shy but unusually determined adherence to Christian principle. Nevertheless, the certainty of this personal definition has bemused critics and readers alike into accepting his poetry as an extended cumulus of mysticism whose individual cloudlets they need not too carefully penetrate. Alternatively and more seriously, his work has been granted the trappings of high regard but has not been closely read and interpreted. The finished surface of it, the reiterated symbolism, the rareness of personal reference, have been sufficient to persuade many that it was all of a high-flown piece, impressive in the mass rather than in individual poems, devoted to a rather esoteric Christianising of the inheritance of myth. Some, even amongst reviewers, have not been certain that they could go as far as that: when Vernon Watkins's first book, *The Ballad of the Mari Lwyd*, was published in 1941, the anonymous reviewer of *The Times Literary Supplement*[1] referred to "the mystery which pours its darkness and strange potency through almost all his verses" and, while clear that "a realm beyond time's imagery" and the "heavy and complicated folds of myth" were the poet's repetitive concern, felt that "passion" was perhaps the single word that best characterised the rhythm and rhetoric which were constantly present. My purpose in this essay is to demonstrate that throughout Vernon Watkins's early published poetry (in which category I include everything he wrote up to 1948, the year in which *The Lady with the Unicorn* appeared) there is visible a dichotomy between mythic inheritance and Christian belief, a dichotomy which in certain key poems stands revealed as antithesis.

It is equally true that in other poems, few of which appear in his first book, he finds means of reconciling a "religious system" which is derived from the Platonists with some, if not all, of the tenets of the Christian Church. I shall put no weight, however, on any argument which relies on the chronological order in which poems appear, or even on their presence in an earlier rather than a later book.[2] A poet like Vernon Watkins, who often made hundreds of drafts of the same poem, kept back rigorously poems which even in their final form failed to satisfy him, and omitted others from their compositional group because they did not suit the plan of the volume he had in mind, is not to be tied down in this way except after an exhaustive analysis of all surviving drafts and worksheets, an analysis for which I have had neither time nor opportunity. What I set out in the pages following is no more than an *exposé* of the themes to be found in Watkins's published poems, largely unadorned by deduction from biographical information or about personal development.

It must be confessed, in any case, that Vernon Watkins himself, despite a number of broad statements made at poetry-readings in his later years, was at no great pains to elucidate either his sources in reading or the development of his thought. The pointers he gave were few, and of these the first important one concerns a time when he had already left Cambridge and entered the bank:

> In my twenty-third year I suddenly experienced a complete revolution of sensibility. I repudiated the verse I had written and knew that I could never again write a poem which could be dominated by time.[3]

It is dangerously easy to leap from this to an impression that the poet has indicated, albeit in other words, his acceptance — perhaps in terms as dramatic as those which were compelled upon Saul on the Damascus road — of the Christian doctrine of the immortality of the soul, and that this "revolution" might fairly be equated with the sort of evangelical conversion which overtakes some, at least, of those who have been brought up in the intellectual convictions of the Christian faith. The use of the word "sensibility", however, should make us pause. Despite its possible fitness for the emotional aspect of such a conversion, its aesthetic overtones make it reasonably plain that the poet is speaking, as the context confirms, of a change in his intentions towards poetry, of a change in his conception of poetry's purpose for him, and of nothing else. The connection with Christian conviction must be made with care. In the later years of his life Vernon Watkins sometimes introduced his public readings with a brief explanation of his meaning in refusing to be "dominated by time", the words of which settled themselves either in the form which follows[4] or in something very like it:

> A poet gains strength from the acceptance of death. The conquest of time lies in this acceptance, the refusal to be raised except by the true God.

The last phrase suggests strongly that "the conquest of time" was bound up with and indeed dependent upon a *Christian* acceptance and the implication is that this was so from the moment when this "revolution of sensibility" became effective. The poems reveal that these statements telescope the poet's real development: that there existed also a kind of acceptance based upon pre-Christian theories is plain, though whether this acceptance preceded the Christian kind or was always co-existent with it seems to me dangerous matter for dogmatism, for the reasons already given above. It must be enough for the present to assert that the story of the poet's development was not as simple as he would have had us think.

Vernon Watkins's failure to chart correctly the poetic course he had taken need not delay us long. Not merely was he antagonistic in general to the exegesis of a poet's work by critics: he made scant use himself of opportunities to explain to the reader, just possibly believing in the secrecy or esotericism inherited from the bardic tradition but more probably convinced of the greater essential simplicity of the symbol than of the transcendental truth behind it. Did not Jesus himself believe that he could best reach the multitude — and not merely the multitude, his disciples too — by means of parables? To attempt to paraphrase a work of words and symbols that had in the first place been chosen with the utmost care was, in Vernon Watkins's view, almost inevitably to falsify the original vision. In 1954, writing of *The Death Bell* in *The Poetry Book Society Bulletin,* he remarked:

> I have been told that the occasional expositions of my poems which I have read on the air are more obscure than the poems themselves, and perhaps this is inevitable. A poet is able to throw

light on the source of a poem, but he cannot simplify it; he can
only make it more difficult.

The truth he was after had been caught, if at all, only in an endlessly
mended net of words and symbols, and after so much labour he could
not reasonably hope for some other, more casual, prosier fortune.
The poems had to speak for themselves. And, in respect to the
exegesis I attempt here, they must do as much again.

In the first place, then, what do the early poems tell us of Vernon
Watkins's "conquest of time"?

The images that carry his meaning recur very frequently, but are
not for that reason more easily understood. One of the first to appear is
that of the fountain, whose pipe gives out water without stop (water is
here the symbol for the passing minutes) into a pool which retains
within its stone lips just so much of the water as we, with our limited
vision, can see and comprehend.

> I cannot tell what art
> Set the grave spring to start
> In whose old pipe and stop
> Time plays no part.
>
> But where green eyes look up,
> Eyes that are blind with sun,
> Uncertain fingers grope
> Around the vine-leaved cup.

These two stanzas — indeed the whole poem, 'From My Loitering',[5]
from which they are taken — offer exposition rather than explanation.
The poet does not know *why* the provision of those who have gone
before helps him to master time: the origins of life are hidden, but the
"grave spring" stands both for the vast seriousness of time (which is
not to be understood as inessential because mastered) and for the
passage of the water of life through the hands of the dead. Those who
accept this, who are "blind with sun" — that is, live the moment to the
full — partake, however uncertainly, of the recurrent myth. What
they hold to the water is "the vine-leaved cup".

A number of other fountain poems elaborate this theme with
different emphases. The sycamore, too, is a recurring symbol,
probably because its wind-borne seeds or keys are amongst the most
obviously successful in perpetuating the genus. For Vernon Watkins

its long life and fertility make it, perhaps of all trees, the best guarantor against time's victory that his eyes provide. But it is rarely a sycamore seen, more often a sycamore formally rather than naturally placed, one with roots gripping the stream of time and taking perpetually from it — but by implication old when the passing water is young, crested with the foam of the immediate minute.

> Centuries made me firm.
> Far I have spread my roots.
> I grip the flying stream.
> Aching, I drop my fruits.

'Sycamore', from which these lines are taken,[6] makes its ultimate point in contrasting the sleep "below" of "small-statured" — that is short-lived — man, unable to answer the tree's challenge.

> Who sleeps? The young streams feed
> My boughs. The blind keys spin.
> Hark, he is dead indeed.
> Never shall fall again
> My natural, winged seed
> On this small-statured man.[7]

That Man is deaf to the lessons of naturalness, of Nature, is Vernon Watkins's frequent lament. But other poets have mourned as much over this for purposes widely different: we no more than glimpse his reasons until he puts before us the paradox at the heart of his position, the acceptance of death as the *necessary* end of life and its equally necessary beginning. Light cannot be perpetuated without the womb of dark. 'Mother and Child', although it may be misread (by stressing the later implications that "white" had for Watkins and by reading "fallen from light" as inevitably after Vaughan and Wordsworth[8]) as one of the many Madonna and Child poems, does no more than celebrate the natural miracle of continual regeneration.

> Let hands be about him white, O his mother's first,
> Who caught him, fallen from light through nine months' haste
> Of darkness, hid in the worshipping womb . . .
>
>   O what secrets are set
> In the tomb of each breath, where a world of light in eclipse

Of a darkly worshipping world exults in the joy she gave
Knowing that miracle, miracle to beget,
Springs like a star to her milk, is not for the grave.

Words like "worshipping" and "miracle", again, need have no
Christian connotation: they are entirely within the good-and-evil
mystery of Watkins's view of myth. But the development of the
essential paradox is still obscure here. It lies in the phrase "the tomb of
each breath", which counterpoints each moment of life as both
leading to death and coming from it, and in the antithesis of the
"darkly worshipping world" (the world of the tomb of death and
preparation) with the "world of light" which at that moment eclipses
it. The "secrets are set" here but are not explained.

In 'Thames Forest', one of Vernon Watkins's finest sustained
poems and amongst those published one of the earliest, dating in its
first version from 1933,[9] the concept of the "thread" or "life-skein",
which places man and his thinking into relationship with the natural
regenerative processes, carries the explanation a stage farther. The
stanzas following are the heart of the poem.

Darkness of the sycamore flies across the river.
From a pattern of foliage see the spirit struggling
Through meshes like memories, woven of their terror,
Wondering, emerging.

Thought, like a thread, still glitters on his fingers.
Still from the dark earth, mythical and gleaming,
Draws he the life-skein, flying ever forward,
Wound by a dead hand.

Light on the wet ground, lighter on the leafmould
Dances that energy, rising to the sunbeam.
Black flies the shadow, asking of the dead leaf
Garment for burial.

Stilled on the charmed world, upward the life looks,
Stunned by that oracle speaking from the tree's root:
'One that is strange-born, one that dies to-morrow
Dances to-day here.'

Dumb roots are whispering; light breaks in darkness;
Frail fibres grasp there, clinging to the close clod.

Under the warm green vellum of the meadow
Trance-wise the seeds break.

Light is a great pool. Look, the clouds are flying.
Of all forms living, man alone deliberate
Scrawls on a leaf the impression of his going.
These leaves are numbered.

The energy of the dactylic stresses in the first three lines of each stanza is so deftly prevented from beating too hard by the halt and balance of the short last line that it satisfies Vernon Watkins's own *diktat* perfectly:

> In a perfectly resolved poem form and belief are so closely identified that they are indistinguishable: the form is the meaning.[10]

In these Sapphic stanzas[11] the deftness of the imagery, too, — the chrysalis opening to make the gnat-dance possible, while sycamores and turf shadow the longer natural processes — persuades us that the connection is made, that man and his purposes can be satisfactorily described in these terms. "Thought, like a thread" is "Wound by a dead hand" out of the "meshes like memories" which are part of "the dark earth, mythical". In other words, Man, who alone "scrawls on a leaf the impression of his going", has made "numbererd"[12] leaves of story about his gnat-dance in the sun and out of those dead leaves the thought-thread rises again in each re-generation. The secret is in the thread, in the thinking connection Man has made for himself with the endless re-birth of the natural world. His life is sewn round, in the dark period of begetting, with the web of myth.

Whether we accept what Vernon Watkins calls "the conquest of time" in any other terms than those of self-persuasion is irrelevant. There are no other terms for this than those of faith, and the acceptance of myth is a kind of faith. He is conscious, undoubtedly, of his own good fortune — as a poet, his rare good fortune, he would have said — in being able to devote *time itself* to this pre-occupation.

I have been luckier than
All others in one thing,
Devoted secret time
To one love, one alone;

> Found then that dying man
> Exulting in new rhyme:
> The river standing,
> All but miracle gone.[13]

If the river can be made to stand, not flow, then miracle is present. The new rhyme which runs into the future can be grasped by that same, finite, dying poet who has already absorbed the past. But that past does not live with him as history, either as a series of objective events learned or as lessons derived from particular cycles of experience. It is present with him always, as an enduring, generic concept. It lies in his mind less as an anchor-chain whose links are barnacled with myth than as a form or pattern laid down from the beginning, an ideality mothered by "the vessel of ages", of which all transient and time-created beings are pale and insufficient replicas. Vernon Watkins's mare and foal poems set out this concept most explicitly, perhaps for accidental, natural reasons (ponies are, after all, a frequent sight on the headlands and commons of Gower) but more fundamentally, in the end, because the identity of the Mare Goddess with the Earth Mother fastens to natural world that life-skein which too much "pure thought" of the Platonic type might separate from essential myth. Watkins, despite his use of Plato's terminology, did not envisage the ideal forms behind the replicas as having an abstract and mathematical perfection. Thus his poem, 'Foal',[14] begins:

> Darkness is not dark, nor sunlight the light of the sun
> But a double journey of insistent silver hooves.

This "double journey" is not merely an awareness of the necessary interlocking of light and dark, of death and life, of prance and preparation, but something both vaguer and more precise, memory's apprehension, personal and generic, of the first form from which the present one is "dropped".

> And whoever watches a foal sees two images,
> Delicate, circling, born, the spirit with blind eyes leaping
> And the left spirit, vanished, yet here, the vessel of ages
> Clay-cold, blue, laid low by her great wide belly the hill.

The foal, "amazed by the movement of suns", is intermittently aware of "His blue fellow"

And he slips from that mother to the boundless horizons of
air,
Looking for that other, the foal no longer there.

So he plays in his morning, "fulfilling the track / Of so many suns",
but sometimes "vanishing the mole's way" (as his "blue fellow" has),
and his mother, the mare, "eluding the dead hands", urges him to
play to the uttermost.

Two aspects of this picture need additional comment. Earth, with
"her great wide belly the hill" is an intermediary as necessary in the
mare / foal concept as that less emphasised Earth in 'Thames Forest'
from which the gnat-dance began. "That indolent fullness rounded
under the ray" — to quote from a later poem, 'The Mare', which
otherwise has little to add — that rounded belly of the mare pregnant
is no more than the visible fruitfulness of the light which is balanced
cyclically by the incipient fecundity of darkness.

In the darkness under the violet's roots, in the darkness of the
    pitcher's music,
In the uttermost darkness of a vase
There is still the print of fingers, the shadow of waters.
And under the dry, curled parchment of the soil there is
    always a little foal
Asleep.[15]

The womb of Earth, the belly, the pitcher, the vase, is needed because
it is easier to understand the cycle of plants from seed through leaf,
flower and fruit back to germinating seed again than it is to carry long-
winded man or beast, in natural rather than theological terms, past
the obstacle of death. Arguably, however, there is another and more
powerful necessity for it. Unless, figuratively, the mare is Earth (and
for reasons deeper than the deep-delved mythology of the Earth-
Mare Goddess, whether her name be Demeter, Rhiannon or any one
of a dozen others) there can be no return to the mould, to the pitcher,
so that the dying replica may be replaced by the "little foal / Asleep".
Without this return the genus horse (or for that matter, the genus
Man) could evolve separately and divergently, collecting blood and
myth along the way.

I have written that this is arguably more important for Vernon
Watkins in this context than any other aspect of the Earth-Mother
because it introduces the second matter which needs comment, a

matter upon which decision is not simple. What was the nature of the replica or copy for Watkins? Was it a constant return to an original, which existed in the mind concurrently with the live image? Or was it a design for perfection, reached by abstract thought in each generation and therefore subject to evolutionary changes? Plato put into the mouth of Socrates[16] the assertion that the mortal achieves immortality by the constant replacing of that which perishes, not by the separate continuity of the individual mortal element, and Vernon Watkins, using the images of the fountain, the waterfall, the foal, obviously embraces the broad terms of this idea.

> The waterfall by falling is renewed
> And still is falling. All its countless changes
> Accumulate to nothing but itself.[17]

But the waterfall, later in the same poem, is "always changing" . . . "Its voice is new and ancient". It is still a waterfall, but is it the same waterfall in shape, volume, depth of fall?

Contradictory answers emerge. A poem in the same volume, 'The Immortal in Nature',[18] makes it reasonably clear that the generic form, the original, is unchanging:

> Think of Donne
> Who could contract all ages to one day,
> Knowing they were but copies of that one:
> The first being true, then none can pass away.

On the other hand, the waterfall is "always changing": "new and ancient" are unified, made one by memory. The original, the "true", is apprehended by that memory, and this must surely imply, not the memory of the individual, but the collective memory over the generations, which is myth. Myth is something which grows with each life, with the numbering of the leaves: it is not given at the beginning and rests unchanged: it evolves as Man evolves. The human spirit struggles out into the brief sun, as 'Thames Forest' has it, "Through meshes like memories". The natural order, and the part of the spirit in that order, are governed by that memory.

> Time is for us transfigured into colours
> Known and remembered from an earlier summer.[19]

It might perhaps not be worth emphasising these contradictions further were it not that here we reach the marker for that dichotomy between the dominance of a mythic inheritance and the weight of Christian belief to which I referred at the beginning. If some of Vernon Watkins's poems appear to work out this dichotomy logically, Christianising the unchanging pattern and leaving myth to influence lives lived at a level from which this pattern is not visible,[20] it must also be said that the contradictions remain. 'The Replica', for instance, is not an early poem. If time brought *some* logic to the dichotomy, the aberrations can still be seen.

It is time now, in any case, to relate what has been said to Christian dogma in its orthodox form. While Plato argued immortality for the just soul (on the ground that disease in or injury to the body could not induce that soul's corruption and that therefore nothing could destroy it), the Christian Church postulates the immortality of all souls, irrespective of their virtue or lack of it. It is, indeed, this *separate* continuity of Man which differentiates him from beasts and flowers, which have no more than a generic continuity. Vernon Watkins shows no sign of accepting a Platonic immortality for the few, though his references to immortality of any kind are remarkable for their infrequency. Indeed, as we shall see, he often gives the impression that the effect of a Christian vision is a higher quality of life within the mortal generation, and that this should be sufficient. As for the uncertainty surrounding the nature of the replica, it will appear that, as time went on, he emphasised more its identity as the "first form", laid down by God at the creation of the world. It can be argued that this clarification in itself marks the poet's adoption of a more fully Christian position, though such a contention, already referred to as of doubtful worth in the present state of knowledge, would involve him with Christian Fundamentalism rather than with any more modern form of Christian teaching.

What is perhaps surprising, as we begin to examine Vernon Watkins's "Christian" poems, is that he makes no use of the superficially similar paradox which is at the heart both of Christianity and Platonism, the need for death so that life may be ensured —

> The Christian Paradox, bringing its great reward
> By loss; the moment known to Kierkegaard.[21]

Or rather, not that he made *no* use of it, but that the use he did make belonged to a range of human feeling (like Kierkegaard's, his losses were *personal)* which was in the end antipathetical to any confrontation by means of theory. It is easy enough to show that Christ's death on the Cross and his earlier saying,

I am come that ye may have Life, and have it more abundantly,

bears only a momentary resemblance to that generic immortality celebrated in some of Watkins's poems:

Dancers perish:
The dance goes on.[22]

Christ died once and for all. The sacrifice unto death was to be valid for *all* subsequent generations. It was a sacrifice made in atonement for sin, that is, for the unsatisfactory quality of Man's life as lived thus far. It was a sacrifice which ensured a new quality of life, as well as immortality (that is, a separate individual continuity), for those who believed in Him. Here, indeed, was another totality of belief whose initial similarities were sufficient to ensure a poetical confrontation with the doctrine of the Platonists. But it was not a confrontation that Venon Watkins either sought or reached. This was partly because, as the continuing ambiguities suggest, the endless regeneration of the natural world still fascinated him and he was inclined to write at different levels, celebrating that glory at the lower and at the higher introducing aspects of Christian belief which did not so much confront as offer a counter whose relevance was less than direct. Partly was it, too, that the power of Christian belief was, at the first, profoundly emotional, so that the poet was not concerned so much with a theoretical confrontation as with a penetration of those other "religious" levels by discrepant symbols.

The worth or otherwise of these generalisations will appear as we examine more closely the poems in Vernon Watkins's first three books.

The Ballad of the Mari Lwyd opens with 'The Collier', a poem which most readers treat as though they had read only as far as the lines:

In the wood of the desk I cut my name:
Dai for Dynamite.

What is treated, unperceptively, as a cap-and-muffler theme is, in fact, a very complex development of the Joseph allegory, and although it is in other respects marginal to my thesis, I feel bound to discuss it briefly here because it may be one of the very rare expressions of Christian doubt in Watkins's poetry. What we learn from it depends less on the interpretation of Dai's ultimate fate[23] than on the meaning of the two lines

> They changed words there in darkness
> And still through my head they run,

If we link these with the implications of the two stanzas previous, that "Jack was not raised up" though "he interpreted their dreams" and Tom "shivered his leper's lamp" in vain,[24] we may reasonably argue that the Divine protection which encompassed Joseph is seen by the poet as being of no avail underground, that the life of the collier is, in some way, beyond the arm of God. This note has a fainter echo in 'The Ballad of the Mari Lwyd', in which the Dead adjure the Living to recognise their oneness with "Cain the farm / And Dai of Dowlais pit" and go on to imply that

> Men of the snow-deep mountain-top
> And soot-faced mining men

are tragic rather than separate.

> Do you not hear like an anvil ring
> The smith of the rock of coal
> Who fell on his steel like that great king
> And sundered body and soul?

Perhaps, again, it was the collier Vernon Watkins had in mind when he wrote of "fidelity to the unfortunate dead",[25] if only because in the more closely structured poems of regeneration death is seen as a necessity, not a misfortune. Yet it is Love which produces such fidelity and it may be that death by accident (as in a pit disaster) is a breach rather in the replica succession than in one of the walls of Christian trust. If this should be so, then the "fundamental" preservation which sorrow discovers to be available for some rather than all (and here the Joseph narrative, as an Old Testament allegory, may fairly be thought part of this incomplete Providence) can give way, as we shall see presently, to a re-interpretation of the succession in terms of the Love which Christ was and which, if perceived by Man, may alter the quality of the apprehension of it.

'Griefs of the Sea' may be set against 'The Collier', first in the sense that the pit, which Vernon Watkins does not know and therefore fears, is replaced by the sea, with which he has long come to philosophical terms, and second, that the griefs of the title, perhaps for the reason already given and perhaps because, unlike the colliers, the sailors are distanced and anonymous, are contained by, ultimately conquered by, that Providence which failed the pitmen. In this poem it is the myth of the inscrutable sea-god that makes it "fitting" to mourn, the untruthfulness of that myth that is to be held against grief.

> For the sea turns whose every drop is counted
> And the sand turns whose every grain a holy hour-glass holds ...

Yet this poem, in appearance a counter to 'The Collier', has its own way of equivocation. The force of the rhetoric with which the poem ends — the word *counted* which proposes for the smallest drop of sea the same Divine care that "numbered" Man's leaves in 'Thames Forest', the application of the adjective *holy* to the aeons of time in the sandgrains — leaves the reader with an impression that Providence has been powerfully proposed. Yet closer examination shows that "the riderless horse" throws off "All things that are not sea". There is no sea-god, no other rider either. The sea is a symbol, arguably a symbol of Divine purpose, but a symbol which in its own right is to be sufficient for the poem. "The riderless horse" must do without a discernible rider, a fact which makes the impetus of the closing lines mis-leading.

The first firmly Christian poem in *The Ballad of the Mari Lwyd* is 'Prime Colours', which essays a confrontation with the mythic powers. In this the "winged horse of myth" is not free: it

> Seems now a circus horse, paid to be clever:

"The huge, high landscape" has, over the centuries, been falsified, shut within books (in another, later poem Watkins wrote: "Tenuous life, I have wronged you . . . Out of dark books I accused you"[26]): it is, indeed, the seemingly burdened ass, the ass with Jesus on his back, who is free:

> The ride from Bethphage will last for ever.

Myth is equated here with knowledge, which is less a satisfactory definition than a description of the bookwork by which Vernon Watkins made its acquaintance:

> Swift, chattering swallows, flying in cloisters cool,
> See through their darting eyes the imprisoned school,
> Cramped, figured scribes, distorted by possession:
> The upright man is always out of fashion.

The keys to the poem lie in the primacy of humility and a return to first innocence.

> Swallows come back to their first house of mud
> Knowing no wider rainbow can be made;

and the ass, knowing nothing save what he is told, stops time by going down slowly from Bethphage to Jerusalem. There *are* only the five colours ("innocent light") — the colours of the rainbow which God gave Noah to symbolise His covenant with Man — and these five, which the poet calls "prime", go back into the original white, the white of God's purity and awfulness.

There will be more to say about "orignal white" later. For the moment I want only to note that 'Prime Colours' appears to argue against myth, though not always clearly, on the ground that it is man-made, a tricky decoration of a simple original, a knowing encrustation intended to diversify and beautify what cannot in itself be surpassed. Christ is the real time-stopper, says the poet, and it is in humility, in the lowly things, in mud, in dust —

> White dust to resurrect the moving dust,

that the real life-thread lies. This argument moves precisely in that direction I indicated earlier as likely: in repudiating myth Watkins was bound to associate Christ's gift of life with the reiteration of an ordained pattern, which in the ass and the swallows had been there from the beginning. No other position would conserve so easily that part of the Platonic concept of immortality which did not concern Man.

It is not unfair to observe at this point that 'Prime Colours' is not a particularly successful poem. The connection of the symbolism of colours, only partly developed in it, with the separate symbols of the swallows and the ass is not clear: the alliance lacks inevitability and force. More importantly, perhaps, the form of the poem "states": it neither presses nor prophesies. No doubt this is inevitable if it is humility that must interrupt the overbearing tricks of the circus horse. But it is difficult, nevertheless, to feel this as anything more than a counter-poem, the uncertain stand of a poet who has not yet found means to match his Christian belief imaginatively with the already flighted symbols of myth.

In *The Ballad of the Mari Lwyd* (if we leave out of account for the moment the title-poem itself) there are only six poems with any kind of Christian reference, and two of those are equivocal. By the laxest count there are fifteen which expound some aspect of the conquest of time by myth. It would be unwise, as I have already suggested, to deduce from this an unequal balance of interest or belief in the poet. The right deduction, if we must make one, is that Vernon Watkins had not then sufficiently shaped the wheel that was to carry his Christian cart: it travelled much less well than the horse of myth. *The Lady with the Unicorn,* published in 1948, contains a variety of long-lined verse-forms which carry both mythic and Christian concepts with a new and startling ease. If we use this for contrast, it becomes plainer that the poems written before 1941 demonstrate less an imbalance in the poet's belief than a relative lack of success in the writing. In the case of both books what we are attempting to judge is the balance of the poems that came to publication, and it is apparent that the later years of the war and those that followed it provided Vernon Watkins with metaphored vehicles for his Christian belief that moved as fast and as sweetly as the prankish horse of myth.

Nevertheless, the earlier days of dichotomy are discernible, and reconciliation of the different levels of belief did not proceed straightforwardly. I have been unable to find any poem earlier than 'The Replica', published in *Cypress and Acacia,*[27] in which a *rationale* of such a reconciliation is attempted. Here the waterfall is used as the symbol of Platonic immortality:

We know it lives by being consumed, we know
Its voice is new and ancient, and its force
Flies from a single impulse that believes
Nothing is vain, though all is cast for sorrow.
There hangs the image of our life, there flies
The image of our transience. If you ask
Where may divinity or love find rest
When all moves forward to a new beginning
And each obeys one constant law of change,
I cannot answer.
                         Yet to man alone,
Moving in time, birth gives a timeless movement,
To taste the secret of the honeycomb
And pluck from night that blessing which outweighs
All the calamities and griefs of time.
There shines the one scene worthy of his tears,
For in that dark the greatest light was born
Which, if man sees, then time is overthrown,
And afterwards all acts are qualified
By knowledge of that interval of glory:
Music from heaven, the incomparable gift
Of God to man, in every infant's eyes
That vision which is ichor to the soul
Transmitted there by lightning majesty,
The replica, reborn, of Christian love.

This is as clear a statement as one may reasonably hope for. The use of
the word "replica", the Platonic term, sets the Christian pattern and
the organic myth side by side. Generic immortality is not invalidated:
it is all that beasts and birds and trees and flowers can hope for, that
continuity which, in that they are faithful to it, gives their mortality
point and purpose: it is still all that Man can hope for, unless he "sees"
and all his acts are qualified "By knowledge of that interval of glory".
Unseeing, he serves his generation only as an unknowing replica of
what God first laid down, and "all is cast for sorrow".

It should be noted, however, that in this poem it is only the
Christian who conquers time. It is knowledge of the "blessing" (which
every child may grasp at, since he is born with the vision of the replica
of Christian love as well as the replica of his own mortality) "which
outweighs/All the calamities and griefs of time". There is no
necessary contradiction here of the comments on Man in 'Thames
Forest' and 'Griefs of the Sea', which were equivocal at best, but that

there is a distinct move away from the message of the fountain and sycamore poems[28] cannot be doubted. The reference of such time-conquest as the Christian achieves to a personal immortality, however, remains vague. 'The Replica' still leaves the impression that for the man who "sees" time is conquered because his acts are differently valued within his life-span. Christian belief may still be understood to be a consolation, a palliative, within the generic structure. This may not at all correspond with what Vernon Watkins intended: but it is as far as the poem takes us. Only in 'The Yew Tree',[29] amongst early poems, have I discovered a statement which removes the omission and claims that immortality which Christian doctrine hopes for. And here it is not knowledge of Christ but His crucifixion itself that raises Man up:

>   . . . soon, bodily
> Reaching to God, I hear that good thief say:
> 'Lord, for no wrong Thou diest, but justly we.'
> That word kills grief, and through the dark-boughed tree
> Gives to each dead his resurrection day.

Such resolution of the two levels as 'The Replica' achieves does little, however, to explain either the means or the impetus to that resolution in the poet. The sole clue, indeed, is afforded by the phrase "the one scene worthy of his tears", for it was grief that drove Watkins to burnish the Christian replica and put it alongside the original. Whether this was a specific grief it is impossible at this point to say. A careful reader of *The Lady with the Unicorn* will notice no fewer than thirteen poems which are overtly about death (many of them about individual deaths), besides others which touch on it — a high proportion even for a Welsh poet. It seems possible, even likely, that the early death of schoolfellows — and I couple with this the death of 'The Collier' and other like unfortunates — compelled Vernon Watkins urgently to question the regenerative power of myth, to see that Plato's immortality of the just was more realistically the immortality of the famous, the long-lived or the lucky, and to demand for those who had fallen out of the mortal-immortal process, for the lost through no fault of their own, the same immortality earned by the survivors. This demand crystallised in the idea that a life, if once earning the truth and validity of a place in the replica-chain, must retain that truth and that validity for ever. In 'Green Names, Green

Moss' — where "these twin tenements, / Obscurity and Fame"
mislead — the plea is made despairingly:

> Yet every moment must,
> Each turn of head or hand,
> Though disfigured by dust,
> Incorruptibly stand;
> If they are nothing now
> Then they were nothing then.[30]

But the early poems are less specific: few in *The Ballad of the Mari
Lwyd* do more than hint at this development. 'The Windows of
Breath', the only serious exposition, other than 'Prime Colours', of a
Christian attitude to be found there, opens with a successful image
which the poet later thought untrue to his real intention:

> Shine out
> Where dawn breaks in the hand,
> Windows where thought
> Piercing and writing like a diamond
> Traced the first sea, the unconsidered sand;
> Windows where grief
> Touched the first fold, when light's first characters
> Narrowing at dawn a lifetime's distances
> To the cool pillow's cheek
> And impulse of belief,
> Discarding constant blood-knit presences
> Parted in light oblique,
> Stole the black silks of camphored elegy
> And white mortality,
> The lamp-shroud, falling cloth, the taper's hood:
> Windows where good
> Sprang to chill dust, veiled light and visionary,
> Formed the foretelling tears
> I hear and see.

Even within the limits of this quotation the loss of force after the first
image is plain; grief — that "good" should spring "to chill dust" — has
a large enough place but an insufficiently striking one; the poem
completed is relatively unshaped and undoubtedly obscure. Dylan
Thomas was friendlily rude about it: "a serious failure, I think — I
mean it is a serious poem which fails . . . It's altogether too ponderous

and stuffy for me; it *is* a camphored elegy — mothballs".[31] I doubt,
however, whether it was Dylan's criticism that moved Vernon
Watkins to re-write the poem years later (an exercise unique for him
with a poem he had been certain enough of to publish). Far more
probably he saw it, from a distance, as obscure because several-
minded when it should have been single. When he re-wrote it in
October/November 1946 (for the second edition of *The Ballad of the
Mari Lwyd*, published in 1947) 'Windows' in the plural disappeared
from the title: the poem was re-named 'The Eastern Window', the
first five lines of the original were cut (at some loss in terms of poetry),
and *grief* was given an unchallenged place as the first motif.
"Thought", after all, however "piercing", had led to the kind of
knowledge by which "all is cast for sorrow". In the revised version

> A night full-starred
> Lent to the curtain-folds a scent of shrouds,
> The constant heavens exciting mortal lips
> To match Earth's memories to the moving clouds.
> Then from the night the nursery in eclipse
> Learnt superstition while the head was still;

Myth, appearing here in its guise of "memories", fed on death and
taught superstition. Grief, on the other hand, led to an understanding
of that love of parents and of God against which loss could be
measured and, in so doing, ensured its own ultimate annihilation.

> God rose from this,
> Shook once the hewn foundations of the world,
> Earthquakes, volcanoes, and the bell-like sea;
> His marl-made Adam into chaos hurled,
> Left grief a mammoth on the spiny scree.

Matthew, Mark, Luke and John blessed his bed and "that fourfold
waking" was "Fairer than Earth".

In the same way "thought" was excised from a later stanza of the
first version. 'The Windows of Breath' introduced the temptations of
Job:

> He in Job's vision threw
> Fixed thought into a moving wilderness;
> In terror's heart, too terrible for fear,

He built upon the spiral ear,
From nerveless rock wrenching the blood's bright way,
The luminous involutions of the fall,
Commingling mortal with immortal day,
Tracked with beasts' ways, the birds' grave ritual.

"Thought", unseated at last by the incessant removal of its marks, had to go, and only the last four lines, in which "the fall" is associated (for the only time in Watkins's poetry, to the best of my knowledge) with the regenerative immortality of the lower orders, survived the revision. Nothing was to blur, in this more radical analysis, the part played by the love which was learned from grief. Both versions have the same climax, though the earlier has marginally more force:

Out of night's dumb looms where the blind Shades keep
Their crooked shuttles whence all patterns run,
Out of death's fold and shade, the coil of sleep,
Breath flies, and love's born hands surround the sun.

Speculation about the grief or griefs which first set Vernon Watkins upon this course towards the realisation of Christian love is out of place here, even though he has left us, in the poetry, some limited evidence upon which to speculate.[32] What cannot be doubted is the strength of his motivation when he says

I toil to set the dead at rest.[33]

However withdrawn he may have been, in terms of personal relationships, he was intensely moved by the cutting of the cord, by the abrupt termination of a life he had even partly known. This probably was, indeed, that aspect of reality, of the immediacy of life and the dangers to it, that broke through his mythologising, as it does towards the end of 'Sea Music for My Sister Travelling'[34]:

Sandgrain, doomed grain, cluster of seaweed, carrion,
Root of the starry tree
Under the dolphins of the dead
In whistling night, confusing memory,
Cannot rend from me the doom
Of these real boards, real wreck, uncertain room
Tomorrow and forever.

There was no system that could remedy this or the fear of it, no regeneration for those who did not complete their part in the chain. Nothing but the healing of a God who knew persons, who felt for the leper and the sick of the palsy, would serve. The leper, indeed, became Watkins's symbol of Divine intervention: he proposed at one time to call his first book of poems 'Gratitude of a Leper' but was afterwards dissuaded, possibly by Dylan Thomas's ribaldry in a letter from Laugharne Castle, dated 22 May, 1941, in which he asked:

> Any more about your leprous collection? Perhaps the volume should be surgically bound. I do hope it comes out this summer, just before the gas.[35]

The poem which was to have given the book its title was never published, though the "bled boy, leper" of Dylan's next begging letter[36] was not the man to defer often to an outside opinion. Perhaps he felt the poem too personal, too direct:

> And because I am healed by the Instant, the period
> Of the planet is subject till death to my listening soul.
> I am shaken by a deluge of light. The glory of God
> Entered by a beam in the night, and my flesh is made
>   whole.[37]

The wholeness of the flesh is, nevertheless, peculiarly complementary in concept to that of the replica, the repeated wholeness of the first pattern, and the union of the two is quietly symbolised, in the later "leper poem" that he did publish,[38] by the movement of a symbol often used before:

> The withered hand which time interred
> Grasps in a moment the unseen.

God, intervening, mends the pattern, with mercy and love.

But the evolutionary process so described appears to have little relationship to the way in which Vernon Watkins discovered how to present his Christian belief with as much *élan* and surface brilliance as he had more than once given to myth. It was the symbolism of 'The Music of Colours' which made this breakthrough possible. The first poem of what became an intervalled series, 'Music of Colours — White Blossom', opens his second post-war book, *The Lady with the*

Unicorn, and Vernon Watkins recounted its genesis in the simplest terms. It was suggested, he wrote, "in winter by a fall of snow on the sea cliff where I live. I walked out on the cliff and found that the foam of the sea, which had been brilliantly white the previous day, now looked grey".[39] That the sea, "the riderless horse" which in his "other" moments carried the mythic spirits, should be so outshone set off in his mind that train of thought which he had followed earlier: the purity of the newly fallen snow, the immediate replica, so to speak, was more impressive by far than the whipped-up furies of the foam: the riderless horse became again the circus horse, accoutred in the doubtful trappings of the ages: it was knowledge of and recognition of the initial pattern, subsequently purified by the sacrifice of Jesus Christ, that brought a special glory into the natural world:

> I know nothing of Earth or colour until I know I lack
> Original white . . .

It was a recognition, too, of an imperfection personal and general amongst humanity, of identification with the regenerative processes of nature and myth.

We have seen already how in 'Prime Colours' the single origin of the spectrum was introduced, albeit in rather a half-hearted way. 'Music of Colours — White Blossom' presents it without doubting, begins with a celebration of it as in and behind all things, conceives of no other truth or possibility:

> White blossom, white, white shell; the Nazarene
> Walking in the ear; white touched by souls
> Who know the music by which white is seen,
> Blinding white, from strings and aureoles,
> Until that is not white, seen at the two poles,
> Nor white the Scythian hills, nor Marlowe's queen.

That repeated "white" lifts the archaic and echoing syntax of the last two lines, uses it, indeed, to suggest the endless regeneration of the original vision, of the "cloud of witnesses" who have "touched" it. But this white is not to be found in nature:

> White will not be, apart, though the trees try
> Spirals of blossom, their green conspiracy.
> She who touched His garment saw no white tree.

In nature, as in myth, "original white" is nearest in the seeming darkness, from which white may be born again

> From the crushed, dark fibre, breaking in pain.

Darkness is always the darkness of birth and possibility. It is this which explains the poem's ending, where — after a magnificent stanza lauding the white of Leda, taken by Jove — the argument seems, on the surface, to have slipped away to the old levels of regenerative myth. But the

> I know you, black swan

with which it concludes makes again the point that natural whiteness is further from "original white" than is the potential of blackness.

> The mound of dust is nearer, white of mute dust . . .

The black swan is the continual augur of possibility. And the form of the final statement — the "I know you" — associates the poet firmly with that knowledge. It was through grief and darkness, not through the near-whites of nature or human satisfaction, that he had perceived the single, yet multiple, pattern of Christ.

The other two poems in the same canon present a different emphasis. 'Music of Colours: The Blossom Scattered',[40] although it reiterates of "original white" that it was

> Not space revealed it, but the needle's eye
> Love's dark thread holding, when we began to die

imagines a tree, "created on the Lord's day", from which the petals "for time's sake" are shed abroad. Those

> Who know the music by which white is seen,
> See the world's colours in flashes come and go.
> The marguerite's petal is white, is wet with rain,
> Is white, then loses white, and then is white again
> Not from time's course, but from the living spring.

Here "original white" has become something that the Christian can see in flashes in nature's colours, and the whites of the natural petals know, as the poet does, that they are "of whitest darkness made", that they are

> White born of bride and bridegroom, when they take
> Love's path through Hades, engendered of dark ground.

They know, in a word, like Orpheus and Eurydice, that there is no music without loss, no white without an initial dark. The white that "flashes" may indeed for a moment, most of all at dawn, at the fledging of "pure spirit", be "original white", and Leda, in this poem rehabilitated, cries after Jove's visitation.

> 'Heavenborn am I. White-plumaged heart, you beat against the sun!'

This second 'Music of Colours' poem, then, by a slight change of emphasis, has raised myth almost to the old ambivalence, introducing the "music of absence" theme (the beauty of Orpheus's singing to the lute as he searches for Eurydice) which in the third poem, 'Dragonfoil and the Furnace of Colours',[41] embraces all nature, running like a faun through the rainbowed flowers. Single, bicoloured, parti-coloured, but never the full white, the blooms speak always of Eurydice lost:

> Yet the turf tells me: she it is, no other,
> Touches the rose-blaze, gathers what became her
> Music. Forgetfulness holds her like a girdle
> Silent. Only by absence is the song made
> Audible. Orpheus, learning above Lethe,
> Knows every note there.

This flower-summer, "this perennial wonder / Of fireborn blossoms" is

> True for this moment, therefore never dying,

a declaration that both re-asserts, for the lower orders of nature, the place of the immediately mortal in the replica-succession and echoes the demand made for Man, in 'Green Names, Green Moss', that even if he fails to discern "The replica, reborn, of Christian love", he should, with memory's support, be immortalised in the mythic chain.

The "magic surface" of myth grows, extends. It is justified by the original Creation. But

> All that is made here hides another making;

even at dawn the human spirit is blind to it.

> Waking entranced, we cannot see that other
> Order of colours moving in the white light.

So the bow of the 'Music of Colours' curves from poem to poem, from a triumphant perception of "original white", through a more hesitant assertion that *some* can see that white in nature's flashes of colour, to a paean of praise for the summer glory which *all* know and remember, even though it be the glory of a lower order. And of this last poem it must be said, if Vernon Watkins's assertion that "the form of the meaning" be accepted, that its regret, its sense of absence, is no more than an occasional question, posed as much by the coloured glories of mortality as by any more consistent mysticism. The irregular dactylic stresses of the four-and-a-half line stanzas (five-and-a-half in the central section) are more joyous and subtle than those of, say, George Meredith's 'Love in the Valley' (which, although dissimilar in stanzaic form is not unlike in stress and spirit) and the half-line poises each stanza for the next, keeping mystery (as in 'Thames Forest') and the faintest of regrets on tip-toe among the rioting flowers.

> Dust drops from campions where the hedge is hottest. ·
> Foxgloves and grasses tremble where a snake basks,
> Coiled under brilliance. Petals of the burnet-rose
> Flash there pulsating: do the gold antennae
> Feel for the white light?

The question has no separate impetus. It has been formalised in the delight of the moment.

With the 'Music of Colours' sequence all sense of an earlier dichotomy disappears. Christianity and myth are now established at different levels on the same tree, a point made symbolically in 'Zacchaeus in the Leaves'.[42] First

> The myth above the myth,

Pan above Zacchaeus;
Zacchaeus climbing,
Mounted above his youth,
Alone in time
Seeking the heavenly death.

Then, with Jesus approaching, Zacchaeus

                    . . . crouching,
Watching the myth
Moving, the myth
Move to the zenith
Not found in youth:
'If His eyes see us,
If His eyes see us,
Dazzled above men,
Though we are buried then,
The myth above the truth.'

The sycamore, most constant among trees, both lifts and drops its keys upon "small-statured man".

This is not to say that the use of a single symbol, as here, ensures that there is, among the poems Vernon Watkins wrote in the forties, a permanent accommodation or relationship between Christianity and myth. If the direct confrontation between the two attempted in 'Prime Colours' was rarely repeated, poems like 'The Song of the Good Samaritan' and 'The Healing of the Leper'[43] see the memoried and regenerated myth as tolerable only when the parallel replica of Christian love shines clearly in view. *Per contra*, I have said nothing so far of what is undoubtedly an attack, on myth's behalf, upon the materialism of a so-called Christian society. I refer to 'The Ballad of the Mari Lwyd' itself. Vernon Watkins once said that "a ballad must be hammered and beaten and knocked into shape until it is as hard and anonymous as a pebble on the shore".[44] I am not going to claim that he broke his rule with the 'Mari Lwyd'. The 'Mari Lwyd' is not, in the strictest sense, a *ballad* at all: it is a dramatic poem, with speeches by rival parties and comments by other, supposedly more objective, voices. In the arguments of the contestants there is a serious imbalance and the third party comment is by no means neutral. The scheme of the "ballad" is briefly as follows: those who on New Year's Eve carry the Mari Lwyd, the wooden horse's head, seek to gain entry to a house by outwitting those inside in a rhyming contest. If the householders fail to answer, the Mari Lwyd party must be admitted and plied with food and drink. Vernon Watkins made his Mari a skull[45] and its carriers the Dead. In his Note to the poem he wrote:

> I have attempted to bring together those who are separated. The last breath of the year is their threshold, the moment of supreme forgiveness, confusion and understanding, the profane and sacred moment impossible to realise while the clockhands divide the Living from the Dead.

This is less disingenuous than incomplete. By intention the poem is another stratagem to "conquer time" and the Dead are, as always in the Watkins legend, the intended conquerors. "I make them three times as human and cunning and violent as the living",[46] he said on one occasion when introducing the poem, and again stopped short of the recognition that he was introducing an imbalance foreign to the *natural* occasion of which he was making use. For despite their savage, soft and cunning attack the Dead are defeated: they are not admitted, even for a moment.

The Living, who have cast the Dead out, as the Prologue tells us, "from their own fear, from their own fear of themselves, into the outer loneliness of death, rejected them, and cast them out for ever", waver between scorn and fear. They

> face the terrible masquerade
> Of robbers dressed like the dead.

The Dead, moreover, are no longer what they were at the moment of death.

> Good men gone are evil become

— they are beggars, drunkards, lechers, "Men of the night with a legion of wrongs", blasphemers, their "red throats parched for gin". The "banished Poor", they have nothing to offer that the Living desire:

> They give what none has asked

except "Froth from an old barrel", an unwelcome, stirred-up past.

Moreover, like the two thieves who died with Christ at Golgotha ("that skull-shaped hill") they represent the blasphemy of good and evil in His presence:

> Those blasphemous hands can change our mind
> Or mood with a craftsman's skill;
> Under their blessing they blast and blind,
> Maim, ravish and kill.

With these "devils" who "have smelt our kitchen-smoke" the Living feel they have nothing in common: indoors there is neither forgiveness nor understanding. Huddling by their fire and in front of the loaded table, they argue only by vilifying: their successful materialism challenges the claims of the Dead in one way only:

> What can you give for the food we store
> But a slice of starving sky?

Yet that the Living themselves have the same dualism as the Dead, the same amorality, is suggested by their self-injunctions:

> The old Nick will keep the flies from our sheep,
> The tic, the flea and the louse.
> Open the flagons. Uncork the deep
> Beer of this bolted house.

They differ from the Dead, then, mainly in being alive and possessing, and their total unwillingness to recognise any communion with those outside is based on a determination to keep out imagination, the past, the questioning of "virtue", and the fear of death. The materialism of the so-called Christian society they represent is challenged by one of the supposedly neutral voices, which evokes

> The breath of a numb thing, loud and faint:
> Something found and lost.
> The minute drops in the minute-glass;
> Conscience counts the cost.
> What mounted, murderous thing goes past
> The room of Pentecost?

The use of the word "room" here, although not untrue to the Biblical account of the "rushing mighty wind" and the "cloven tongues like as of fire" in "the house where they were sitting",[47] suggests the confinement of the evangelical Gospel in a materialist society. And if "room" should be interpreted as the "place vacated by" the Gospel's inspiration, the indictment is sterner yet. It is significant, for either interpretation, that the Mari, the duality of death and imagination, "goes past" it. Certainly Vernon Watkins, who in another poem[48] wrote that

... the dead live, and I am of their kind.

had no part with the possessors. That this possessing society, arguing only from the "things" that they possessed, successfully kept out "the banished Poor" was no more than a recognition that his was a minority view.

On the other hand, the poet's claims for the Dead, with which the greater part of 'The Ballad' is occupied, enlarge themselves with the twists and turns of the argument. It is no part of my business here to tease out all the obscurities of mythical or biblical reference[49]: I confine myself to setting out the nature of these claims.

In the first place, the Dead are both good and evil, not as separate souls but as a collective force (the strength of myth).

Those Exiles carry her [the Mari], they who seem holy and have put on corruption, they who seem corrupt and have put on holiness.

So goes the Prologue, setting out both the mortality of the individual in the chain of immortality and the immortality in which mortality has a share. The poem follows this by confounding it with a duality of good and evil, set as a refrain throughout:

Sinner and saint, sinner and saint:
A horse's head in the frost.

In the second place, a recognition of this duality, in which the Living share, is necessary before life can be lived in the fullness of understanding.

And now you must let our Mari in:
She must inspire your feast.

The word "inspire" is crucial. In this sense

> Our Mari tries your faith.

Her carriers know the charity that is born of self-knowledge: the Dead, behind their claims first to bless and then to curse, understand that, in this duality of good and evil, they are one with the Living. That is why they both curse by contraries —

> Hell curse this house for a badger's holt
> If we find no man devout.
> God singe this doorway, hinge and bolt,
> If you keep our evil out.

— and cry revengefully:

> Know you are one with Cain the farm
> And Dai of Dowlais pit;
> You have thieved with Benjamin's robber's arm;
> With Delilah you lay by night.
> You cheated death with Barabbas the Cross
> When the dice of hell came down.
> You prayed with Jo in the prisoners' fosse
> And ran about Rahab's town.

But they have more to offer than self-knowledge, and it is this "more" that the Living reject with fear and trembling. The Dead claim for their Mari that

> . . . She knows all from the birth of the Flood
> To this moment where we stand

They themselves have hidden with David in the cave of Engedi, seen (always in the half-darkness) the battle-strength of Samson, and watched, from the caves of Harlech, the seven men who carried the head of Bran as they themselves carry the Mari, feasting for the allotted seven years.[50] They have brought the Mari from "white Hebron",[51] Ezekiel's Valley of Dry Bones and the glass castle of Arianrhod:[52] they were present at Golgotha and the Mari, older than they, remembers the pagan ceremonies that preceded Christ's coming.

> She saw dark thorns harrow
> Your God crowned with the holly.

This time-conquering "holiness" (which is the holiness of the myth that grew from the original Creation, not a Christlike holiness) is the special gift of death and of those who have accepted it:

> In the mouth of the sack, in the stifled breath,
> In the sweat of the hands, in the noose,
> In the black of the sack, in the night of death
> Shines what you dare not lose.

But the Living wish to lose it, nevertheless. The Dead comment on their "faith in the pin of the tongs / Laying your fears at rest" (fears particularly associated with "the ash of the grave") and catching in a single symbol the time-hinge of the Old/New Year[53] and the attempt of the Living to grasp and disperse their fears of ashy death, urge that "the pin goes in to the inmost dark / Where the dead and living meet". In that dark, they assert, both "beat with the selfsame heart".

All this the Living seek to ignore. The gifts of forgiveness, self-knowledge and vital or "religious" imagination which the Mari has to offer are stubbornly rejected. The door remains closed and at length, after several seeming retreats, the rabble outside goes away. One of the neutral voices comments:

> You have seen a god in the eyes of the beggar.

The Dead, all the same, have had two-thirds of the talking-time and even more of the imaginative force allotted to them. The imbalance of the poem is plain. It is no part of my thesis to suggest that this imbalance was fully calculated: the weight is where, given Vernon Watkins's already outlined preoccupations, we should expect to find it, if we once accept the total omission of Christian values from the thinking of the Living. But that omission could hardly be other than calculated. If there was "a god" outside, there was no God within — certainly not in the room where the table groaned with food and drink.

The pattern of mythic and Christian themes in Watkins's early poetry is therefore much more varied than might at first appear. Kathleen Raine in her article 'Vernon Watkins: Poet of Tradition' suggests that his "initiatory knowledge" of the tradition of imagination and "inspiration" came not from Coleridge or Blake, Plotinus or the Platonists, Heine or Holderlin, but from "the vital memory of the Welsh bardic tradition".[54] It would be pleasant, from a purely Welsh point of view, to think that this was so, and there is no question at all that he was acquainted with Arthurian legend, the Mabinogion and such Welsh poetry as was available in translation from a very early age. But "the Welsh bardic tradition" would, in Vernon Watkins's youth, have been much more difficult to approach without far more than a smattering of Welsh,[55] and Kathleen Raine's argument, examined more closely, appears to centre in the Taliesin poems, the first of which was included in *The Death Bell* (1954). Watkins's knowledge of and interest in the poems of Taliesin, long since available in English in the translations of Lady Charlotte Guest and J. Gwenogvryn Evans, plainly antedates this by many years. How else should the claims of the Dead whose Mari masters time echo some of the details of Taliesin's most famous poem?

> I was in Canaan when Absalom was slain;
> I conveyed the Divine Spirit to the level of the vale of Hebron;
> I was in the court of Don before the birth of Gwidion.
> I was instructor to Eli and Enoc;
> I have been winged by the genius of the splendid crosier;
> I have been loquacious prior to being gifted with speech;
> I was at the place of the crucifixion of the merciful Son of
> God;
> I have been three periods in the prison of Arianrod;
> I have been the chief director of the work of the tower of
> Nimrod;
> I am a wonder whose origin is not known.

Chronology, therefore, may be no barrier to Kathleen Raine's thesis, and the attraction of the Taliesin theme to a poet already in love with the conquest of time is sufficiently plain. But when she infers that it is "the elusive figure of Taliesin" that "unites pre-Christian with Christian themes" for Vernon Watkins and that there was a "deliberate baptism of the bardic spirit"[56] she may be convicted of not having read his work carefully enough. It was grief, not the bardic spirit, that brought that baptism, grief that first brought down the winged horse of myth and found it a circus entertainer. And baptism, if that must be the term, had been in no sense deliberate: first suffered in childhood, it had advanced its power no more rapidly than death.

> Even as a child I began to say: How far?
> Parting the curtain, the winding-sheet of the dead.
> The loom of the hand has the pathway of every star.
>
> Disappearance of the proud horses! Circling in dread,
> Stampeding in light, he heard the mythologies shrink,
> The rushing stars, their reverberant, thundering tread;
>
> From a little worn-away trough where asses drink,
> One by one, and above them, finding the sea,
> Swallows pass, and their world ripples over the brink.[57]

NOTES

1. 25 October, 1941.
2. There is a *prima facie* case for Kathleen Raine's suggestion that "Mr. Watkins has been for a long time moving from Pagan rite to Christian sacrament". 'Vernon Watkins: Poet of Tradition', in *The Anglo-Welsh Review*, No.33, Summer 1964, reprinted in *Defending Ancient Springs* (O.U.P. 1967) but it is scarcely strong enough to face up to the biographical complications it might involve.
3. 'Poetry and Experience', a lecture-reading dated October 1961.
4. Notes for a reading at Ammanford, undated.
5. *The Ballad of the Mari Lwyd*, p.19.
6. *Ibid.*, p.25.
7. Whether "small-statured man" here is the conscious precursor of the Zacchaeus symbol Vernon Watkins later favoured I do not know. But it is at least interesting that Zacchaeus, "the chief among publicans" (or tax-gatherers), who was "little of stature" (St. Luke, c.19, vv.2-3), climbed a sycamore tree to see Jesus pass through Jericho, and it was this incident which the poet used in 'Zacchaeus in the Leaves' to provide a Christan reversal of the message of 'Sycamore'.
8. *Light* here is the symbol for Life, both in its sense of the period of human existence and in that of the understanding and enjoyments intrinsic to it. "Fallen from light" seems to me to refer solely to the child's genesis as seed in the living world and his subsequent period in the womb. It has none of the significance of being "heaven-dropped" which we might infer from Henry Vaughan's 'The Retreate' or Wordsworth's 'Intimations of Immortality'.

9.   'Poetry and Experience', p.2. Watkins records that "two years later, when I met Dylan Thomas, ['After Sunset' and 'Thames Forest'] were still incomplete. He did see both poems in early drafts on the very day I met him, for he came to my house and asked to see "any poems I had". When he had seen two or three, he asked if there were any more, and I dragged in a trunk from the next room."

10.   'Theory and Act', a typescript article, undated.

11.   The Sapphic line proper consisted of eleven syllables or five feet, arranged as trochee, spondee, dactyl, trochee, trochee. *Sedibus gaudens variis dolisque* is a Latin example of the line. Horace created what may be called "the Sapphic stanza" by using the Sapphic line three times repeated, followed by a shorter fourth line consisting of a dactyl and either a spondee or a trochee. John Heath-Stubbs ('Pity and the Fixed Stars', *Poetry Quarterly,* Spring 1950) was correct in representing Vernon Watkins as *experimenting* with the Sapphic stanza in 'Ophelia', though the phrase would have been much more appropriate to 'Thames Forest', written three years before. It should be obvious however, that Watkins' first three lines are preponderantly dactylic rather than trochaic, and that the stanza acquires movement and urgency because of this.

12.   The line "These leaves are numbered" reads like an attempt to equivocate, to have it both ways. It suggests, not a consciousness of the ages and generations of history, but the incursion into the argument of the poem (to which it is extraneous) of that Divine control superimposed upon 'Griefs of the Sea' and its personalising in God's love for every individual soul: "Are not five sparrows sold for two farthings, and not one of them is forgotten before God? But even the very hairs of your head are all numbered" (St. Luke, c.12, vv.6-7).

13.   'A Prayer against Time' (*The Ballad of the Mari Lwyd*, p.38).

14.   *The Lady with the Unicorn,* pp.43-44.

15.   'The Foal'.

16.   In *The Symposium* or *Supper.*

17.   'The Replica': *Cypress and Acacia,* p.87.

18.   *Ibid.*, p.53.

19.   'Music of Colours — Dragonfoil and the Furnace of Colours', *Affinities,* p.83.

20.   *Ibid.* The theme of the poem is that Man is so "entranced" by the colours of the natural world that he cannot see "that other / Order of colours moving in the white light".

21.   'Discoveries' (*The Ballad of the Mari Lwyd,* p.68).

22.   'Touch with your Fingers' (*Cypress and Acacia,* p.78).

23.   John Heath-Stubbs, *op. cit.*, p.20, calls him "the youthful survivor of a pit-disaster". It appears at least equally possible that Dai under his "linen sheet" is *dead,* a climax which would validate the denial of the Joseph allegory in the verses preceding.

24.   The negative response to the leper's lamp here is underlined by the gloriously contrary declaration of other leper poems. 'The Healing of the Leper' begins:

          O, have you seen the leper healed,
          And fixed your eyes upon his look?

There is the book of God revealed,
And God has made no other book.
(*The Lady with the Unicorn*, p.77).

25. 'Fidelity to the Dead', *ibid.*, p.40.
26. 'Fidelity to the Living', *ibid.*, p.40.
27. p.87.
28. e.g. 'From my Loitering', 'Sycamore', 'The Age-Changers', 'A Prayer against Time'.
29. *The Lady with the Unicorn*, p.101. 'Four Sonnets of Resurrection', *ibid.*, pp. 58-60, merely pose a question and the ultimate resolution appears to be in generic immortality.
30. The later extension of this idea is illustrated by the quotation from 'The Immortal in Nature' on p.108.
31. *Dylan Thomas: Letters to Vernon Watkins*, p.76.
32. For example, "I set one grave apart" ('Three Harps' in *Cypress and Acacia*, p.16). But since this, in point of date, may have referred to his father, it may throw no light on early losses and their effect on the poet.
33. 'Crowds' (*The Lady with the Unicorn*, p.63).
34. *The Lamp and the Veil* (1945), p.34.
35. *Dylan Thomas: Letters to Vernon Watkins*, p.102.
36. *Ibid.*, p.103.
37. Poem in manuscript.
38. 'The Healing of the Leper' (*The Lady with the Unicorn*, p.77).
39. 'Poetry and Experience', p.7.
40. *The Death Bell*, pp.26-28.
41. *Affinities*, pp.80-83.
42. *The Lady with the Unicorn*, pp.90-94.
43. *Ibid.*, pp. 95-98 and 77-78 respectively.
44. Introduction to *Three Ballads*, broadcast 14 January 1953.
45. His Note to the poem in the first edition described it in practice as "a white or grey horse's head modelled in wood, painted and hung with ribbons". The corresponding Note in the second edition goes as follows: "It was a horse's skull. Sometimes it was supplanted by a copy, a white or grey horse's head modelled in wood, painted and hung with ribbons, but in all examples of the true tradition the skull itself was used. The skull had been chosen and buried when the horse died, and the burial-place marked, so that it could be exhumed for the ceremony. After it, the skull was kept, and used again on the next thirty-first of December, and so year after year."
46. 'Poetry and Experience', p.3.
47. The Acts of the Apostles, c.2, vv. 2-3.
48. 'Gravestones', *The Lady with the Unicorn*, p.74.
49. An extended examination of such obscurities is attempted in Dora Polk, *Vernon Watkins and the Spring of Vision* (1977). To this work I am indebted for such explanations as I offer.
50. The interpretation of the "caves of Harlech" reference is a matter of doubt. "The dead sea of Harlech", in another place, suggests that Cantre'r Gwaelod and its drowned lands may have been intended, but Harlech was the extreme northerly limit of the lands supposedly lost.

51.   Hebron was Abraham's chosen abode after Lot had first taken the lion's share (Genesis, c.13) — therefore perhaps the place of sacrifice in a sense deeper than that Abraham built an altar to God there. It was there also that God promised Abraham a son. Abraham, as the first man in the Book of Genesis to hear and obey the voice of God consistently, may have bestowed on Hebron — in the poet's view — the blessed associations of the word "white" (c.f. Welsh *gwyn*; also Taliesin's placing of the Creation there: Polk, *op. cit.,* p.119, quoting Lady Charlotte Guest's translation).

52.   "The room of glass", the constellation Corona Borealis, to which the souls of dead kings repaired to await resurrection. Polk, *op. cit.,* p.50.

53.   The Mari, in her guise of The White Goddess, was also the Roman goddess Cardea, "the hinge on which the year swung". Once the mother of Janus, the two-headed god of doors and the first month of the year, her later attributes were hostile to his. But Ovid says of her: "Her power is to open what is shut: to shut what is open". Robert Graves, *The White Goddess,* pp. 68-69, and 178.

54.   *Op. cit.,* p.20.

55.   Robert Graves' *The White Goddess,* for instance, was not available until 1946, *The Development of Welsh Poetry,* by H. Idris Bell, not until 1936.

56.   Raine, *op. cit.,* p.33.

57.   'The Song of the Good Samaritan', *The Lady with the Unicorn,* p.97.

"The Black Spot in the Focus":
A Study of the Poetry of Alun Lewis

Raiders' Dawn[1] is an obsessive book. I do not mean *obsessive* for the reader, though that too may be true, but for the poet. Very, very few of the poems in it are not concerned, in one way or another, with the threat to Love. Yet somehow, in the minds of many critics, the theme has been fragmented, even diminished, by being seen against the onset of war, against a portrait of Alun Lewis in uniform and the much more varied impact of the stories, and even, separately, against his wartime marriage to Gweno Ellis. It is time that the poems were read carefully and together, so that the real essence, both of *Raiders' Dawn* and *Ha! Ha! Among the Trumpets*[2], may be distilled.

The problem may be indicated, in one of its aspects, by the following quotation from David Shayer's article on 'The Poetry of Alun Lewis' in *Triskel Two*[3] (an article which in many matters of textual detail is a useful introduction):

> Gweno and the war came together: the realisation of almost intolerable joy was almost exactly paralleled by a confrontation with the real possibility of death. There is a poem by Graves ('Pure Death') which expresses the dilemma exactly:
>
> > We looked, we loved, and therewith instantly
> > Death became terrible to you and me . . . .

However well put that may be, it was not the position of Alun Lewis, except in that his new and personal love afforded ancillary agony to the main debate. In that sense it cannot be described as *wrong* in itself. Rather it falsifies by concentrating on the personalised aspect of a much wider picture. That is what I mean by the tendency to fragment in much of the criticism at present available.

Alun Lewis was a Socialist of the most idealistic sort, what is still called in our rather feeble echoing way an International Socialist. It may have been somewhat late in the day, even in his teens and early twenties, to hold high ideals which the League of Nations had let resoundingly fall, but Lewis was a tenacious idealist. It was, in a way, his tenacity — what, obversely, we could call his failure to adapt — which brought about his ultimate defeat. We have, I think, to see him as a man whose political and social faith had grown out of a family doctrine which had only recently separated itself from a religious tradition with deep roots in the previous century of Wales. Conscious knowledge of oneself and unconscious or unrecognised powers have to be kept apart, however. If Lewis was a Welshman by birth, by emotional attachment and by radical sympathy, it is nevertheless true that at the beginning of his work as a poet he stood with his back to Wales, looking outwards. Being both human and young, he saw the great battles to be fought for the faith as "out there", in the wider world, and he had the all-too-familiar difficulty in applying to those close at hand the Love about which he was prepared to speak loudly at a distance.

In Section VIII of 'Threnody for a Starry Night'[4], in the midst of the "individual defeat" that was already his when War attacked his hopes, he writes:

> For we maintained
> The state must wither in the end,
> And soon forgot
> That fire withers most
> Armies as cities, frail as summer flowers.

He was then understanding more clearly, realising that the battle was always where one was. "We were the daylight but we could not see." It was, of course, a natural concomitant of growing older.

This poem, nevertheless, may be seen as an evocation of a miracle that does not yield either to age or to mortal enemy. Love's "milk teeth" may be "smashed"[5], the original innocence may be irrecoverable, the odds may seem forever stacked against the good and war make its terrible inroads most of all into the lives of the blameless, but, contrary to even the blithest expectation, Love is not defeated. It may appear even as the worm that transforms the appearance of death[6]. Over-imaged as this poem undoubtedly is, and to an extent confusing, there can be no doubt that it expresses what was to Lewis nothing less than a faith — a faith already savaged by war and sad experience but one that was to survive for what little time was left.

We need, I think, some definition of this Love which was the poet's talisman and, as often, definitions are difficult. Alun Lewis's vision of Love contains that kind of caring and suffering for mankind, individually and *in toto*, which Christian love attempts: it contains the full human affection which two persons, man and woman, may feel for each other: it contains eroticism and lust: and it contains, if less commonly, comradeship and sentiments of home. I hope to show that some of these elements have been neglected. They can certainly be peeled away from each other, like the skins of an onion, but Lewis was much more concerned with his failure to integrate them — that is, with the contrast between personal experience and the often-stated ideal. We must certainly ask at this stage: Was Alun Lewis a Christian? One of his grandfathers, Melchizedek Evans, had been a miner turned parson turned Unitarian minister[7]: the other was, according to Alun's sister Mair, "a Bible-black, God-fearing man who never kissed his children, whose house on Sundays was like a morgue, and who persuaded mother, against her judgement but to save family irritation, to have us all sign the pledge when we were four years old."[8] That description, of course, is in the language of revolt and carries its own assumptions. The Unitarianism of the Lewis household, during the childhood of Alun and Mair, was a very much laxer faith: Unitarianism, indeed, throughout the late nineteenth and early twentieth century, was often the creed of those who were gradually leaving Christianity for humanism. And certainly the Lewises had abandoned Christian observances, except in the most occasional sense. Art — an art of living as well as enhanced aestheticism — had taken their place. The word "beauty" had taken to itself an absolute value. So that when Alun Lewis wrote to Brenda Chamberlain that he wanted the Caseg Broadsheets "to reach the people — with beauty & love"[9] he was not so much indulging in a rather unattractive kind of preciosity as reaching into a haversack of long-held beliefs. I doubt whether Art survived the traumas of war, except in the narrower sense useful to the writer, but Love did. And this Love must be examined further.

If Christianity was no longer a matter of observance, it was still present in the Lewis household as myth. Alun Lewis plainly knew his

Bible well and, if God was a figure of some dubiety — the creator of pain as well as joy — Jesus was a revered teacher, in whom and from whom the principle of Love took its origin and impetus. All this is worth saying because Alun Lewis's ideals were, at the very least, post-Christian. The word he uses in several of his poems for the integration of ideals at the very centre is *soul*— a curiously religious term which is often at odds with the Keatsian Romanticism of his imagery. In Section VII of the poem already quoted, 'Threnody for a Starry Night', we find lovers with "the soul's sweet fern seed on their bodies"[10], a state of sexual integration which the tragedy of the times finds insufficient. In 'Postscript: For Gweno' it is "Our soul" — not only the love they have for each other but the beliefs and concepts they have in common — which "withstands the terror"[11]. The overtones of a no-longer-accepted belief come through.

Section I of 'Odi et Amo', though the theme of it is obscurely phrased, appears to suggest that the fullness of love began in a peace, "in the / Stillness of the heart in the white breast"[12], in which sensual and caring elements were at one and that the worst shock to its confidence is the record of history, whose "living weal" demonstrates the need for something more — the will to bear suffering, to carry "the stigmata / Of the christ in us". There are moments when this theme is treated literarily or inconsequentially, as in 'The Defeated', with its opening quotation from the Welsh:

> More love was there never
> By Euphrates and Tigris
> Than in our proud country[13]

— a state that, as Caesar observed of the Celts when they were continually defeated by the Germanic tribes, unmans the warrior. Love and its opposite cannot co-exist. But perhaps this poem begins the look-back, not so much to a grandiloquent Wales as to the remembered, but previously disregarded, workings of Love in a poor community. It may indeed not be "literary" at all, but a move away from world theory towards local practicality and practice, something which is not really apparent in Lewis's writing until his second volume, *Ha! Ha! Among the Trumpets*.

But if we presume to call Lewis's Love post-Christian, we have to realise too that it comes unsupported by any real theological apparatus (for which biblical images are no substitute). It is an agnostic who circumnavigates God in the prologue poem 'The Grinder':

> Who carved the round red sun?
> Who purified the snow?
> Who is that hidden one? You do not know.[14]

What the poet, the "grinder of words", is looking for, he asserts, is a precise outline of "Existence in its native nakedness"[15]. If he cannot find it or make it out, at least the details he is able to put together "can warm the night". A good deal has been made of this in the context of Lewis's reason for writing at all: his poems, it is said, challenge darkness. And with this I would not disagree, provided darkness be better defined than it has been in most critiques. But I want to emphasise the word *warm*. There is here an echo of an earlier poem, 'Atropos to Ophelia', in which Ophelia is urged to

> Give of your warmth, then, to the sable stranger[16]

— the elucidation of which must wait for a while. But this is basically what Lewis wanted Love to do, to warm the world. And if you ask the question, did he really, more than occasionally, believe that Love had done, could do and would do that job, he himself answers with the question which the wind in the olive tree in Gethsemane garden poses in 'The East'. If pain and grief and passion are meant to refine and improve man

> Must
> Such aching
> Go to making
> Dust?[17]

There is a difficulty here, of course. As soon as one speaks of a meaning and a purpose *outside* man, one is precluding the humanist answer: it is apparent that Lewis is not considering Jesus as humanist teacher banking on the psychological force of example but is looking wistfully at Jesus the Son of God calling upon a divine promise. And the poem is called 'The East' — the beginning, traditionally. Undoubtedly this is an early poem and too much may be laid upon it: but it is, nevertheless, difficult to see the Love of which Alun Lewis continually speaks as having less than some residually superhuman, if not divine, quality. Its persistence in the face of the denials of self-betrayal and war suggests that it rested on something more than an inexperienced human opinion. It had, in its way, been laid down as a faith.

Perhaps the only full expression of this Love, if characteristically oblique, is to be found in the poem called 'The Madman', an appellation which, in the well-known Shakespearian phrase, should clearly be associated with "the lover and the poet". There is, in stanza one, some attempt to justify the title by phrases like "The shattered crystal of his mind" and "dangerous splinters"[18], but the poem goes on to show that the quest for an "ultimate beauty" has nothing destructive about it. In the face of life's immediate twists and turns the so-called madman may appear helpless —

> His laughter has the sound of weeping

— but his singleness of purpose enables him to disregard all minor madnesses and point his dreams at "God's terrible silence" —

> His weeping has the sound of laughter.

But the sensual has no place in these dreams:

> He knows life is a beautiful girl who loves no one
> Yet makes the mirrors glitter and men mad.
> And he has lived a lifetime with a virgin,
> Peacefully, like Josph of Nazareth.[19]

Indeed, it is important to understand the sensual as temporary, as deflowering without saving the bloom or the pollen. Absorbed in natural wonders, the madman sails on "without a compass" "through the clashing ocean of love": his phallic mast is a rose-tree lapped in leaf which sucks up "the salt sap of his timeless grief"[20]: his *seed*, a favourite Lewis word to which we shall come back, is dispersed in wonder: the "glittering constellations" are his progeny.

But all this is encompassed by darkness, a darkness against which and into which his dreams point fingers. Somewhere in that darkness is the continually frustrated completion of his dream, "the maddening ultimate beauty of the . . . angelic faces". Now it is apparent that an unsensual Love is the means to the quest and beauty is the ultimate sought after. But both are one in the end: the beauty is "angelic" and situate in "God's terrible silence". It is also clear, I think, that the poem is telling us that neither from the temporary nor from the long-lived mutations of the natural world can one draw evidence about human perfectability, which I take to be what *beauty* means in this context: it is, in the end, a matter of faith and desire, by the latter of which words I imply not wishful thinking but a positive and effortful willing. This seems to me particularly clear from the last section of 'Threnody for a Starry Night', where

> The white brain crossing
> The frontiers of darkness
> To darkness and always
> Darkness pursuing,
> Finds asylum in a dreamless
> Traumatic anguish where the planets
> Stay at the stations where they gathered
> In darkness of Creation;[21]

The "white" brain — that is, one unaccustomed to dealing in darkness — arrives by constant *pursuit* (a better word than the *dreams* of 'The Madman') at the dream*less* but anguished position which was God's when he was about to make man. This is not something divinely given: it is achieved by effort and imagination:

> And in the dark the sensitive blind hands
> Fashion the burning pitch of night
> In lovely images of dawn.[22]

Not only is there something here very like Vernon Watkins's belief in the dark as that out of which light comes, as life from death: there is also a strongly Pelagian, perhaps even humanistic, element. Love as the means to the perfectability of the world needs human effort to make it work. Amidst it all God stands afar off in his silence.

I have spent a little time on what seem to me a few key poems not solely because they suggest some of the outlines of Love but because, too, they introduce the *darkness* which has engaged the attention of several critics. This *darkness* has been associated with a world at war, with Love under duress, with personal separation and the pains of death, and, most commonly, with the gloom that settles on the poet's spirit as his spiritual problems mount. I do not seek to discredit these associations entirely, least of all the last one: if I did my own title of 'The Black Spot in the Focus' would be meaningless. But it does seem to me to be important to emphasise that darkness is present in the early poems written before the outbreak of war, many of them before even the beginning of the poet's love for Gweno. What does it seem to signify?

In general it may be likened to the experience of being alone, standing alone, without the help of lover, comrade, history, myth, standing alone without certainty of God, to put a question or questions to "Existence in its native nakedness"[23]. In 'The Captivity' it is, more conventionally, the darkness of the imagination, into whose safety the princess escapes from the hated attentions of Pharaoh:

> My heart is escaped in its night.[24]

But even here aloneness is the key: the conditions of living are entirely hateful: the heart can reject them. 'Horace at Twenty', another early poem, looks to the night for salvation:

> But I lie alone, alone, Lalage;
> The darkness has made me whole.[25]

But perhaps this confident note is heard only in poems that are not merely early but derivative. Interestingly, 'Atropos to Ophelia', which might have been similarly described, is in a different section of the book, along with 'The Madman' and the few Welsh poems. The darkness here parallels much more closely that in 'The Madman'. Hamlet is the unknown "sable stranger"[26] to whom Ophelia gives her ignorant love: what that experience of loving may discover may be no more than an emptiness, a series of meaningless antitheses:

> His birth and his death shall be one thing, and then no thing,
> The womb and the coffin shall be one place, and then no place.

That is the risk that Love takes. But it has to be taken: Ophelia's love may be "ignorant as sunlight on his limbs" but it is "warmth". Darkness is the meaning of living: it has to be penetrated, whatever lies beyond. It is also, of course, the risk that we take alone, with Love as our only conceivable asset. In passing we may note the stylistic likenesses between this poem and 'The Madman', the correspondence between the sun of Ophelia's love and the "white brain" crossing the frontiers of darkness in 'Threnody for a Starry Night', and the word *warmth* which we recollect again from 'The Grinder'. It should be plain, in retrospect, what Alun Lewis thought the poet's job was: to take "Such odds and ends as likely you possess"[27] and get such "sparks" out of them as may *warm the night*. Love is what we have, and can apply. Meaning and purpose may come from that Love, or they may not. Darkness has to be challenged because it is *there*. Life cannot progress on any other terms.

It may be noted, too, that darkness is sometimes the nature of experience itself, something that happens but is not understood, or something in which change takes place without its being noticed. In 'Destruction', another key poem which I shall come back to,

> ... my love knows nothing of that grim destruction,
> For the night was about her, blinding her when she crossed[28]

What his Love crossed (and he is not here, despite the sound of it, speaking of anything other than his own idealistic belief) was a viaduct, a symbol of the poet's qualified altitude in his narrow Welsh valley: the viaduct was destroyed by the bombs (obviously a metaphor for the compulsion on him to leave home at the onset of war) and the poet, entering the "sidings" in "the neutral city", does not know, has not adjusted his ideals to, the fact that he can never go back. Darkness or night may therefore imply the non-apprehension of immediate meaning. One may suspect, of course, that *night* was too frequent a word with Alun Lewis during his period of apprenticeship as a poet, but that suspicion is enough to prove my point. Darkness is not a concept characteristic only of the later poems.

Before I leave this issue, I should like to say a word or two about 'The Sentry', if only because it has been facilely assumed that *Night* in this poem means *Death*.

> I have begun to die.
> For now at last I know
> That there is no escape
> From Night.[29]

The poet has begun to die only in the sense that in his living he is permanently conscious of mortality. Night is that darkness of

meaning we have spoken of: he hangs "sleeplessly" "from the hidden
roof" of Night, which, in a later image, is "the cold shore of thought".
The burden of the poem is that war has made the challenge to Love
inescapable, that the poet has left behind both "the beautiful lanes of
sleep" (that is, the happy assumptions he had about the omnipotence
of Love when "barefoot") and

> The lovely bodies of the boy and girl
> Deep in each other's placid arms[30]

(that is, the assumption that Love means no more than the integration
of two personalities in a fully sexual and caring relationship). The poet
knows now that more is required and that his station is to face the
night of meaning or meaninglessness alone. No reader should be
misled by the title — 'The Sentry' — and the first four lines into the
belief that the poet foresees his death in combat, or anything equally
simplistic.

Mention of the concepts of Love that have now been found
insufficient compels me to go back and identify in the poetry that
precedes 'The Sentry' the several attacks on it suffered by the original
ideal. The earliest attack was not that of hatred and war. The first
attack came from Lust, from the erotic urge. We have seen how
carefully unsensual 'The Madman' was: it becomes obvious from the
rest of the pre-war poetry that the nature of a caring love, one that
sought not only an integrity between individuals but a concern
diffused over all mankind, was undermined by the existence in the
poet himself, as in all men, by a destructive urge whose qualities were
impermanence and unloving. This needs looking at carefully,
because there appear to be two stages of the experience of this. Robert
Graves apparently commented to Alun Lewis on "the disturbingly
sensual vein . . . that interfered with the poetry of the poems",[31] and
most critics have commented on the Lawrentian stimulus it shows to
a good deal of phallic imagery. We have a lot about the *seed* and
"mating simply in the ferns"[32]. I cannot prove that this belongs to an
early period of Lewis's writing but I would suggest strongly that it
does. The second section of 'Threnody for a Starry Night' offers a little
hindsight on his early dilemma. "The boy who climbed the creaking
stairs"[33] to sexual experience and afterwards suffered "in khaki"

> . . . disapproved Christ's chastity,
> Chose warmth

> Of loins, afraid to burn
> Obedient martyr to a rigid creed . . . [34]

The word *warmth* again earns our notice. Warmth is the necessary link for Lewis between his caring Love and sexual Love. Credal Christianity seemed to him not to provide it. But the poem goes on to point out that his choice had not in the end separated him, in the face of the horror that had overtaken his world, from the caringness of his Love. He

> . . . found
> Christ crucified bequeathed
> His agony to us.[35]

Rather, indeed, did he now wonder *how* erotic experience could be made to care. Looking back, he felt that sex had "rifled" his soul in a "sordid attic"[36].

It is possible, therefore, to distinguish two phases, the first in which the young Lewis is bursting with a desire for sexual experience and, by implication, reviling society for not making it possible, the second, in which the lack of identity between sex and Love has already made him deeply anxious. His poem called 'The Desperate' must serve as an example of the first. Men and women are urged to

> Fling wide the sluice,
> Release the seed;
>
> And Love, poor Love
> Must bear the ache
> Of lust grown holy
> For the soul's sweet sake.[37]

This poem plainly has its didactic side: lust must be made "holy" so that the integrity of "soul" may be achieved, that is, caring Love and sexual Love be made one. But even here there is a price to be paid: caring Love — such as love of parents, perhaps — will be put upon, required to suffer: though whether this is a temporary phenomenon — society being required to accommodate a freer expression of sexual Love so that the spiritual health of the young may be ensured — or whether there is an appreciation that no such accommodation will eradicate the ache of Love, the poem is too compacted to set out.

The erotic vein does not disappear with the emergence of anxiety (nobody needs telling that) and perhaps David Shayer is right in calling the poem which begins

> Stars seem gilded nipples
> Of the Night's vast throbbing breasts[38]

"decadent"[39] — though I think we have to be very careful, even in a poem which seems to consist of nothing more than strong visual images of Love, fear and war, that Alun Lewis is not giving us a cryptic version of his more argumentative preoccupations — the stars as indicative of Love rather than hate (the alternative image is that of "warriors' nodding crests"): they are all we can judge the unknownness of Night by. And though there are ostensibly *three* 'Songs for the Night', thematically they are one and the second has

> Beauty's face is pinched with dread . . .

The individual image, therefore, may well be subordinate, even in what seems like a dissociated whole.

But that is not to say that Lewis's sensual desire is not, for the most part, to be taken at face value. 'Fever', for example, is full of sexual images: the universe becomes "a rain-swollen toadstool", the "I" of the poem clearly choosing the homosexual alternative even as he lies beside the sleeping loved one.

> Oh my love! Why did I dream this dream in my bed; feeling
>   your nearness . . . .[40]

It is significant that the love by whom he lies is "like the sunlight" — a likeness we met before in 'Atropos to Ophelia': in other words she offers him desire and caring integrated and yet he finds himself lost in the "trembling mirage" of a different desire. An unrestrained sexuality, he demonstrates, can be destructive of the loving relationship. In 'Lines on a Young Girl' he is already setting "a desperate value"[41] on "much-mothered" innocence, while 'Valediction' pictures the ego shut out by desire not merely from the normality of life but from the glories of the vision open to "The Madman"[42]. There are other, wryer poems like 'The Encounter' and 'The Swan's Way', but the two most interesting are 'Mid-Winter' and

'A Separation', both of which seem to me to have been less than fully understood by critics thus far.

Let us take 'Mid-Winter' first, because it has an apparently Welsh and personal setting and because it seems to contain most of the elements of the evolving view I have been describing. The countryside and the sea-shore are deeply frozen: old Dafydd tells the poet:

> "The waves freeze as they fall. It is indeed
> Funny to hear that silence, 'tis indeed!"[43]

Since the released wave later appears as the symbol of sexual desire satisfied, as the passionate wave that

> Answered the moontug, leaped, and in high poise
> Tense in a timeless wave contained itself,
> Then broke, ah broke, and shattered and seethed all white
> Up the green and purple pebble beach — the reach
> Of desire that rushes white from the swirl of pain[44]

and the mountains, the meadows and the grasses are held in the ice of the loved one's absence, it may not be unreasonable to see, since it comes in Dafydd's words, a comment on the society that imposes such chastity and the unnaturalness of "that silence". But the poem does not end with the arrival of the beloved, the Cytherea or Aphrodite of the rain's blessing. When she comes, her soul is troubled, overcome with memories of a journey "Through the chasms of time and pain": she is "silent, hesitant, engrossed". The poet exhorts her to lie in his arms, "In the warmth of the flesh", "In the curve of the wave". Dafydd's thatch leaks and "the river runs again with gladness to the sea". Ostensibly there is satisfaction, even happiness, in what the poet or narrator imagines is a caring as well as a sexual relationship: he asks her to tell him about "the stress of the rocks"[45] and her "soul's escape" but he does not really want to know. His solution, behind the satisfaction of the flesh, is to forget "the dry and hidden bone", forget the stone on which the wave shatters. But Cytherea has "a madness" (note that particularly) that "word / Or kiss or loving pity" cannot dispel. There is no answer here. Desire has satisfied itself again upon the ache of a more demanding Love.

In 'A Separation', a complex poem in very simple language, male treachery is more apparent. *She* becomes what *He* wishes. This is a full and loving relationship on her part, "a gesture / Of faith"[46]. But *He* lusts after her as she was before she was changed and, not finding her, directs his desire to a new mark. *He* says that he "aches unbearably" and that the refashioning of the loved one is something he can forget: "in hollows of Night" (the word capitalised) — that is, the speculative unknown — he continues to search for what he tells himself was the original source of his physical passion. That is his excuse. *She* knows that she can never reach him, any more than the waves that fall and break can reach the moon that calls them: her gesture is therefore one "Of faith and of failure". The blame here is very firmly a male blame: Alun Lewis was not the man ever to point elsewhere. If integrity was what was needed to make a Loving world, then the integrity he had to begin with was his own.

This slur on "the heart" — for it is the heart that "lies on its side / And aches unbearably" — is not solely a feature of the early poems. 'Encirclement', for example, one of the poems from England in *Ha! Ha! Among the Trumpets,* has the poet, like other men, seeking in "distant footfalls / The elusive answer of love"[47]. In other words, what is unknown is romanticised and lusted after, and it is an effort, needing "the heart's blind strength"

> To reach the mild and patient place
> Where the lamplit room awaits a stranger
> And suffering has sanctified your face.

It is an effort — to paraphrase again — to make the deadly romanticism of the meeting with the whore yield to the love which suffers or enable the two somehow to coincide. It serves no particular purpose to identify this theme further in the later poems. We need not doubt that it was always there. It was indeed this especial treachery that Alun Lewis regarded as the ultimate murderer of his ideal of Love.

Thus far I have spent a good deal of time on early poems because it is important to realise that Lewis's concept of Love, as it appears in his poetry, manifested itself first as a world-idealism and was not formulated against and because of the stress of war. What I have tried to show, too, is that within a poetry prolific of imagery there is a consistency of symbol which marks out and identifies the existence and growth of that concept. This is not a matter of special pleading on my part: it is *there.* Alun Lewis, commenting to Robert Graves on the difficulty of maintaining a stance in criticism and philosophy in war-time, declared: "But at any rate I know where I stand in love . . . "[48]. If the certainty there expressed is, in the poetry itself, riddled with doubts and qualifications, no one need question the intensity of the preoccupation.

The time has come now for a brief look at the development of Alun Lewis's concept of Love in its philosophical and idealistic aspect against the background of pre-War Wales. We need not be surprised that as a base for a world development he found Wales unsatisfactory. In part this was due to the inability of man, especially when young, to realise that the practical application of any creed ought to be with the believer in the spot where he actually is, and in part, no doubt, due to the unwillingness of those he encountered to accept him as any kind of prophet (we may recall that even Jesus Christ had this difficulty amongst his own people). It was probably also due to that inbuilt propensity in all those who take to themselves a world faith to think, that the battles to be fought are "out there", away from the personal obstacles the individual is likely to encounter on known ground, by large battalions of which the believer will become a faithful and much less vulnerable member. Accordingly we may note Lewis's belief that the people of Wales did not look outward: they were locked in contemplation of their own narrow habits. In 'The Rhondda'

> Circe is a drab.
> She gives men what they know.[49]

Her mine-shaft swallows up "their hands and eyes" and the women have accepted it all. There was no room for idealism, for energy even, in wider causes. This was what Alun Lewis meant when he wrote to Jean Gilbert in January 1938:

> We are a long way from the world in Wales, and there is a kind of apathy about things. The poor accept their lot and the well-to-do their comfort. And the farmers pray only for rain. I would like to wake them up. I mean, too, that I would like to wake myself up.[50]

That last sentence is characteristic. Lewis did recognise that it ought all to begin with him, but easier ways of thinking had ruled his youth.

Of the other two poems that are relevant here much the better known is 'The Mountain over Aberdare'. It would be unjust not to see this, in its most literal aspect, as a poem inspired by a particular view on a wet evening and as an effort to encapsulate the familiar as seen from a distance. But the method — or rather, the mixture of methods — the poet uses to achieve his end reveal his mind. The almost-aerial viewpoint perhaps suggested the Auden manner, though one cannot be sure that a young poet who had been reading Auden might not deliberately choose a viewpoint which would bring that manner naturally into play. I am more interested here in the feeling that this *generalising* manner, which is also Auden's, is a way of thinking progressive thoughts at a distance. In this sense it epitomises Lewis's difficulty with his Welsh background. He cannot be entirely impersonal: Aberdare is "my father's home":[51] he knows something of its individual history — it is "The place for which the Quakers once / Collected clothes". But then the poem becomes landscape and social analysis with, towards the end, some very curious perspective effects.

In passing, I may perhaps say that I regard this as a faulty poem in which Lewis's rhythmic instinct fails him more than occasionally and in which the adjectives are frequently one too many. But I am bound to defend it against some of the strictures of critics who have treated this poem in isolation. We are dealing here with a poet who was already obsessed with one theme and was evolving a symbolism appropriate to it. Accordingly, any analysis which treats 'The Mountain over Aberdare', or any other of Alun Lewis's poems, as a totally separate entity is bound to miss something. John Stuart Williams, for instance, knowing of Lewis's left-wing stance but doubtless not having studied all the poems together, considers 'The Mountain over Aberdare' as a poem "of protest"[52] (I believe the definition of *protest* would have to be very careful to make this true) and therefore regards as inappropriately "poetic" the passage which begins:

> ... hymns
> That drift insidious as the rain
> Which rises from the steaming fields
> And swathes about the skyline crags
> Till all the upland gorse is drenched
> And all the creaking mountain gates
> Drip brittle tears of crystal peace ... [53]

"Crystal peace", he says, is meaningless, and the clichéd "tears" is saved only by the unexpected adjective "brittle". But "crystal", which we have encountered already in 'The Madman' ("The shattered crystal of his mind"), is, as David Shayer has pointed out[54], the symbol for the higher clarity of mind which the poet seeks (it occurs again in 'After Dunkirk'[55], in which, however, it indicates a hardening brought about by time rather than the mood imposed temporarily by Nature). Nevertheless, it stands for self-detachment and is the almost-expected adjective here for the "peace" which is achievable at the level of the mountain-top (in the poem 'Destruction' it is to "the eyries among these Welsh mountains"[56] that the poet's *soul* flies for its idealistic food). "Brittle"[57] is self-guarding: it recalls the "dangerous splinters" of the mind of 'The Madman' and is especially defensive of "tears" in the poem under survey. "Crystal peace" is an attempt at self-detachment that the poet is aware realists would laugh at, and it is not accidental that the movement towards it begins in hymns (as the poet himself does ancestrally). But as soon as the mood moves back to the individual "curtained parlour" (and it does so very suddenly) the "tiny funeral", which the poet observed in perspective, becomes "Huge grief, and anger against God". This, to my mind, is where the poem goes wrong: the Auden-like perspective has held until this point and the sudden subjective surge downwards, in which God is obviously to be contrasted with Christ, still about in the dark alley, as are his betrayers, is intuitive and visually impossible. One sees what this is intended to do — to suggest that a Christian humanism is down there struggling with venality, with politics or myth (dependent upon what "the tales" are that the colliers are listening to) and with the unaccountability of God. But it is all at odds with the later attempts to keep the visual in perspective — the dusk, for example, veiling "the cracked cottages with drifting may". Perhaps the most important thing to notice is that at the end the whole scene becomes subject to the gloomy verdict of time: the poet watches "the clouded years"[58]: it is "a lost age" — a mood that darkens and swallows belief, foreshadowing, indeed, the ultimate shock that time was to give him in India.

Plainly it is right to criticise 'The Mountain over Aberdare' in its function as a separate poem, and the criticism of John Stuart Williams and others as applied to the words and the rhythm are often entirely valid. But for my purpose it is additionally helpful to know *why* the poem fails and, more particularly, to discern the place it has in Alun

Lewis's view of himself and his native society. He wanted to distance himself from what he knew, to generalise about it like an outsider. But in the end he had to put something of himself into the scene, and the pity is that he did so by a series of dubious and rather cinematic pictures that were much closer up than he was, his sound apparatus even being sensitive enough to pick up "the clink of coins".

If 'The Mountain over Aberdare' is gloomy, 'Destruction' is gloomier still. It is also later: the war has begun, the poet is leaving his valley or has already left it, the Love that he has not known how to use as it should be used must operate in "the neutral city", [59] The poem begins with the dreadful fixity or unchangingness of Wales: his village "sinks drearily deeper / In its sullen hacked-out valley": the poet is equally fixed:

> This is the street I inhabit.
> Where my bread is earned my body must stay.[60]

He, however, is fixed at a level somewhat above "the dismantled pitshaft": the symbol he uses is that of the eight-arched viaduct. I can imagine a critic of a certain sort making a meal of this in terms of Lewis's middle-classness or even in his acceptance of a place in a meritocracy. But Wales's middle-class then were only one step away from their working-class origins and Lewis's inherent radicalism, let alone socialism, would certainly have precluded such meanings. His elevation is in terms of idealism: he calls it "this viaduct of my soul"[61] and makes it clear that his "rails" are *fixed* no less than are the lives of those on the valley bottom. Indeed, his elevation is subject to stresses that the much-walked roads below escape. Goods trains cross this viaduct with an excess of noise and heat, rocking those fixed rails: engine-smoke "blows higher" — and obscures — his good intention. In just the same way, when war comes, with the bombers' "impersonal drone of death"[62], he is confused by the noise in a way that those with no particular ideals have not to suffer — so much so, that he does not even realise fully that his "place" in the valley is no more and that his confused Love is being *rocked* "down empty sidings / Between dark tenements . . . / To the street she must inhabit" in the neutral city. There is a great deal more one could get out of this prolonged metaphor — the "dark tenements", for example, the piled-up, unknown people instead of the unchanging colliers — but we must go back to the defeats the poet records in Wales. First, his disappointment and inertia were such that towards the end his moments of "crystal" detachment became rarer and rarer. Then he remembers the treacheries to which his ideal of Love was subject. Down in the "dirty bed" of the "poisoned river"

> . . . a girl lies dreaming, diffusing attar of roses.[63]

Why did this urge to cheap romance, this "destructive impulse", mar the poem that he was trying to make of life?

> And I in bitterness wonder
> Why love's silk thread should snap,
> Though the hands be never so gentle . . . [64]

This destruction was like the stone from a schoolboy's sling (again from down below) which killed a swallow flashing under his viaduct's arch "to the inaccessible eaves". What was the good of thinking high thoughts when there were impulses in oneself which answered the follies and vulgarities and evils below?

It was a Love already very troubled, then, that Alun Lewis brought into the threat and conditions of War, though nobody should imagine that these few poems are a microcosm of what he thought of Wales: his native place was just the first place of failure: there were to be many others, for the failure he ultimately recognised was in himself.

War and other places, indeed, were to bring about correction. When he was away from Wales he could see the people better. In 'A Welsh Night' he recognised that blind habit, that fixity of which he had complained and which he still recalls, for "This village" is still "buried deeper than the corn"[65], is not the enemy of Love. The old Garth mountain now offers "a sermon of patience" and from the blacked-out houses

> Faint strokes of thoughtfulness feel out
> Into the throbbing night's malevolence,
> And turn its hurt to gentler ways.

This Love he sees, both for the present and the absent, knows nothing of the meaning of Life (it is "blind . . . beneath the angelic planes"): it takes to itself "all known and suffered harms", accepting what comes, not knowing whether it is Life or Death, or, indeed, whether Life *is* Death. The village "wears the darkness like a shroud or shawl". The poet is recognising that he has been misled by his own frustrations: Love has no more to do with world-wide concepts than it has with thoughtfulness across the table at home. The instinct of the people, as it is shown in duress, is towards Love, which is in truer accord with the only possible basis for his philosophy.

Indeed, it was not only in the context of Wales that Alun Lewis's view of Love needed amendment. 'The Crucifixion' makes it plain that "this surrender of self to a greater statement"[66] is now dubious in his eyes. Jesus Christ, putting away *life* and *people* and their insistent demands and moving serenely towards a supreme martyrdom, "suffering suffering only", seeking for an immediate consummation of life, may well have been mistaken, even in his own terms as the Son of God. Did He not, by breaking his Self up, convulse His Father with pain? Could one, in effect, seek the complete denial of Self except at the cost of other Selves? This was not the way Life was to be improved. There was not even an example in it. Perhaps the "natural preoccupations,/ Duties, emotions, daily obligations,/ Affections and responses" were the true means of expressing Love after all. 'Sacco Writes to his Son', again, has echoes of this conclusion: Sacco urges his son Dante to "Reject this death" — that is, his own — in favour of Life: it is within the life-span that happiness is to be found:

> .... remember in the play
> Of happiness you must not act alone.
> The joy is in the sharing of the feast.[67]

In that apparently very personal poem 'Goodbye', when the girl turns her face away

> .... afraid to speak
> The big word, that Eternity is ours[68]

we sense immediately that she is right to be afraid. Self is the seat of Love, its limitation in time:

> Everything we renounce except ourselves.

And the poem, which up to that point has been circumstantial, launches away on a voyage of the Self's delight in the world and ephemerality, its unthinking acceptance of mortality:

Selfishness is the last of all to go ...

What began as personal has now become didactic: it develops as an attempt to establish a true basis for Love. The instinctive movements of one Self towards another — the emerald ring he gave the girl and the patches she sewed onto his old battledress — are truer than any words about eternity. The whole emphasis of Alun Lewis's philosophy has deserted grandiloquent statements, world-views, political or religious martyrdoms, for the deliberately realistic, limited exposition of what the Self that seeks to Love can do, not merely for the one it Loves best but for all others for whom there are "Duties, emotions, daily obligations, / Affections and responses"[69]. It is an exposition of the possible community, in part created by, but also improvable by, a purely human and Self-based Love. That Love improves the condition of Life beyond the time-span of the one life is not clear from 'Goodbye', but 'Song' tells us

> That Life has trembled in a kiss
> From Genesis to Genesis,
>
> And what's transfigured will live on
> Long after Death has come and gone.[70]

It is difficult to believe that the abandonment of world-view was totally unconnected with Alun Lewis's greater experience of himself as a writer (with the writer's necessary preservation of self). However that may be, he inevitably becomes a poet more interested in time and place, limited and conditioned and interested in describing those limitations and conditions. There is a marked increase in the poems of occasion. And, of course, he was better able to reassess the familiar. On embarkation leave at Penbryn he could at last distinguish those emotions he had let come between him and the "grinding-stones of fact" and was able to begin

> ... a search for those old country gods
> A man takes with him in his native tongue
> Finding a friendly word for all things strange,
> The firm authentic truth of roof and rain.[71]

It was with such a diminished positive of Love that Alun Lewis left Britain for India.

I have, of course, allowed my exposition of the Love which was central to his thinking to enter its third phase, when it had been affected by the spiritual impact, if not the experience, of war, by absence from home, by uncongenial service and by separation from his wife Gweno. My concern has been to set out, first, the original concept (perhaps never wholly untried), second, the concept attacked by Lust and the knowledge of personal treachery, and third, the already doubted concept found inapplicable in Wales and modified by absence and the onset of new experience. I must now go back to consider briefly the part played in the movement towards the third phase by the assault of war and death — in a word, to look at those poems which constitute the most prominent part of *Raiders' Dawn*. We are back here in the obsessional stage of the writing and though, towards its end, description of the outward scene becomes more important for its own sake, critics who miss the persistence of the central vision have not begun to understand Alun Lewis. To take just one example, A. Banerjee, in a comparatively recent book entitled *Spirit above Wars,* alleges that Lewis had not developed a consistent vision, had not come to grips with the fundamental problems presented to the individual by the war. "Rather", he says,

> his poems seem to be a record of the life of a man who was hurled from one experience to another, leaving him bewildered and depressed. The poems, are, therefore, 'occasional' rather than constellations composing one sky.[72]

It would be difficult to be more wrong.

Let us briefly examine the title-poem 'Raiders' Dawn'. It tells us that "lovers" — that is, disciples of Love who use words like "Eternity" and believe in the inevitable progress of civilisation down the centuries (this gathers in the theorists and the romantics, you see) — wake up to find that after so much writing and pontificating and living men are slaughtering the babes of the world in their thousands and hundreds of thousands. Beauty (and don't forget that this is the poet's word for the ideal of human perfectability) has taken a very nasty shock. If my paraphrase sounds relatively unlike the poem as you know it on the page, with its concluding quatrain

> Blue necklace left
> On a charred chair

> Tells that Beauty
> Was startled there[73]

it is because there are apparently personalising elements in it which mislead. Lovers "waking / From the night — " does not mean what we are bound at first to think it and the feminine image of "startled" Beauty — the "startled" is crucial — superimposes itself on the intended meaning. If the poem is successful, then, it is irrelevantly so and the short-lined stanzas rhyming first and third, despite the greater lumpishness in the longer middle section, help to diminish the shock which the poem intends.

This is didactic but not personal. What wounds him both in his belief and as a man is War's demand that his Love accommodate another and terrible destructive impulse beside which the schoolboy's stone that killed the swallow under the eaves[74] may seem merely irresponsible and childish. He is clear-sighted enough to know that no accommodation is possible: he lives with two incompatibles. Perhaps this is the moment to cast an eye back on Lewis's pacifism, on his argued abandonment of it in letters, and the poem 'Parable', with its scapegoat symbolism and its very simplified recollection of a pastoral peace. It was "within the glades of Love"[75] that he sought to recover that peace and in another and "febrile glade" that "grey elders" determined upon their ritual sacrifice to combat "the sabre-toothed shaggy hunter". Bitterly his "wounded beast"

> . . . . gave witness with his blood
> According to the word of God.[76]

Whether Lewis intended this Old Testament irony as a direct comment on that God who stood unknown beyond the darkness — and there is a line in 'Christmas Holiday'[77] which might bear this out — or whether he was pointing at the endorsement of War by the Christian Church is not clear. That he was critical of the ability of some Christians to accommodate the two incompatibles is, however, demonstrated by the poem 'To a Comrade in Arms'. This man whom he addresses as "Red fool, my laughing comrade"[78] can hide his "woman's love" and his "man's madness" — that is, the conflict between the two — under a cheerful countenance. But the poet has two questions for him: first

> What foe will you make your peace with
> This summer that is more cruel
> Than the ancient God of the Hebrews?[79]

and second, when he is dead

> What vow shall we vow who love you
> For the self you did not value?

The meaning of these last two rather difficult lines is that this Christian, whose eyes "are frantic / With love that is frustrate" has torn his Self in two (observe the new importance of the Self) and made it difficult for those who love him to know in what direction their undivided love should now look. This is a rhetorical question, of course: few soldiers could have had any kind of undivided love to offer, let alone the poet. What the poet is saying is that his comrade sets a bad example for those who know what Love means, and leaves his friends, those of them who are still seeking to love him in a personal sense, uncertain what part of the torn Self they should love. This theme is continued in the poem 'Finale', where the *poseur,* "fascinating to the young ladies, / Male, seductive, sardonic for the occasion"[80], enjoying his role as a hero but still troubled by the "inscrutable demon of self-knowledge", is "Crucified on a cross of fire" and ends up as a translated Christ of "the heroic age". In this case the soldier portrayed has no choice: the "confused dishonesty" (again the matter of ideal or example is important here) of his role is resolved by the "last simplicity" of Death and the soldier is content that it should be so because he sees no other way out.

If these glances at others are few, it is plainly because the poet's view of himself differs only in inessentials. 'Odi et Amo' is a poem in which he works out the dreadful accommodation of Love and Hate in a hard-won victory for the former. In the first section he recapitulates the stages of Love, its beginning in

> . . . . stillness, in the
> Stillness of the heart in the white breast,[81]

its learning, Christlike, how to bear "the livid / Weal of history", and its physical stimulus, from "the loins in passion", to examine the nature of loving and gather "all eternity / Into the milky ways of night?" He recalls, then, the vow made at the beginning of the war, "Fiercely blindly to endure / With all the stubborn faith of man" until "the peace / That was dreamed of in the beginning" should return. The second section shows him being taught to hate and kill,

>   . . . . my cheek
> Stroking the rifle butt; my loins
> Are flat and closed like a child's.[82]

But in the third section "love's dark roots writhe back" (dark because they have spread themselves in the Night) and in a scorched and corrupted world where "the love songs of Ophelia" (the ignorant Love that was to be "sunlight" on Hamlet's limbs) and "the laughter of Lear" (the madness of the soul beginning its search from helplessness) cannot be heard, the poet is able to declare:

> My soul cries out with love
> Of all that walk and swim and fly.
> From the mountains, from the sky,
> Out of the depths of the sea
> Love cries and cries in me.

This is the dreadfully-experienced Love that has lived with Hate and it flowers with "all the unbearable beauty of the dead" because it is fed and sustained by the faith of those gone before who believed in and were exemplars of the perfectability of Man.

Sometimes, too, the poet is able to re-establish the calm needed for Love by absorption in Nature — "the flash and play of finches" in 'The Soldier', even though they are indifferent to him and do not set forth "the holy mystery" of human Love: sometimes, however — in 'Lines on a Tudor Mansion' "the soft silk flash of the swifts" — Nature with its "own instinctive life" is seen as completely in tune with men who have lost their faith and their ideals and are in process of being shaped like "the coward cruel brute"[83]. Men and birds live in the moment, have short lives, have no time or respect for a "grey assured house, surviving change". This is a poem of Love defeated, in which Alun Lewis sounds for the first time like many other war poets. It is also the poem which, identifying the soon-to-die soldier's vision with

> . . . . the fleeting sunlight in the forest
> And dragonflies' blue flicker on quiet pools

most foreshadows that much later poem 'The Jungle'.

For the most part, however, Lewis accepts that Love as he once envisaged it is no longer possible: Soul lives on, not knowing how to accommodate together loving and killing. 'After Dunkirk' begins:

> I have been silent a lifetime
> As a stabbed man[84]

— a very telling figure for the kind of terrible wounded pause into which his thoughts had fallen. He notes that recovery is marked by

> A growing self-detachment, making man
> Less home-sick, fearful, proud,
> But less a man.

Love is distanced, weakened. He feels his nature is moving, slowly, on a fatal slide. The poem ends, however, with a hope, never to be expressed again, that action, the hour of battle, which for some has already recovered "the heightened vision" of "the worn and beautiful faces of the half-forgotten"[85], will reinstate Love in its fullness and that in the presence of Death "the smiles of dying children and the joy / Of luckier babies playing in the cot" will somehow be balanced.

Poems of "less a man"'s land predominate. Love is getting farther away all the time and Death is nearer. This land is peopled, as in 'From a Play', by "little men grown huge with death"[86] who, despite their "innocence" — that is, their killing at another's instruction — have participated in slaughter. These now see their

> . . . faint familiar homeland haloed
> In a rainbow of disease.[87]

The disease, of course, of *their* seeing. 'Autumn 1939', an earlier poem, is a more literary version of this. The "old jaundiced knights" who tell themselves that they fight for Love no longer know what Love is. One by one "the warped old casements shut"[88]. A number of poems in *Ha! Ha! Among the Trumpets,* from 'Infantry' down to 'The Jungle' repeat this theme and develop it. Men long removed from the spheres of Love

> Think lightly of the themes of life and death,
> All mortal anguish shrunk into an ache

Too nagging to be worth the catch of breath.[89]

The poem which leads out of *Raiders' Dawn* into the rather larger number of *occasional* poems in the second book (though I would wish to insist again that this, too, is intensely thematic and that those who miss this have become lost amongst the descriptive trappings) is undoubtedly 'All Day it has Rained', which introduces for the first time the temporary cessation of personal Love, which is linked with an indifference towards the Self. But we have often been so mesmerised by the introduction of Edward Thomas — described, incidentally, with less than accuracy both as to literary preoccupation and manner of death — into the last few lines that we have missed the point, which is, that, in the absence of Love, chance particulars and observations become important — the children shaking down chestnuts in the woods, the shaggy dog who followed the poet — and the mind is prepared to accept, without evaluation, happenings which are incidental. The reader is left to decide, I think, whether the search for Edward Thomas, in which these incidentals appear, is "inflated" in the same way. If the response is "Impossible!", what we have is a poem about dullness, boredom, a collective lack even of instinctive love from which the poet is suddenly seen stepping purposefully and unexplainedly in an individual literary direction.

The real always fades into the meaning,[90]

he writes in that very late poem 'The Assault Convoy' and this is what we should be watching for throughout Lewis's work. Where even the vestiges of Love remain and their standards are being applied, the particulars are deployed only to lead towards the central evaluation.

There is no time now for a detailed consideration of the Indian poems and I propose therefore to summarise the later story of Love diminished. First there was the terribleness of distance to add to the weight upon Love: in 'The Departure' the poet, less than a man, is carried by the

> . . . deep sad rhythm of the process
> Of the created thing awaking to the sound of the engine.[91]

It is the woman at the dockside, Love unchanged, who knows what is at stake. Now and again Lewis feels that Love in its fullness is not beaten yet: on the troopship

> The simple donors of goodness with rugged features
> Move in the crowd . . . .[92]

But more sadly, when he writes of

> The gradual self-effacement of the dead[93]

he is facing the fact that there will be no "eternity of grief", whatever Love may wish, and perhaps that "the good is oft interred with their bones". No, not *oft*, perhaps *always*. This theme recurs, particularly in 'Shadows' and 'Home Thoughts from Abroad'. The first comes to the gloomier conclusion:

> He chooses best who does not choose
> Time and all its lies;
> Who makes the end and the beginning One
> Within himself, grows wise.[94]

Love and the perfectability of man are not abandoned: another verse in the poem tells us that they will survive. But individual man does well not to think about affecting history and changing the world: he has between birth and death to do what he can of good and should accept those terms. The second of the two poems blames the West (from India, of course) for "the dark inherited disease"[95] of faith in progress or purpose: the "bridle paths" of home all end in that dark: Love is found "in the gap of centuries" and there is an "itching warmness" (you will remember that *warmth* from Lewis's earliest poetry) in the hand of the society from which these exiled soldiers come. 'Peasant Song', again, if more lyrically, puts the question: does good survive the individual life?

> But if I should go
> And you be left behind
> Among the tall red ant hills and the maize
> Would you hear my plough still singing
> And, bearing endless days,
> Somehow give praise?[96]

The struggle goes on, as you see, but Love is fighting a losing battle.

There is a momentary lift of heart in 'To Rilke' when the approaching India is seen as a new opportunity in which

> .... a perception
> Of what can develop and what must be always endured
> And what the live may answer to the dead

may set to work again. But it does not last, not even within the poem. The "devoted", the ones who are "known by their faces", have little chance "within the darkness of India" where "the wind disturbs" the "lamp".[97] Indeed, this is followed by 'By the Gateway of India: Bombay', with its Forsterian echoes, in which the loosening of Lust is the only way to mitigate the unansweringness of the Marabar Caves universal. It is stating the obvious to say that India was a shock to Alun Lewis, but it is important to understand why. It was the final blow to his hope of a progressive Love working within his own lifetime: in 'Karanje Village'

> ... the people are hard and hungry and have no love[98]

The "little Vishnu of stone" warns him that "Love must wait". The time-scale is enormous. The "singing birds of the soul" must not hope for a change discernible in the time "of the flesh". He warns Gweno that he is "seeking less and less of world". That well-known poem 'The Mahratta Ghats' confirms a part of this. The Indian peasant will never lift himself up to the red, newly-turned soil high on the ghat — no, not in a thousand years. The "landless soldier" it is who sees, against a vast time-scale, what the India "which burns and withers in the plain"[99] accepts unthinkingly. In 'The Peasants' the soldiers, with their sense of history, die while the men and women in the fields look on. And this does not necessarily refer to their possible death in battle: they carry their sense of mortality, of the length of one life, down the road that passes those fields.[100]

All this throws a more frequently recurring emphasis on personal Love and there are some important poems like 'In Hospital: Poona (1)' to demonstrate it[101]. But the *positive* there set out is not unchallenged in other poems. "It had been easier, not loving", says 'Ways',[102] "Love being gravel in the wound". 'Motifs', seeing "the world" as "These desultory palms, this tepid sea", would let that world go: the poet feels bound to

Conceal my heart's great love and love's great fear,
And would forget you, if I could, my dear.[103]

The only way to stay unwounded till death is to be detached, uncaring. 'The Jungle' has been taken as a key poem, and so it is, if only because it recapitulates much of what other poems have said. But there is nothing new in it except a stronger identification with predatory Nature. What it does is to kaleidoscope all the stages of the fall from Love, even to recalling the "old temptation to remould the world"[104]. It goes back to Auden and the West as he might have seen it and it encompasses Love defeated in the Indian void, when the soldiers' training is totally successful and they prefer as Beauty realised

The dew-bright diamonds on a viper's back

to the slow poison of a meaning lost

And the vituperations of the just.[105]

It looks again at the divided heart, its Love and not-Love, its ability to forget even instinctive Love (as in 'All Day it has Rained'). And, recognising the belittled and diminished humanity of the soldier, "the killing arm", it ends by wondering whether what Love he has shown, early or late, will in any way add to the music of the world-soul when he dies (that is, whether his death will make more loving a world he couldn't change when he was alive) or whether Love ends with Death and is only reciprocated within the life-span. I have tried to show that these stages of the fall from Love and the many questions that accompany it have all been touched on before, in other poems, and the jungle is just another and geographically appropriate version of darkness or Night, the uncharted region in which ideals and principles have to find or lose their way to an ultimate purpose which may no longer be called God.

That the way was lost is more and more apparent. India was winning its war of attrition. Those who see Alun Lewis as a left-winger appalled by social conditions and no more are missing a great part of the truth.

Love could be had for nothing.
And where is love now?[106]

he writes in 'Observation Post: Forward Area'. If he thought he had changed and could leave it all alone, he was mistaken:

> The black spot in the focus grows and grows . . .[107]

he writes, but cannot leave off looking. One of his later letters contains these three sentences:

> There's a maniac in me that cries out only for to be sensitive to hurt. He's more concerned with poetry than normal natural happiness and patience and he drives me to odd places. I let him, too. I'm dull and platitudinous when he's away from me and I welcome his return with a secret exultant trepidation . . . .[108]

That is how the writer decribes the idealist in him, the idealist who is facing the end but is the most potent part of him still. Do what he would, the writer could not survive him.

NOTES

1.   First published March 1942.
2.   Published posthumously in 1945.
3.   Ed. Sam Adams and Gwilym Rees Hughes, 1973. p.132.
4.   *Raiders' Dawn*, pp.38-39.
5.   *Ibid.*, p.36.
6.   "The soldiers' frozen sightless eyes
       End the mad feud. The worm is love."
7.   Mair Fenn in 'Outward Challenge and Inward Search': *Poetry Wales*, vol.10 no.3, Alun Lewis Special Number, pp.29-30.
8.   *Ibid.*, p.29.
9.   Letter of 14 April 1941, printed in *Alun Lewis and the Caseg Broadsheets*, ed. Brenda Chamberlain, p.7.
10.   *RD*, p.38.
11.   *Ibid.*, p.45.
12.   *Ibid.*, p.24.
13.   *Ibid.*, p.29.
14.   *Ibid.*, unnumbered page, but strictly 11.
15.   *Ibid.*
16.   *Ibid.*, p.92.

17.   *Ibid.*, p.93.
18.   *Ibid.*, p.85.
19.   *Ibid.*
20.   *Ibid.*, p.86.
21.   *Ibid.*, p.39.
22.   *Ibid.*
23.   'The Grinder'. *Ibid.*, unnumbered page (11).
24.   *Ibid.*, p.74.
25.   *Ibid.*, p.80.
26.   *Ibid.*, p.92.
27.   *Ibid.*, unnumbered page (11).
28.   *Ibid.*, p.90.
29.   *Ibid.*, p.20.
30.   *Ibid.*, p.21.
31.   Letter from A.L. to Robert Graves dated 2 May 1942, printed in *The Anglo-Welsh Review* vol. XVI no.37, Spring 1967, p.12.
32.   *RD,* p.30.
33.   *Ibid.*, p.35.
34.   *Ibid.*, p.36.
35.   *Ibid.*
36.   *Ibid.*, p.35.
37.   *Ibid.*, p.50.
38.   'Songs for the Night', *ibid.*, p.66.
39.   *Op. cit.*, p.130.
40.   *RD,* p.49.
41.   *Ibid.*, pp.90-91.
42.   *Ibid.*, p.53. "The madman's silver falchion clove the dusk".
43.   *Ibid.*, p.51.
44.   *Ibid.*, p.52.
45.   *Ibid.*, p.53.
46.   *Ibid.*, p.54.
47.   P.20.
48.   *HH,* quoted in Introduction, page unnumbered but strictly 8.
49.   *RD,* p.88.
50.   *Alun Lewis: Selected Poetry and Prose:* Introduction by Ian Hamilton, p.15.
51.   *RD,* p.87.
52.   'The Poetry of Alun Lewis', *The Anglo-Welsh Review,* vol.XIV no.33, Summer 1964, p.61.
53.   *RD,* p.87.
54.   *Op.cit.*, p.134.
55.   *RD,* p.32.
56.   *Ibid.*, p.89.
57.   *Ibid.*, p.87.
58.   *Ibid.*, p.88.
59.   *Ibid.*, p.90.
60.   *Ibid.*, p.89.
61.   *Ibid.*
62.   *Ibid.*, p.90.

63.   *Ibid.*, p.89.
64.   *Ibid.*, p.90.
65.   *HH*, p.16.
66.   *Ibid.*, p.22.
67.   *Ibid.*, p.23.
68.   *Ibid.*, p.25.
69.   *Ibid.*, p.22.
70.   *Ibid.*, p.21.
71.   'On Embarkation'.*Ibid.*, p.30.
72.   *Op.cit.*, p.137.
73.   *RD*, p.15.
74.   *Ibid.*, p.90, in the poem 'Destruction'.
75.   *Ibid.*, p.30.
76.   *Ibid.*
77.   *Ibid.*, p.40. The cock feels "God's needle quiver in his brain" and his is the signal that has men tumbling out of bed to "start the war again".
78.   *Ibid.*, p.27.
79.   *Ibid.*
80.   *Ibid.*, p.28.
81.   *Ibid.*, p.24.
82.   *Ibid.*, p.25.
83.   *Ibid.*, p.26.
84.   *Ibid.*, p.31.
85.   *Ibid.*, p.33.
86.   *Ibid.*
87.   *Ibid.*, p.34.
88.   *Ibid.*, p.68.
89.   'Infantry'.*HH*, pp.18-19.
90.   *Ibid.*, p.72.
91.   *Ibid.*, p.26.
92.   'A Troopship in the Tropics', *ibid.*, p.33.
93.   'Song', *ibid.*, p.35.
94.   *Ibid.*, p.51.
95.   *Ibid.*, p.52.
96.   *Ibid.*, p.63.
97.   *Ibid.*, pp.37-38.
98.   *Ibid.*, p.42.
99.   *Ibid.*, pp.43-44.
100.   *Ibid.*, p.57.
101.   *Ibid.*, pp.52-53.
102.   *Ibid.*, p.47.
103.   *Ibid.*, p.65.
104.   *Ibid.*, p.70.
105.   *Ibid.*, p.68.
106.   *Ibid.*, p.58.
107.   *Ibid.*, p.69.
108.   Letter of 3 October 1943 to Brenda Chamberlain.Printed but wrongly dated in *Alun Lewis and the Making of the Caseg Broadsheets*, p.39.

The Caseg Letters: A Commentary

In 1970 the late Brenda Chamberlain edited and published twenty-eight letters from Alun Lewis either to her then husband John Petts and herself or to herself alone under the title *Alun Lewis & The Making of the Caseg Broadsheets*. It is not my intention in this article in any major sense to re-tell the story of the six Broadsheets published between 2 December 1941 and 11 June 1942: for this Brenda Chamberlain's book is quite sufficient evidence, even if odd details of it may be added which, in some way, illuminate the attitudes of Alun Lewis himself. What I want to do is to make full use of the holographs of the twenty-eight letters now lodged in the National Library at Aberystwyth in order to throw more light on the poet himself and, by no means incidentally, on the manner in which Brenda Chamberlain saw and executed her editorial function.

In the first place, I am bound to applaud the personal modesty of Brenda Chamberlain as editor, in deleting Alun Lewis's most complimentary remarks about her own writing, especially when they involved comparisons. Similar approval should be accorded to the deletion of his less favourable comments on contemporary writers, still living or recently dead. These are not many in number, but I shall follow Brenda's example in not making them public. It is difficult, again, to quarrel overmuch with her decision to omit most references to Alun's personal life with Gweno, his wife, harmless as most of them are: the primary aim was then, and as far as I am concerned still is, to demonstrate the writer as a writer and not in those aspects of his life which, while those who loved him are alive, are not merely rightly termed "private" but are of peripheral concern. Nevertheless, it will appear that this part of the editorial function was not well executed, however sound may have been the intention: at least one serious alteration of meaning results from deletions. If little that is new about Alun Lewis's poems emerges from the passages suppressed I will set down almost at random, one small point. When, in the poem 'In Hospital: Poona (1)', he wrote

> And like to swan or moon the whole of Wales
> Glided within the parish of my care;
> I saw the green tide leap on Cardigan,
> Your red yacht riding like a legend there

the "red yacht" is not, as may perhaps have been imagined, simply a colourful symbol to be linked with "green tide" and "legend", but a reality which, symbolically or otherwise, could be linked to Gweno. The letter of Tuesday, November 4, 1941, refers to the "red-sailed yacht" that Gweno's father possessed at Aberystwyth.

If all the deletions were as justifiable as this, entangled as it is in less quotable material, there would be small cause for complaint. Unfortunately, I have to go on to say that the editing in other respects is distressingly bad and that, if the various letters were not at some time accidentally confused, liberties have been taken with the material which are seriously misleading and entirely regrettable.

Let me, however, quote what is good and worthy first. If Brenda Chamberlain is not here now to answer criticism, at least her absence makes it possible to make public what Alun Lewis said of her creative work, both in poetry and in art.

On 21 February, 1941, when the two had not yet met, Alun wrote to Brenda thanking her for an engraving or line-drawing of "the woman with the ear-ring", which she may have sent him to illustrate a story. After a long evaluation of it he added:

> *But there is so much more in your block than in my story: I will write it again, differently with more possibilities & less definition one day.*[1]

In the next letter, dated 14 April, he was acknowledging the receipt from her of an "exquisite tete-de-femme". And "so joyous was I inside me with the rhythm it set up", he went on, that he could not write about it in detail. There followed this passage:

> *... briefly, I think you are a great artist. I'm sorry if that upsets you, or sounds too enthusiastic. Also I'm not technically qualified to judge.* It seems possibly [sic] that your real genius is at the moment confined to the use of a strong black effect, darknesses and infinitely subtle spiritual expressions through a *bold* line. I don't

see the delicate economy of line of that little hunchback who painted & drew in the brothels (I can't remember his name, silly[2]). *But I think you are, in this phase of your growth, a master. I am moved more deeply than I can say, in joy, & wonder, & mystery.*

About Brenda Chamberlain's poetry he was as expansive and even more detailed. What needs to be noticed here, in preparation for further comment at a later stage, is the confidence with which Alun Lewis came to his judgements, in the realms both of art and poetry, especially in a correspondence with someone he had not yet met. On 2 June 1941 he wrote as follows:

> *Then your mountain ponies poem, Brenda; I can see that as a broadsheet, it cries out for you to come. Only I would like you to alter the poem, if you will believe me when I say that there are some weak lines in it that dim & blur the real poetry it has. Look, this is how it should go. I am sure of this myself. I can see it from outside, absolutely.*

There follows a detailed re-arrangement of the poem, with the alteration of a few words and phrases. Then he went on:

> *I love this poem: the skates too, which is a far more difficult one to do, for you are dealing with an emotion that is most dangerous to touch — cold pity (almost self-pity, transmuted & harmonised with the Earth).*
>
> *The other I don't like half as much. You'll let me say that, will you? It doesn't hurt you, please? "Massive delicacy" spoils Tryfan because its a combination that overbalances — the first word crushes the second — like a rock on a Japanese lantern.*
>
> *There is a simplicity in your poems that is very cool and soothing, like your mountain lakes, a kind of innocence, naivety that I do not find in your engravings where there is more criticism of life, more exploration of human flesh & blood & emotion. That is, perhaps, why you write poetry, because it expresses a different, younger self. They're not as sure & masterly as your engravings, but they have something which the accomplished artist almost invariably loses with study & mastery of technique (in its broadest sense of understanding & collating both subject and expression of subject) — innocence is the nearest I can get to it.*
>
> *I wouldn't say any of this if I didn't think you were, although I've not met you, my friend, as John is, to whom I can speak my thoughts, whatever they be.*

In an undated letter which Brenda sets in the same month he wrote:

I'm returning your prose vigil without delay owing to a sudden posting order. I leave here [his home in Aberdare] for the infantry tomorrow — at Gloucester Barracks, foot-slogging. *And I've got so many jobs to wind up here & kit to blanco or hand in that I've got no proper time to think or speak of it critically. I think it has very fine visual powers and turns of great simple strength: only I feel that the lover motif comes in too late: you shouldn't have 'concealed' it; if you were going to bring it in let it come early, to balance against death as the pony does. But I can't say. It's very fine and fresh.*

That "can't say" is perfunctory, a faint concession to anyone who might think him too free with criticism. But he was no less free with praise. In a letter from Morecambe dated by Alun '19th' and editorially 'August 1941'[3] he wrote, addressing them both:

I was very pleased to find Brenda on the next page to me in Life & Letters. It's a very sweet refreshing poem, yours, with a strange and lovely effect on me of home & love & children & loneliness & pride. Achieved with such economy of image & word too.

In a letter of November he was prepared to broaden his June comment on Brenda's poetry. He had by this time spent a night with Brenda and John at Llanllechid: it was the only occasion on which he and Brenda were to meet. In recounting his subsequent travels round Wales to raise support and interest in the Broadsheets, he delivered himself as follows;

I stayed the week-end at Llanybri, a hamlet lost in Carmarthenshire, with Lynette & Keidrych Rhys. Lynette is doing very fine work — her poems are becoming very rich & powerful & she is painting some fine things. She has a prodigal & worldflung imagination with a depth of personal & historical myth (she is South American by birth — Aztec) to draw on & a Catholic strain that provides ritual & mystique. It is interesting & exciting to read her poems & then yours — *both of you surpass any other woman poet I've read* — *yet* you are so utterly utterly different. I hope you will publish your poems — not just yet, though. They are very beautiful & pellucid — but occasionally there is an echo of someone else — the poem about the adder, for example, is too like Lawrence's poem Snake: and Dead Climber has echoes of the Bible: And really, Brenda, your poetry must never echo anyone but yourself. That is the sole condition of its virtue. *There is no other Brenda Chamberlain living — & I don't think there has been one ever before.* That is the great truth you must create through.[4] Do you understand? *I am anybody: but you are yourself. Selflessly yourself.*

That the style is not a little fulsome must not obscure the note of caution, the "not just yet" which holds sufficiently back. And the paradox of the ending (which, unless he is stirring in aesthetic independence with a dose of spirituality, has little meaning) is the preacher's way of concluding, the "I" who is "anybody" being the poet as reader or observer, a nonentity before the completed work of another.

From this point onwards, Alun Lewis, although still ready to offer criticism, was also concerned to help Brenda Chamberlain to get her poetry published. A postscript to a letter editorially dated 'December 1941' ran:

> *Horizon would like to see your poems, Brenda: I told Connolly you were more important than Anne Ridler or Kay Raine & he raised his worldly brows!*

Two months later, in February 1942, he commented again:

> I'm delighted Tambimuttu is printing your Climber & Ponies. Good for him. When you send to Connolly, send him a lot — send the whole series of Love-Songs & Green Heart. You're not an easy poet to understand, Brenda; one must discover you gradually, moving from poem to poem, as along a grass track leading to the long grass-levels of the mountain-tops where the air is & the heavens & so much, so little else. And may I in the friendship of poetry warn you of one thing? <u>Words.</u> I found myself using the same adjectives a lot over a period of, say, two years. 'Terrible' I used, and 'lovely' — ordinary words which cannot be used often for their poetic value lies in lifting their ordinariness — <u>once</u> or twice at most — into a higher order of feeling. You use 'tormented' too often, sometimes in association with natural things that are naturally not tormented — e.g. tormented waves. I suggest that your imagery & the words that express it are reaching the stage where they must change *& grow and become something wider, deeper & more sinuous-reaching in their roots, less oppressed by mountains.*[5] Also that you will discarded [sic] 'flat' words such as 'tinctured'. Rilke, even in translation, is a

rich source of words for the same fundamental thoughts as you
work in.

The work of Lynette Roberts had by this time fallen from Alun's
favour, and Brenda continued to earn a substantial meed of criticism.
In July 1942, during his last months in England, Brenda had sent him
a poem and Alun acknowledged it as follows:

> *Thank you for your fine long letter and for the poem, which I admire very
> much but would like to see it shortened & the first few lines cut away
> entirely. Without the written description in your letter it's difficult to
> know what the poem springs from. If you entitled it "To a Shepherd whose
> Dog has died" or something less clumsy but equally obvious, I think it
> would be better. And try the Listener, yes? (They've just taken a poorish
> poem of mine, after much rejection).*

But from the latest letters come only praise and advice. On August 22
1942, Alun Lewis wrote:

> I've been looking thro' Tambi's anthology & I think it's pretty
> good — Streets ahead of most of its kind. Your Green Heart
> reads extremely well, *Brenda. You've made a big mark with that, I
> feel. Good, good.*

A letter which plainly antedates that,[6] of which I shall have more to say
later, perorates in a manner which, although a little forced, essentially
repeats the wish that Brenda shall not be too much "oppressed by
mountains".

> *Well, I must away now, Lady, to mount my guard. I hope your pony is
> well now and the mountains your comfort & your strength. Keep on
> writing poems; and when you will come into the streets where also there is
> much danger & fortitude.*

A postcard from, Penbryn[7] on his embarkation leave said merely:

> I hope you've received Tambi's book by now. I do like your
> Baltic poem very much.

As has already been said, Brenda Chamberlain's deletion from her
printed text of the passages which most lauded her work does her

great credit, but it should also be apparent, even from some of the paragraphs quoted above, that there were other omissions which were less justified, some plainly in error, some the result of misjudgement. There is no obvious reason, unless its last sentence was deemed to be "cruel", why this passage from the very first letter of all should have been left out:

> Your letter was lovely. The soft ringing showers of frost-leaves & the white peaks in the sky are in my visual memory now as well as yours. Here [Longmoor Camp] the country is all in miniature & evergreen, little wooded rolling hills and sandy green woods with small blue lakes & red houses. It isn't Wales at all at all; it's the civilised comfortable south, bourgeois and vitamin-conscious. When I hunger for the mountains I know it's a long time since I felt the discomfort of wildness & hardness & want. The South will get all that from the Luftwasse, I expect: it's a pity for the children & the mangling of bodies: but its effect on the mind will be ultimately good.

Omissions in later letters grow more frequent, as though increasing haste were a factor in the judgement. The mutilation of the following passage from Alun's letter of February 1942 is the more regrettable because the reasons seem insufficient:

> Today I've been under a rood, or in the streets all day *Scrubbing Gweno's scullery*, typing like a fiend at an outrageous roaring short story, listening to Welsh ballads on the wireless at lunch, to Beethoven's violin concerto on the gramophone at tea, *picking a costume with Gweno for our little two days in London at the end of the week, supper with mother & daddy* — and then back home on a silver night with the heavenly twins serene above Orion.

Even less justifiable is the omission of the passage which follows from the letter of August 22 1942, significant as it is for our knowledge of the deep taproot of Alun Lewis's life and understanding. When he wrote it he had been commanded overseas:

> *I'm going on leave first, this week, and will spend a few days in Penbryn, Cardiganshire, with Gweno: it's the country we lived in as children, and a deep homing instinct takes me there now. The rest of my leave I shall be at Aberdare, except for a day at Aberystwyth at Gweno's home. So I'm afraid Llanllechid is outside the orbit of the practicable.*

And later in the same letter there is this delightful miniature of an Indian summer of happiness, again needlessly omitted:

> *Gweno has been with me here at Southend for nearly three weeks and we've had a very happy time, boarded by a delightful old German chef-and-gardener and his comfortable pious wife. They call us "the children" & feed us on spinach and kohlrabi and marrows. And cake with a hole in the middle!*

There is a sad echo here of the "first" in History that was built on his landlady's rice pudding, all of seven years before.[8] Such halcyon feeding had then, too, preceded a time of parting and unhappiness.

There are other passages that are either mutilated or omitted, of course, that might have been read without offence to anyone. But they are not so very many, and if criticism had only this to chew on, it could well depart without a meal. Unfortunately the editing, in its other aspects, takes us deep into muddle and misdirection. Brenda Chamberlain obviously meant well: she corrected some, but not all, of Alun's errors — her text has "Carneddau" for his "Carneddi" several times, "Nos da 'chi" for his "Nos da 'ti", but, inconsistently, "Wrexham" for his "Wrecsam". In places she altered awkward constructions, rescued a word or two that had been miswritten ("articulate" for "inarticulate" will serve for example) but apparently did not dare to correct the occasional mishmash of personal pronouns of which Alun was guilty. Less justifiably, she omitted very, very many of the *verys* with which Alun expanded and brightened his adjectives. As a result his style has a sobriety and a measuredness that is not true to the real ebullience that often broke through.

So far, nevertheless, she might easily be forgiven. But worse is to follow, dropping sadly to *much worse*. The text of *The Making of the Caseg Broadsheets* is full of unnecessary errors: it would be tiresome to indicate more than a few. Some appear to be misreadings of individual words in Alun's letters (whose haste?): whole phrases are omitted: occasionally the involuntary alteration loses for us a distinctive Lewis word or image — in the letter of November 18 1941, the holograph is as follows:

> Don't buy Lilliput, please. I look as if I've been boiled in oil & all the other poets look deprave and hard.

Brenda Chamberlain's text has "I'm boiled" and "depraved": one

mistake, one correction. In the letter editorially dated January 1942
Alun wrote:

> So I should be a cheeryble sort of person, *really,* shouldn't I?

The "cheerful" of the text if featureless by comparison. Again, the
Southend letter of 26 July 1942 has the following:

> . . . I've been racing around "Garthend" all day & looking for my
> luggage at several of the ugly railway orifices of London all night
> . . .

"Railway offices", as in the Chamberlain text, takes out of the
mundane details what little literary interest there is. Undoubtedly the
errors increase towards the end of the book. It should be said,
however, that straightforward spelling mistakes are in evidence very
rarely indeed. Someone — the printer's reader, probably — went over
the whole thing and made *words* of what was there, though he seems
not to have had access to the holograph letters themselves. The
printed text was certainly not checked against the letters or what I
have to say later could scarcely have occurred.

For when we have noticed briefly the omissions indicated and those
that are, and when we have ticked off the alterations of punctuation
without cause and the very partial attempt to underline the book and
magazine titles that Alun Lewis forgot to underline, there are graver
matters at bottom.

That the twenty-eight letters in the National Library should have
been twenty-nine or thirty is plain enough: one or more is missing
from the beginning of the correspondence. But this may well have
been a carelessness totally unconnected with the subsequent editing
of the book: indeed, it may well be relatively blameless. Page 26 of
Alun Lewis and the Caseg Broadsheets, however, prints three lines only of
a letter, allegedly dated "sometime in November" and the first sent
from Woodbridge in Suffolk. This letter is not amongst those in the
National Library twenty-eight. It is possible, presumably, to suppose
that this letter, present when the original editing was done, was
subsequently lost. But what are we to make of the presence of a letter
amongst the twenty-eight which is neither printed in the book nor
referred to in any way? Dated only "Tuesday" it is obviously later than
the one dated 26 July 1942 and earlier than the "spinach and kohlrabi

and marrows" letter of 22 August — more than three weeks earlier, indeed, for Gweno had not then come to Southend. It is as well to say, perhaps, that there is no intrinsic reason for the letter's omission.

The peculiarities continue. On page 7 of her text Brenda Chamberlain printed a letter dated 25 April 1941. The holograph letter carries the date 25 August 1941, as clearly as Alun Lewis ever wrote his dates. As a result this letter appears much too early in the sequence, alleging, amongst other things, that Allen & Unwin were using John Petts's engraving of Alun for the cover of *Raiders' Dawn* and that they might consider publishing the Broadsheets in book form, all of which clearly belongs, from the evidence of other letters, to a period five months later. This error is compounded by the fact that the letter's postscript is printed on page 18 of the Chamberlain text, attached to the letter dated October 1941. The postscript which really belongs to this October letter is omitted altogether and the letter's text in the book, though editorially dated "October", is introduced by a passage in which it is allocated to September. How errors of this sort could occur, and at what stage some of them happened, is almost a matter for creative fantasy.

But the gravest of all the peculiarities remains to be outlined. The last two letters in *Alun Lewis and the Making of the Caseg Broadsheets* reveal a very serious transposition. These letters are dated October 3, 1943 and February 7 1944, four months apart. In Brenda Chamberlain's printed text the first of these two letters is short: almost the whole of its real message has been added to the second. The paragraph which follows heads the transposed passage:

> I want to wish you fortitude and independence of spirit & a certain physical immunity from the hurt of things, Brenda. They are what I wish for myself when I'm sane. There's a maniac in me that cries out only to be sensitive to hurt. He's more concerned with poetry than normal natural happiness and patience and he drives me to odd places. I let him, too. I'm dull and platitudinous when he's away from me and I welcome his return with a secret exultant trepidation . . .

Two closely written pages follow, transposed like the paragraph above. On the third page there is a paragraph about Alun's brothers, which Brenda deleted, another which she allowed to remain in the earlier letter to which it belongs, and the peroration, which is made to appear the end of the later letter.

> Well, Brenda, God bless you. I hope we meet again some time
> . . . I hope to see you both say in 1948 or 9. I don't expect to be
> home earlier, if ever. Good wishes, Yours ever, Alun.

A superficial suggestion might be made that the entire transposition
was brought about by the artistic "rightness" of this farewell, with its
admission of possible death. But to base such an enormous editorial
liberty on such a flimsy ground would be indefensibly culpable. I
think there was another reason, an infinitely greater one, which it is
outside my purposes here to comment on. Even against the possibility
of this, however, Brenda's action seems extraordinary. It is perhaps
no great matter that her transposition makes it appear that 'The
Orange Grove' was to be published in the autumn of 1944 rather than
that of 1943: there are other ways of checking this. But to confuse the
tone of the two letters is a positive disservice to an understanding of
Alun Lewis. The first, that of October 3 1943, presents a firm picture
of the poet waiting, biding his time, the poetry active in him in terms of
the sensitivity quoted above but rarely emerging in written poems.
His attitude to India has changed:

> It's a world I wouldn't have believed in if I'd stayed at home. It's
> infinitely more wasteful, vaster, fundamental, and tragic than
> the closed & highly organised world I left. Its poverty is deeper
> and more imperviable, its people more various & simple, its
> extremes more extreme, its perfidies and selfishnesses more
> obvious & blatant. I no longer think the Indians guiltless. I think
> they're getting what they deserve, and I feel no compunction
> about being here as a soldier, for I am sure that it's in India's
> interest that the Japs should be repelled. There is a vast field for
> human effort here, unlimited possibilities of improvement in the
> simple necessities of life — food, health, schooling, housing,
> clothing, hygiene, medecine [sic]. It's fascinating to see these
> possibilities. They presented themselves to the Russians in 1917
> & they were enthralled. If I were a young Indian I should wish
> for nothing except to serve my country. As I am not a young
> Indian I observe in a detached but warm way the flux & reflux of
> it all and it profoundly affects the way I think and the things I
> wish to write. I think you'll understand what I'm trying say if you
> read . . . The Orange Grove . . . I haven't written much except
> that story. I've written a few poems, but for a long time now I've

done nothing. The Army absorbs me & the mere physical efforts we expend in our training dull me a lot. I'm waiting really. I've not even reached the stage of being inarticulate. I'm quite passive and do not wish to write yet.

This is clear enough. Alun Lewis had stopped trying to identify himself with something too big for him and alien, inescapably cosmic in its repercussions on the observer. It is the difference between a poem like 'Karanje Village' with its

. . . little Vishnu of stone,
Silently and eternally simply Being,
Bidding me come alone,
And never entirely turning me away

— in which it still seemed possible for the poet "alone", as an individual, solitary, to add his identity, so to speak, his understanding, to the eternity of India — and the recognition of his separateness, the inevitability of his observation from outside, which we see in 'The Mahratta Ghats'.

Who was it cried to see the falling star?
Only the landless soldier lost in war.

The tone of the letter of February 7, 1944 is recognisably different. Alun Lewis was basically depressed, his being divided. On the one hand there was the holding-in, the restraint, the "hard mouth" which the Army had made for him:

God knows where happiness & spiritual safety lies: not here, not with me, not now. Perhaps you will find it by Tryfan: I would like to dream of me being there, but I can't let[9] myself any more than I can become a poet now, or let myself be. I'm on a hard rein, blinkered, mettlesome; I watch lest I bolt, and I look at the froth & the sweat of my noise and clumsy living and I sigh very quietly and regret myself & let it all go on in its inevitable crashing drive into the headlines and the oblivions of this mammoth world . . .

On the other hand, there was the overwhelming depression which he acknowledged had come over him ever since his last leave, which he spent in the Madras hills:

Since then I've gone steadily downwards and a growing obscurity & introversion has come over me. As usual with such neuroses we don't do anything to stop them until the 'thing' has a very strong grip on you & then your realisation[10] has a quality of hysteria in it and you tend to go wronger instead of righter. I've been fortunate this weekend, my very dear friend Dick Mills came up from South India to spend two days with me and I was able not only to talk but to do myself some good with talking & feeling my words struggle into will. And my dear batman took it on himself to speak fatherly to me: which has helped me greatly. And I'm coming on! I talk lightly as I can of a bad business: not the first time it's happened: but just now I can't afford to have it: it's a critical period in my little existence and more depends on my balance and brain than ever has before. So I don't mind sacrificing my writing & the wilder genius that wins itself out of these catacombs if you stay deep in the toils. I want to emerge straight & now, at whatever price. I'm telling you what I haven't told anyone else . . .

. . . Dick Mills says my mind is tentative in everything, and being tentative is a heavy disability in the Army. It can either be the pliant grasp[11] or the stammer and falter, depending on [the] climate of your[12] soul & thro' the soul, the nerves; And on the pressure of circumstance & of others. Others — a strange word for those who have entry into one, live in one's thoughts & being, — yet "others" is right in part, for much of the most powerful things within us happen alone in us. I've lived in vacuo too long & I want no more of it. But I'm not my master. Fortunate those who are . . .

I can't write about India, "the heat" sounds so banal, the red flowers too, the beggars, — I'd only be a tourist if I wrote of India. Perhaps again when the river is clear I'll write to you about this country. It's alien to me now but sometimes I'm within it.

I've continued to get the MSS for another collection of poems to Allen & Unwin for all this & that, and it may come into the world in the autumn. It's not a very good book. It's called HA HA AMONG THE TRUMPETS — Job, the last but two chapter.[13] Read that chapter for me, *Brenda*. About the wild ass, the ostrich & the battle charger.

Oh dear Brenda, God be kind to you, poet & painter & woman.
My love and thoughts with you
Ever
Alun

This is how the last letter really ends. If the penultimate one carried the sign "Waiting", this one is marked "Stop". Twenty-six days later Alun Lewis was dead.

It is no pleasure to have to draw attention to these editorial peculiarities, the less since many of them seem to have been protective in character. The amalgamation of the last two letters certainly was. What we are to make of some of the earlier changes is much less certain. Before we leave the Caseg letters, however, it may be possible to offer one or two observations on Alun Lewis that are more positive, wrested less from dead editorial hands than from the substance of what he wrote — not so much "pulling paper through water", as he wrote of certain poems intended for the Broadsheets, "as though translation had sogged them",[14] as enquiring more acutely into the mind and the assumptions of the writer.

One of the developments that these letters comprehend is the growing acquaintance of Alun Lewis with Wales. In the most overt sense, of course, he knew it only too well. Childhood in Cwmaman and holidays in Penbryn had made him party both to the depressed radicalism and essential democracy of the mining village and to the rural fraternity, spatially wider but no less depressed economically, of the tenant farmers of the Cardiganshire coast. But, like many successful families, the Lewises were self-satisfying: graduates from a family of this sort (and there are many of them still about) were insulated, not merely by knowing little at firsthand of the camaraderie of misfortune but by deliberately emancipating themselves, according to the fashion of the time, from the cruder conditions and time-honoured beliefs of their background. Religion, for instance, was not a matter for practice: it could be amalgamated, in terms of need, with a wider idealism and non-materialism in which Art might assume the more important role. Nevertheless, second-hand though proletarian Wales had been to the child, to the adolescent at boarding school, to the very young man, it was present before the eyes, it flashed through in moments of imagination from grandparents, more distant relatives and acquaintances: in the end it became that responsibility to which idealism called Alun Lewis, even though he understood its shape so little. It nagged at his "privilege": it called him incessantly towards a truer democracy.

But for long there was something in the way, something born of the emancipation. Ian Hamilton suggests this in his Introduction to *Alun Lewis: Selected Poetry and Prose:*

> If Cwmaman was the source of Lewis's responsibility, then
> Penbryn encouraged the dream that recurs time and again in his
> poetry, of isolation in a benevolent, undemanding Nature.[15]

My personal belief is that the antithesis created here between
industrial background and rural is as misleading as the emphasis on
the unthinkingness of holidays at Penbryn. What is really to be
observed is the growing belief in the romantic separatedness of the
writer — the detached observer, the sympathiser with deprivation,
perhaps, but the separated mind which must preserve itself and
afterwards may find power to draw others to a like freedom. That this
was, in its early basis, unusually but by no means uniquely naive and
that it leads directly on into a deep morass in which "the purpose of
the writer" flails helplessly about is not my main concern here. I want
to show only that in taking this road Alun Lewis was parting from the
traditional feeling of Welsh writers that they were, and should be, part
of the community about which and for which they wrote, and to
suggest that this parting was the result both of the "emancipation"
which his generation suffered (which meant broadly the acceptance
of English social and artistic values) and of his schooling at
Cowbridge, a boarding school on the English model, where he was
taught and influenced most of all by Eric Reade, an English master
who was himself an Englishman. Neither of these last points has
pejorative implications: I simply note them as influences in Alun
Lewis's development. But there was never complete victory for such
influences, as there was for a time in Dylan Thomas: Cwmaman was
always there, in the depths of the imagination, like a hunk of hard
cheese in the stomach that the "civilising" digestive acid failed in the
end to dissolve: in the end it had to be accepted, an enduring pain that
could only be borne by a different kind of personal commitment.

Ian Hamilton, of course, and other writers, however sympathetic,
who believe that the writer continually emancipates himself from the
provincial to the metropolitan, from the insular to the European, and
that this emancipation is to be equated with continually increasing
understanding and mastery both of the literary process and of life,
describe with approval this outward march: they are unaware that the
flower they mark is a graft on a different stock. When in January 1938
Alun Lewis wrote to Jean Gilbert, a French historian he had met at a
conference at Pontigny the year before,

> We are a long way from the world in Wales, and there is a kind of

apathy about things. The poor accept their lot and the well-to-do their comfort. And the farmers pray only for rain. I would like to wake them up. I mean, too, that I would like to wake myself up[16]

— and it is quoted approvingly by Ian Hamilton as a sign of increasingly open eyes ("he was clearly beginning to find Wales stifling"), I am inclined to see only the last sentence in that light. The remainder reveals a young man too little in touch with the real ills and resentments of his own country and impressed with himself as already taking a European view. This sounds unkind, but it is not meant to be: Alun Lewis was still very young, of course, and he was moving in the direction in which his assumptions took him.

Even as a historian he had done little or no Welsh history. He had been drawn, through the patronage of Professor Treharne, into research into an obscure aspect of Papal history of the thirteenth century which had no more than faint Welsh connotations. One of the minor facts that emerges from the Caseg letters is that he knew of the battle of Catraeth but had no understanding either of the facts about it or their significance. In a letter to Brenda Chamberlain dated June 2 [1941] he wrote:

> Riders would be fine for the War in Wales sections. The men who went to Gododdin — cattle raiders 15 centuries ago pursuing a tribal feud against the tribes of the Scots border and being massacred at Catraeth.

Such a back-to-front description would have failed him at C.S.E., let alone O Level! But it would be foolish to make too much of this. All I wish to suggest is that his training in history did not provide him with an adequate introduction to his own country.

Instead, he had to walk the long road out, only to turn back on it. Ian Hamilton does not fail to quote

> The world is much larger than England, isn't it? I'll never be just English or just Welsh again[17]

without realising that Alun Lewis was doing just what he implied, adding important experiential correlatives to his central experience. But of the centrality of Wales, however he was separated from it physically, he became more and more sure. His last pronouncement on this aspect of himself as a writer was in a letter of 23 November 1943 to his parents:[18]

> When I come back I shall always tackle my writing through
> Welsh life and ways of thought: it's my only way [this is a
> repetition, almost *verbatim*, from an earlier letter of June 1943];
> but I must get to grips with the details of life as I haven't yet done:
> the law, the police, the insurance, the hospitals, the employment
> exchanges, the slums: I've always enclosed myself in an
> impalpable circle of seclusion, turning away to the Graig and
> Traeth Bach for the aloneness that is somehow essential for
> youth to breathe and grow at all. But I hope I can breathe in
> crowds and in business when I return, for all these fields of
> human life — the greatest part of people's lives in fact — is
> scarcely known to me.

This is a very explicit statement and supremely important. It is only
in "the aloneness that is somehow essential for youth to breathe", true
as this is in part, that he still fails to recognise the influences and
assumptions which had made solitude a prerequisite.

Nothing so revealing as this passage is to be found in the Caseg
letters. In 1941 the process of learning about Wales was only
beginning. Alun Lewis's first moves as a writer had been
Londonwards: this was partly because of the help he received from
Helen Waddell, his English master's distinguished cousin, and his
early introduction to Allen & Unwin, *Horizon, Poetry London,* and
other adjuncts of the literary scene: his period at Longmoor Camp,
too, made London the natural Mecca of his ambitions. While at
Aberystwyth he had edited the students' magazine, *Dragon,* but I
cannot discover that he ever contributed to Keidrych Rhys's *Wales,*
founded in 1937: of all the poets and short story writers who were
young at the beginning of the war, he was the only one absent.
Whatever the full reasons for that face towards London, they
managed to exclude Wales, in a literary context, more effectively than
any that influenced Dylan Thomas and his other contemporaries.

A certain experience of Wales he had (did he not boast to Brenda
Chamberlain that in a fortnight in North Wales he had "swum in all
the cold lakes, Ogwen, Idwal, Llanberis . . ."?) but of its reading
public, its sales outlets, the writers of his own age and situation
(without the Welsh language) he knew next to nothing. Accordingly it
is of some small interest to observe him, when about the business of
the Broadsheets, beginning to remedy these deficiencies. The

account of this is necessarily groaning with the kind of detail interesting only to those who have followed in his train (either in publishing or in editing magazines), but for Alun Lewis it was a brush with reality, the reality of preparing publications for an audience in Wales. Generalities were slowly modified by acquaintance with the possible. In November 1941, after scurrying, on one of his leaves, round West and South Wales, he wrote to Brenda:

> W.H. Smith's in Cardiff have taken 40 of each number — I'm sending the order to Llandyssul — they can send it on direct: the manager of Smith's is an enthusiast & is distributing the prospectus forms to all the right people. I went to my old school at Pengam & they jumped at the idea. I left 2 ½ dozen of No.1 there & you can expect a cheque or order for subscribers' copies + receipts of sale for No.1 sheet. I've mailed a lot of sheets & I'll give you the names, so that if you get a subscription for the series from any of them you can begin with Sheet 2 as they've already received No.1. I'm enclosing a cheque for Subscriptions already received, and will put names and addresses with the other information. Gweno will take two dozen copies of each sheet, & I think Aberdare Smith's will take the same. They've had two dozen of No.1 & will send you the proceeds less one third discount — the same terms as the Cardiff manager asked. With such a heavy discount I feel we must limit our sales through bookshops as much as possible & concentrate on subscribers. So I haven't written to Smith's head office yet . . .

Difficulties over paper, miscalculated costs, postages unreckoned — all these and other points can be checked against Alun Lewis's experience in passages no less mundane than this. It was a beginning, no more.

And there were his fellow-writers to meet. By 14 April 1941 he had already written to Keidrych Rhys and hoped to get help from Gwyn and Glyn Jones. His letter of June 2 reported that "Gwyn and Glyn Jones are enthusiastic, the former offering £2 & promising to dispose of 100 copies at once". Later, in November, when the realities loomed a little larger, Alun was arranging to take 150 copies himself of Sheet 1, send 50 to Gwyn Jones and forward a prospectus and specimen sheet to "Foyle's, Richard Wilson, Llew. Wyn Griffith". In the same month he spent a week-end at Llanybri, as has been mentioned earlier, where Keidrych gave him a list of addresses, telling him that "W.H.

Smith's at Llandudno is a good shop & will sell the sheets". No other writers were, apparently, asked for their support. Alun did, however, when the Broadsheets were foundering, attempt to persuade Brenda to write to David Jones for an extract from *In Parenthesis,* repeating this request when no action seemed to have been taken — a surprisingly early recognition of an Anglo-Welsh work of the first importance. It is plain that the whole exercise, partial success as it was, had been for Alun Lewis an introduction to the poetry of his own country, both in Welsh and English. It was a skimpy introduction, right enough, depending rather heavily for translations from the Welsh on Idris Bell's *Welsh Poetry,* which he had borrowed from a colleague at the Lewis School, Pengam, and making possible, very early in the enterprise, a rather tenuous and facile comment that the Broadsheets contributed towards a "demonstration of continuity, almost of identity, between Wales 16 centuries ago & Wales today". But it was a beginning. In a letter of August 22, 1942, he wrote to Brenda and John to say that he had seen a set of watercolours of Wales in the Recording Britain exhibition at the National Gallery and "was angry to think that you two had not painted Wales as you can, instead of those fanciful Rowntree and Mona Moore fantasies". Identification with Wales was beginning.

It is significant, however, that it was by way of two artists — Brenda Chamberlain and John Petts — that he was able to make this "return" to Wales. If the fact depended, in part, on his having met John Petts in Surrey, where he was working on a farm, the development of the idea of the Broadsheets sprang from Alun Lewis's own confidence in the field of art. The letters that he afterwards wrote to Brenda and John about the project were, of course, letters to artists and it was inevitable that he should argue, comment and suggest within their field. It is, however, the gratuitousness of the comments that impresses, the boldness of a young man made free of this world of art by his education. And it is this very freedom that strikes the reader at once as un-Welsh, as not arising from either the knowledge or the attitudes of the background immediately beyond his home. I must content myself with one illustration out of many possible. In the first available letter, dated 21 February 1941, and addressed to a Brenda Chamberlain whom he had not met, he wrote:

For the woman with the ear-ring I thank you seventy times seven. The two most moving impressions I had were — first: the

Michaelangelo curved sweep of draperies & calf in the bottom of the composition, a great powerful motion that gives passion & purpose to the stillness of her body, and conveys all that has & is going to happen. Secondly the reflection in the mirror, which astonishingly develops the whole complex being of the woman. For her flesh is so real & simple: then the dark remote beauty comes swimming up from the mirror, a part of the darkness between her & her reflection & all round her. I begin to think of what she is thinking, and of what she is. You may have suggested the platonic image as well as the reality, her mind as well as her body. I find it both satisfying & exciting, but I cannot say in words what I feel so sensitively and floodingly. The dark shadow, as of a shoulder, in front of her, alone distracts me with its too obvious outline, — I wish it had more fluidity so that it melted into the dusk & the light under her arm was thereby less bright.

If one dares to suspect him of a deliberate display of artistic erudition, one in which other kinds of knowledge are embedded, at least the ease of it all — and the perfunctory disclaimer about "words" too — may be parallelled in other letters. Somewhere — whether at Cowbridge or Aberystwyth — he had been made free of a kind of knowledge and brought to an appreciative sensitivity distinctly uncommon amongst his graduate contemporaries in Wales.

Another trait may be noted here. I have already, once, referred to his language as "fulsome". Alun Lewis's taste in perorations was curious. If we pass over the "poet & painter & woman" of his last letter of all, we must nonetheless take note of "Good fortune, Good Artist" (14 April 1941), "blessings on the woodfire" (July 1941), "And a Year of Love to Us All" (January 5, 1942), "Brenda of the mountains" (February 1943), and "Good luck to the graver and the spade" (postcard dated 4 September 1942). These have an air of deliberate contrivance, unsalted by humour. Only the "Fare ye well for I must leave you" (March 1942) has the unthinking note of spontaneity. Throughout he is freer with his "love" than one would expect, though I take this to be a mannerism of the same sort as the perorations. There are other signs, here and there in the language of the letters, which confirm the tone of what I have noted already. In a letter of August 1941, which contains a long appreciation of the engraving reproduced on pages 12 and 13 of *Alun Lewis and the Making of the Caseg Broadsheets* (an appreciation which the printed text mauls badly three or four times) Alun ends with the part-sentence:

& you must come & live with it one day when you decide to visit
the south, won't you?

Again, in a letter of the October following, when his only visit to
Llanllechid was in view, he wrote:

I too would love to live with you for a while, but alas, a peep is all
the times permit.

In the second case he is *clearly* using "live" where we should use "stay",
and indeed, after the visit to Brenda and John, "stay" it has become:

. . . after the war, if you can accept me, I want to stay with you a
Summer, please.[19]

There is, in general, a moderation of the rather precious tone when he
gets to know his fellow-artists better, but this is less a mark of the
victory of honesty over affectation than of the pressure of the problems
of a joint enterprise (even when the undertakers were artists) upon a
concept he had evidently cultivated of the unhampered love and co-
operation possible between particular people whom Art had made
free. All the influences that had pressed Alun Lewis towards this
concept I cannot pretend to identify, but that D.H. Lawrence was one
is pretty certain. When he writes of Gweno in his letter of July 1941

. . . I call her with blood of heart & sinew of brain . . .

the mark is there, plain enough. And if a single sentence should not
convince, there is the passage from the letter of 14 April 1941, about
swimming in "all the cold lakes . . . That's when I'm nearest to
complete being with the universe — for swimming is like a starry sky
as well as the groins of rock — naked swimming, that is, in naked
water, green water, salt or simple".
    When, therefore, he wrote, in the same long letter, of the
Broadsheets project as intended "to reach the people — with beauty
& love", it is all of a piece. If we had asked, "What love?", he would
probably have replied that he meant the kind of love that artists and
poets, free and untrammelled individuals, could feel for each other,
the kind which ordinary folk, hog-tied by poverty and circumstance,
could reach out to if they could begin to understand and know the
beauty in life. If this seems an odd doctrine to propagate in time of war

and a naive one at any time, it must be seen as the product of a deal of reading in the Romantics and a very inflated notion of what "being a poet" meant. (A comparison here with Vernon Watkins, the product of similar schooling, and his view of his relationship with Dylan Thomas might be enlightening). In it, whether acknowledged or not, Art has become what Religion once was and Education must be made its handmaid.

From the beginning of the correspondence with Brenda Chamberlain and John Petts, beauty and love were not to feed on themselves in isolation or be applied solely to scenery, to the earth, to objects inanimate. They were to be available for *people*, to affect society. Responsibility, in the voice of Cwmaman, was the driving force.

> The quarry villages like Llanllechid & Bethesda are no different from the mining villages in the South. I wonder when you will turn to the quarry, the pit, the slum street & the bench in front of the Workmen's Hall for your compositions. I think you will, eventually. For in this world the people are as profound and as enduring & as exciting as the great Carneddi. And those who understand 'Art' must learn through Art to understand the people.[20]

It was not that he claimed to be far ahead of his coadjutors in this respect. "I am learning so much in the ranks", he added. His letter of 14 April nevertheless set out, in the context of the Broadsheet idea, his feeling of divergence from Brenda and John:

> You and John are working out your own lives in your own way — up in the mountains where you can work best, a-gathering simples & selling pups, earning your right to live the way that you feel best. I seem to be moving in a different direction — to a closer mixing with society, with poverty & politics & economics, for I see no other lasting way of creating a situation where Art can live in the people. I've been pulled into the war & regimented & bullied & taught to kill. That is the measure of the impossibility of our present society being good arable land for human seed. So I have the deep conviction that there are two urgent needs for me: — one, to write for: the other, to educate The People. In practice, they work together — my writing is an expression of all the conflict, all the hope & faith & despair & love that is humanity.

There are several ideas compressed in this passage. The first is simple enough. The followers of Art have so far opted out of society, like Brenda and John, believing that the quality of life desired is possible only to the few, in a chosen isolation. Alun believed the opposite, that Art must be brought into society, to elevate it, Beauty, as presented by artists, must alter the vision of the ordinary man and woman. One may wonder, in parenthesis, why this should succeed where natural beauty fails and why any kind of beauty, natural or man-made, should be held to preclude violence, sudden death, war or suffering, present, all of them, in Nature and in the very poems of Wales — the 'War in Wales' section — that Alun Lewis planned for the Broadsheets. There is a deal of confused thinking here: a humanistic morality was trying to push its way through an education that had created the illusion that poets and artists might really become acknowledged as the legislators of the world. But confused or not, it was powerful enough at the time. On 25 August Alun Lewis reported that Allen & Unwin might publish the Broadsheets in block form:

> It's tickled Unwin's fancy — after all, it's a _true_ idea, isn't it?

The only significant later development in the theory of an enterprise that aroused in him greater and greater disappointment — "my feeling is that we haven't realised the ideal we envisaged at the start — typographically, artistically or poetically", he wrote on 9 April 1942 — is that Art, to educate satisfactorily, must be brought up to date.

> Leonardo's Horsemen . . . was too archaic for the modern reality
> that WAR connotes.

Keidrych Rhys, as early as November 1941, had been instrumental, in any case, in altering the balance towards the modern:

> He believes and it is _so_ true that the living must be helped before the dead. The Cymrodorion publish Taliesin & the old literature: nobody publishes the new. You know the hardship of trying to get your work published. All the young writers are the same, & we must help them to find a platform & a public. Later, after the war, we'll start a Review . . .

The desire to educate was still there, though mingled with other sympathies. For my purpose, I want to emphasise the curiosity of the re-appearance, in the genesis of the Broadsheet idea, of the seed of the traditional Welsh notion of the writer as educator, as contributor to community life, as commentator and celebrator, enclosed within an alien husk — a husk that would make beauty, or rather what man could make of beauty, the agent of future happiness. Contradictory as this was — for beauty, when realised, would still, without some wider correlating dogma, have contributed more rapidly to the deeper vision and freedom of possibly contentious individuals rather than to the spiritual advance of a community — Alun Lewis might still have modified it satisfactorily, if only in a Welsh context. His Broadsheet idea failed because of his own absence from the Welsh scene and war was soon to carry him away to India, where the application of his writing beliefs faced him with enormous, if not insuperable, problems. His ultimate admission that India was not *his* community symbolises the loose end his creed had come at, and though he was deeply hurt when an instructor at Karachi said to him

> "You're the most selfish man I've met, Lewis. You think the war exists for you to write books about it"[21]

he made no reply. His subsequent rationalisation still lacked something in honesty:

> I hadn't the strength to explain what is instinctive and categorical in me, the need to experience. The writing is only a proof of the sincerity of the experience, that's all.[22]

If that means what it appears to mean, then the writing is for the writer first and for anybody else only insofar as they share in, or may be able to share in, the experience truly told. This is an inevitable regression brought on by his immersion in war, his absence from home and all the more immediate objects to which the writing might be directed. The new presences were Death and Life in a strange form. The latter produced reportage:

> What is Life? Now I'm writing like a little man in Chekov. The remedy is always the same. Discover what is exciting or laughable in the immediate.[23]

The former aroused memory of his more essential self, at work in the place in which he belonged:

> And although I'm more and more engrossed with the single poetic theme of Life and Death, for there doesn't seem to be any question more directly relevant than this one of what survives of all the beloved, I find myself quite unable to express at once the passion of Love, and coldness of Death (Death is cold) and the fire that beats against resignation, acceptance. Acceptance seems so spiritless, protest so vain. In between the two I live. But oh! I'm so terribly anxious to get back, and I hit out violently at any suggestion the poet may make to the contrary.[24]

To create, in these circumstances, was to turn more and more inwards, towards the recesses of the spirit, and to find how little that was ultimately relevant had been secreted there. He was still very young, of course, lacking in the sediments of experience. But he knew enough, in his last months, to believe that, given life, he must begin again, with Wales.

I have space for only one more point. Alun Lewis, in his artistic freedom, believed, as we have seen, in his right to comment, to set standards. More than once he was active in this respect in a field not his own. On 9 December 1941 he had occasion to write:

> I'm sure you know me well enough, John Petts Ffermwr, to take my words in the good humour we share. I know I was trespassing on your ground — but trespassing is a nice occupation & does me good. Do you permit me to walk your mountains now again?

No doubt this potential confrontation was resolved by friendship and humour. But once again the right and purpose of the writer are in question. If he believed, as he did, that politicians and economists had a like leadership to take in the affairs of society, then, if demarcation disputes were to be avoided, the area of the writer's true concern must be clarified, if only by trial and error. Alun Lewis's identification with the sphere of education is already sufficiently plain. But all this was within the compass of the Welsh attitude, in which radical politics and education were natural fellows. The crisis for the writer's purpose arose with the onset of war, in which the Government, and, instrumentally, the Army, claimed the right to *defend* society. Pacifism was strongly represented in Welsh communities, and though Alun

Lewis never claimed this for himself as more than a natural affinity, his early attitudes, even when he regretfully accepted the need to play some part in the war effort, were deeply resentful of the kind of leadership that the Army offered. In May 1939, before joining up, he wrote to Dick Mills, of

> the army, the bloody, silly, ridiculous red-faced army — in its bloody, boring khaki — God save me from joining up. I shall go to the dogs like blazes — it's the only honest way.[25]

When he was at Longmoor, the infinite variety of petty inconvenience and the impersonality of Army life persuaded him, in part, that there was some abstract value in the kind of enforced democratisation that was compelled upon him, and he used it, as we have seen, to try to come to terms with men as they really were, at close quarters, tentfellows. But the officer class, even when he joined it, remained alien to him. It is understandable that he objected violently to the snobbishness, the class discrimination, the sheer brainless vacuity too often represented in the officer's mess, but he seemed unable, until the last few months of his life (and perhaps not then), even to accept the function of leadership which the officer represented in the necessary conduct of war. The Alun Lewis who preferred to eat his sandwiches with the men rather than dine with the officers, who dropped his Sam Browne in the street when attempting to salute a passing RSM,[26] was not so much the clearheaded logician as a Welshman unable to divest himself of the natural prejudices of the society in which he had been brought up. It was the change to a kind of male, class-accented hierarchy that disorientated him as a writer and made him incapable, despite the Current Affairs lectures and entertainments he was called upon to devise, of offering the kind of 'inside' commentary which his Broadsheet enterprise had begun to outline. (Indeed, the Broadsheet enterprise, if only partly successful, was a deliberate attempt at re-orientation, in a context he could accept). He was, of course, frequently in trouble with his superiors and colleagues who, nevertheless, showed him more tolerance in the end than his strictures on them might have suggested. His undated letter from early August 1942 report, one of his "difficulties":

> I'm in a bit of trouble about a story I wrote for *Tribune* which was recognisably written about certain people in this unit. They're

out for my blood: and I'm not one to bear a feud easily. It wears
me out.

Writing impulse and nature were by no means at one. But the point I
am trying to make is, admittedly, obvious enough. The beginning
Lewis had made, in his Broadsheet venture, in taking up again the
traditional Welsh function of the writer within his community was
defeated in the end by the reality of his presence in an Army
community whose basic function he had difficulty in accepting and
whose social attitudes were alien to the environment he knew by habit
and instinct in Wales. He was driven, through many contradictions,
into the position of writer as separate ego, neither officer nor private: it
was a position in which he felt free to offer comment according to his
personal values and from which he turned, inevitably, more and more
inward. There is nothing extraordinary in this: many, if not most,
English writers occupy this position permanently. What this change
in Lewis shows is only that the deep sense of responsibility of his
nature, with its roots in the radical democracy of the Aberdare valley,
could only function fully within the kind of community where such
values were widely shared. There alone it could be constructive,
integral. In making his late declaration from India that he must begin
again with Wales he showed both that he knew this and that the
uncommittedness of the separated writer could never satisfy him.

NOTES

1.   Quotations, or parts of quotations, rendered in italics indicate omissions
      from the text printed in *Alun Lewis & The Making of the Caseg Broadsheets*.
2.   Presumably Toulouse-Lautrec.
3.   The letter is certainly dated "19th". The editorial question-mark printed
      after it should have been attached to the month and year.
4.   Improved by Brenda to "through which you must create".
5.   Misread and misplaced in the printed text as follows " . . . and grow and
      grow and become more, something wider, deeper and more sinuous-seeming
      reaching in their roots . . .". Then "Oppressed by mountains" separated from
      the remainder by two sentences.
6.   Probably early August 1942. Not printed in *Alun Lewis & The Making of the
      Caseg Broadsheets*.

7.   Postmarked 4 September 1942.
8.   Alun Lewis's letter to Professor Treharne, 22 June 1935. *The Anglo-Welsh Review* No.40, Winter 1969.
9.   The Chamberlain text has "find".
10.   "Resolution" in the Chamberlain text.
11.   "Gnash" ditto.
12.   Printed as "the" [soul].
13.   Actually the last chapter but three.
14.   Letter dated editorially 'July 1941'. The printed text (p.14) has 'putting' for 'pulling'.
15.   p.11.
16.   Hamilton, *op. cit.*, p.15. Letter dated May 12, 1938.
17.   *Ibid.* p.54. Quoted from *In the Green Tree*, p.34. Letter to his parents dated April 7, 1943.
18.   *In the Green Tree*, p.51.
19.   Letter of 4 November 1941.
20.   Letter of 21 February 1941.
21.   *In the Green Tree*, p.47. Letter to Gweno dated 30 September 1943.
22.   *Ibid.*
23.   *Op. cit.*, p.31. Letter to Gweno, New Year's Eve [1943].
24.   *Ibid.* p.36. Letter to Gweno, April 1943.
25.   Letter to Dick Mills, May 30, 1939. Quoted by Ian Hamilton, *op. cit.*, p.18.
26.   See 'Second Lieutenant Lewis: A Memoir' in *Memoirs of the Forties* by J. Maclaren-Ross (p.229).

Philosophy and Religion in the
Poetry of R.S. Thomas

In this number of *Poetry Wales* is printed the script of John Ormond's film of R.S. Thomas, with the poet's answers — fuller ones than ever before elicited from him — to some searching questions about his religious beliefs. As I write this I have not seen it, have indeed no inkling of what it contains. I approach my subject, then, with one hand tied behind my back, well aware that what appears on another page may make turgid nonsense of what I write on this. And yet I venture, not solely because I am commanded to advance. What R.S. Thomas has written he has written: his poetry is there to be interpreted. If I misrepresent him, then he will have to pronounce again to put me right. And that won't do any harm, not even to my pride.

I have another reason for advancing across this already enfiladed ground. I have read the poems of R.S. Thomas many times: until I began this study I imagined that I knew them, that I had little more to learn from them, that R. George Thomas, Pennar Davies, H.J. Savill and I (with interlocutory and explanatory remarks from Raymond Garlick) had built up what might be called a *corpus* of only occasionally dissonant views of the philosophical and religious content of his work, at least of the earlier poems. Now another and more concentrated look has shown me how little I understood, how often I was led away by lesser themes and missed deeper implications, and to what extent I had failed to perceive a development from the position set out at the beginning. In the result, how surprising, indeed how vulnerable, is what R.S. Thomas is offering by way of philosophy. I use the word *philosophy* in its restricted sense of the philosophy of religion and intend by it, more specifically, those interpretations of it which see it either as preparatory to religion or as establishing the possibility of religion in a negative way, thus making room for faith. If these interpretations, as glimpsed in this essay, seem to the reader cast unjustifiably into secular territory, a glance at R.S. Thomas's own *Penguin Book of Religious Verse* (1963) will reveal with what latitude he could and did interpret the adjective *religious*. Indeed, such a glance will puncture a little the surprise that might be felt on realising his own unorthodoxies.

Two points must be made by way of preliminary. The first is entirely obvious to anybody who already knows R.S. Thomas's work: it is that the argument is approached, must be approached, from the position and function of a priest of the Church in Wales. That part of the argument which is still alive, indeed, turns back upon and scrutinises that function. The second is that R.S. Thomas's first two books, *The Stones of the Field* and *An Acre of Land,* represent, broadly, the period of conflict, of theory and counter-theory about the place of Nature in God's purposes. The broadcast poem *The Minister* begins the resolution of that conflict. The volumes from *Poetry for Supper* onward are concerned — again, broadly — with the validity of the priest's function in a suffering world.

The title of *The Stones of the Field* (1946) is taken from the Book of Job:

> For thou shalt be in league with the stones of the field;
> and the beasts of the field shall be at peace with thee.

It needs no great imagination to see how the *stones* of an arid Palestinian hillside appealed to him as the symbol appropriate for the "land's hardness" on the shoulders above Manafon. But to be satisfied with thus much perception would be to take the first of many wrong directions, not a few of which are supplied by the fifth chapter of Job from which comes the verse quoted. In this chapter Job is enjoined by Eliphaz the Temanite to commit his cause to God. Although

> ... man is born unto trouble, as the sparks fly upward

yet God

> shall deliver thee in six troubles: yea, in seven there shall no evil touch thee.

But what R.S. Thomas has picked out becomes irrelevant, in his interpretation, to the chapter's prevailing message. The poet's emphasis lies on the word "league", the phrase "in league with". This is his departure-point and the point to which he returns.

It is true that the seventeenth verse appears to lead into the first statement of his argument:

> Behold, happy is the man whom God correcteth: therefore despise not thou the chastening of the Almighty.

If God is in the stones, in the beasts of the field, Nature is His in action, not merely in creation. Nature may therefore be the chastiser, the orderer of a discipline from which Man seeks periodically to escape. The farmer in 'Out of the Hills', the poem which opens *The Stones of the Field,*

> ... has shaken from off his shoulders
> The weight of the sky, and the lash of the wind's sharpness
> Is healing already under the medicinal sun.

Even the mountain has a "cold care". But the man from the "starved pastures" has "dreams clustering thick on his sallow skull", dreams of "the legendary town". They hang there, making a "slow wound" (as in 'The Minister'): he cannot believe that it is the same world over the hedge. But in 'Out of the Hills', although "traditional discipline / Of flint and frost" has thawed, . . . "The earth is patient, he is not lost."

But lost from what? From a league with God (via the stones)? From the good life? From morality? One poem cannot answer these questions. But what the town brings about in the farmer, in 'Out of the Hills', is "the sudden disintegration / Of his soul's hardness": he is guilty of "maudlin laughter": beer sullies and slurs "the limpid runnels of speech". He loses dignity as well as discipline in the act of associating with others — whether in talk, beer or sex (the last is a gloss on other poems). In 'Valediction' there is an indictment of "the shallow stream / Of neighbours' trivial talk". 'An Old Woman' who sees and hears little, passes the hours with "drops of milkless tea".

> And yet if neighbours call she leans and snatches
> The crumbs of gossip from their busy lips,
> Sharp as a bird, and now and then she laughs,
> A high, shrill, mirthless laugh, half cough, half whistle,
> Tuneless and dry as east wind through a thistle.

Such talk with neighbours, then, is not seen as a mark of friendship. Too often it is "spite or guile", a Genesis vision. As for Man

> ... every imagination of the thoughts of his heart was only evil continually.

Two conclusions may tentatively be reached about this. The first is that *solitude* is a pre-requisite of the *league* with the stones of the field. The second is that these views are as much a predicament enforced upon the priest intellectually and socially as observed by the poet to be enforced upon the hill farmer by his physical isolation. In 'Country Cures' he writes:

> I know those places and the lean men,
> Whose collars fasten them by the neck
> To loneliness;

In this sense the development of Iago Prytherch from an observed figure on the skyline to the poet's overtly leagued *persona* was inevitable. It was the isolation in himself, he believed, that made the discipline possible. The hill farmer, in a similar situation, aroused his expectation. His dark figure posed a "gaunt question".

> My poems were made in its long shadow
> Falling coldly across the page.

In 'The Airy Tomb' is to be found a full-scale exposition of this myth of isolation: Twm leaves school, unschooled, for his mountain home, his father and mother die, he continues to live alone, his mind at peace, his body free of "the itch of cattle". "The glimmer of flesh, deadly as mistletoe", is resisted: Twm dies as alone as he has lived, "entombed in the lucid weather". R.S. Thomas presents this as an "odd tale," but its attractions for him are made plain enough by the presence of some of the elements in other poems. Twm is *in league* with the stones of the field right enough. He remains uncompromised.

What is in question is how far this exposition of the virtues of solitude should be read as a means to morality, to what a more down-on-the-valley-bottom pastor would perhaps call "the practical application of religion". In one sense it is obviously impractical: a society which consisted of Twm in the plural would soon cease to exist. But this does not entirely answer the case for solitude. The hill farmer generalised does not come down often, but he *does* come down. Does that patient earth save him? Is he more religious because of his domicile, more moral? Here I feel that R.S. Thomas is locked in his own predicament, which may be partly a sectarian one. He preaches the rules from the Book and is not heard. Yet the people have a morality, or what passes for it: in the Nonconformist chapel of Maesyronnen, well away from his parish, the atmosphere can be dismissed as one of "stale piety": in the unspecified moorland parish of 'The Minister' the democratic practice of "calling" a new pastor becomes Nature as debased by the farmer, the dominance of Job Davies and "the logic of Smithfield". There are rules which are generally understood, if frequently broken. It is the failure of the preacher's moral invective to redeem the rules that so irks the poet. The face of the hillman is, he feels, "lit always from without": he is betrayed by "wilderness within". The desert waxeth: woe to him that hath deserts within! as Nietzsche puts it. R.S. Thomas's acknowledgment of his reading here makes one wonder how much further he was indebted to *Thus Spake Zarathrustra*. "The great Immoralist", as he called himself, is unlikely company for a Christian priest. Yet Zarathrustra (Zoroaster) went into the mountains where "he possessed his spirit in solitude and for ten years wearied not thereof". When at last he was tired of his wisdom and came down, he preached the death of God, the birth of Superman, and life as art. The last of those three messages has some odd echoes in R.S. Thomas's thinking.

But the great burden for the poet is the prescriptive task of the priest. If there is one thing that seeps out of R.S. Thomas's poems it is that to preach morality — that is to thunder incessantly against sex and beer and money — is useless and worse than useless, a wound salted and re-salted. The Bible appears frequently as a limitation, even in a poem like 'A Welsh Testament' whose import is not primarily religious.

> Even God had a Welsh name:
> We spoke to him in the old language;
> He was to have a peculiar care
> For the Welsh people. History showed us
> He was too big to be nailed to the wall
> Of a stone chapel, yet still we crammed him
> Between the boards of a black book.

To escape the dimension of images, yet to be imprisoned in the Word
— this was no state of grace, either for preacher or congregation. The
people are uncouth, unwilling, only momentarily affected by the
Word, even with *hwyl.*

> Who is this leaning from the wide pulpit
> In judgement, and filling the chapel
> With sound as God fills the sky?
> Is that his shadow on the wall behind?
> ('The Minister')

His is not a word that gives Life (and here we see the Welsh heritage of
the Word indicted). It is a man-made encounter, arranged for the
habit and delectation of the people.

> I call on God
> In the after silence, and my shadow
> Wrestles with him upon a wall
> Of plaster, that has all the nation's
> Hardness in it. They see me thrown
> Without movement of their oblique eyes.
> ('Service')

The priest (or the minister) is not so much their intermediary with
God as their weekly sacrifice to him.

Prayer (in the poems) is not answered.

> There is no other sound
> In the darkness but the sound of a man
> Breathing, testing his faith
> On emptiness, nailing his questions
> One by one to an untenanted cross.
> ('In Church')

These admissions, about preaching and prayer, are acknowledged as
personal to the poet, however, only in later poems, of the period of
Pietà. In the earlier debate they are alleged at 'The Minister', where
they appear at all. R.S. Thomas, within the bounds of his first two
books, acknowledges nothing of the sort: he remains in his isolation,
seeking to discuss whether the Nature which has taught him is
teaching others, particularly those of his fellows whom he sees in

similar isolation. And it is important here — in the thesis and anti-thesis which R.S. Thomas sets up — to be clear as to what Nature can be expected to teach.

In 'Affinity' is to be found the most optimistic estimate:

> From the standpoint of education or caste or creed
> Is there anything to show that your essential need
> Is less than his, who has the world for church,
> And stands bare-headed in the woods' wide porch
> Morning and evening to hear God's choir
> Scatter their praises?

The hill farmer escapes the limitations of buildings, of institutional-ised religion (the quality of a *church's* silences is analysed later in the poem 'In Church'): he lacks for nothing, appearances notwithstanding, and the landscape is very firmly God's. But the moments of doubt and contradiction are much more numerous. 'A Labourer' suggests that Man does not love even the earth which nurtures him: in other poems the way of life it shadows is symbolised by "the mixen": it is "the brown bitch fawning about my feet" ('The Slave').

> The dirt is under my cracked nails;
> The tale of my life is smirched by dung;
>   ('The Hill Farmer Speaks')

Thought is impeded by that discipline of frost ('Frost') which 'Out of the Hills' praises: the man in the fields is "blind with tears of sweat" ('A Labourer')

> . . the hedge defines
> The minds's limits: only the sky
> Is boundless, and he never looks up.

What, indeed, can he learn but

> The land's patience and a tree's
> Knotted endurance and
> The heart's doubt whether to curse or bless?
>   ('Peasant Greeting')

There is, after all

> . . . no forward and no back
> In the fields, only the year's two
> Solstices, and patience between.
>   ('Aside')

Thoughts of progress, thoughts of any kind, find no harbourage in his cranium. "There is something frightening in the vacancy of his mind." ('A Peasant'). And as for his faculties of communication, is he Blind? Yes, and deaf and dumb, and the last irks most, ('Enigma'). That lore from "the age of innocence", which his solitude and closeness to God's creation might have collected never passes "the cracked lips".

Yet this predicament is parallel with that of the poet, who himself speaks but is not heard, in his preacher's guise, by the people he addresses. Using his intellect and his memory, the poet has approached his league with the stones of the field by learning *about* them, by reading in "the flower-printed book / Of nature", by distinguishing "the small songs / The birds bring him". He is caustic that the hill farmer has not done the same. And yet he cannot be certain, simply from an insufficiency of speech, that he has not. The later Iago Prytherch symbolises the possibility that the lore he hopes for is really there, not of a kind to be memorised and intellectualised, a lore quite foreign to the city-bred man, even to the poet in his book-lined study.

> Here all is sure;
> Things exist rooted in the flesh,
> Stone, tree and flower. . .
> . . . Space and time
> Are not the mathematics that your will
> Imposes, but a green calendar
> Your heart observes; how else could you
> Find your way home or know when to die . . . ?
>   ('Green Categories')

But Iago notwithstanding, the doubting antithesis will not be denied. The absence of "thought", of mind, worries the poet.

> Is truth so bare,

So dark, so dumb, as on your hearth
And in your company I found it?
Is not the evolving print of the sky
To be read, too; the mineral
Of the mind worked? Is not truth choice,
With a clear eye and a free hand,
From life's bounty?

('Servant')

And yet *not* choice, as the poem concludes. The farmer has none. Nor, when he understands, has the poet. His heart is "capable of the one crop". That is "the bread of truth".

The word *truth* begs all the possible questions. The conclusion reached by the balance of the poems in the first two books is that Man in isolation has *not* been taught, knows little or nothing of God. Is this a failure of Nature? Of God? Is Nature indeed God? How is it that it does not better the Word and the Book, seeing that he believes that it has taught him as poet? But this is a failure that he is inclined, by interest and involvement, to redeem. "You must revise", he tells himself,

Your bland philosophy of nature, earth
Has of itself no power to make men wise.

('Autumn on the Land')

The question must be posed differently, perhaps by going back to the beginning of the argument. What was it that Eliphaz really enjoined on Job? And what, in essence, was to mitigate Job's suffering and temptation? A very early poem, 'The Question', foreshadows this re-thinking and provides a closing stanza that leads into R.S. Thomas's latest answer.

Who can make plain
The thin dark characters of rain,
Or the hushed speech of wind and star
In the deep-throated fir?

Was not this the voice that lulled
Job's seething mind to a still calm,
Yet tossed his heart to the racked world?

It is the poet, not Job, who is satisfied with this interpretation. In part, this "still calm" of the mind is a happy gloss on "the embryonic thought that never grows". Much more importantly, it is an account of what "the stones of the field" can do for the poet. This stillness is the solution which he proposes for Elias Morgan in 'The Minister'. Morgan preaches moralistically, thundering against sex and money, but he lives in "a fool's world".

> They listened to me preaching the unique gospel
> Of love; but our eyes never met. And outside
> The blood of God darkened the evening sky.

In one sense it is quite clear what this means: the minister who

> . . . listens to the voice
> Of God, the voice no other listens to

is in a false position from the beginning. There is no case for this kind of ministering, this priesthood of the sole intermediary. He must speak of what others know:

> O, but God is in the throat of a bird;
> Ann heard him speak, and Pantycelyn.
> God is in the sound of the white water
> Falling at Cynfal. God is in the flowers
> Sprung at the feet of Olwen, and Mclangell
> Felt his heart beating in the wild hare.

Not merely is this God in Nature vindicated, but God in myth, in poetry (as we shall see later), God in solitude, as of saints. If the ministry of the Book did not succeed, Morgan should have listened to the thrush in the cypress by the gate who sang "To a tune John Calvin never heard" and accepted the temptation of the evening sunlight on the wall. Not to do so was to leave himself powerless.

> Protestantism . . .
> You have botched our flesh and left us only the soul's
> Terrible impotence in a warm world.

With the word *Protestantism* (which I once believed to be a careless mistake for "Puritanism") R.S. Thomas associates himself with Morgan's predicament, thereby scoring out some of the needlessly sectarian asides of which he is guilty in other poems. It would have been better for Morgan, argues the poem, if he had listened to "the hills'/Music calling to the hushed/Music within". He would thus have been prevented from letting his mind

> Fester with brooding on the sly
> Infirmities of the hill people.

These folk are not, cannot be, in Job's league. They are reached neither by moralistic preaching nor by Nature itself. Plainly, therefore, the solution offered is not one of successful evangelism: it is a balm for the preacher/priest/minister, a means by which he can bathe his soul in calm in the face of the nominal failure of his mission. Here is the "still calm" of 'The Question' again, the answer for Job, the answer, much more, for the poet himself. Nature's truth is *primary*, he concludes,

>   . . . her changing seasons
> Correct out of a vaster reason
> The vague errors of the flesh.

The vagueness, I fear, is not in the errors. Job Davies was vague neither in choosing a minister nor in taking Buddug under the hedge. It is Nature that *appears* to be vague by reason of the vastness of its scale of operation — a view which R.S. Thomas elucidates and adds to in later poems. But before I approach this, there is another question which 'The Minister' raises in acute form. It is, indeed, another and tangential line of argument.

'The Minister' is a poem which contains some of the most beautiful descriptive passages R.S. Thomas has written. And Morgan is surrounded by much of the imaginative sympathy that the poet feels for his own predicament. But it is also a seriously muddled poem philosophically, if only in using two different kinds of arguments that cross in the same phrase. "The blood of God" which "darkened the evening sky" might reasonably be interpreted as better evidence of "the unique gospel of love" than Morgan's "finger / Before him in accusation" (an interpretation that R.S. Thomas stands clearly convicted of wishing to impose on the unwary): yet it lacks the precise theological colour of Christ's death on the cross. It is in fact being presented as part of a gospel of beauty which the workings of Nature will not easily bear. And a very confused gospel it is.

Morgan is disinherited initially by his distrust. Absurdly (as a representation of the Puritan view) he pulls up the flowers under his window because they are "untidy" and sprinkles cinders there instead. This action is also a symptom of a desire for human ordering, an addiction to the word and the book (both in lower case) as against a wider acceptance. Beauty does not speak to him at all. There are two poems earlier than 'The Minister' — 'A Priest to his People' and 'Valediction' — which emphasise the same distrust, the same blindness. In the first R.S. Thomas explains that the "wantoners" (those whom his moral teaching has not reached) are equally impervious to the claims of beauty.

> How I have hated you for your irreverence, your scorn even
> Of the refinements of art and the mysteries of the Church . . .
> I have taxed your ignorance of rhyme and sonnet,
> Your want of deference to the painter's skill.

These two passages are revealing in a number of ways. In the first place, while underlining R.S. Thomas's awareness of the distrust felt by a Nonconformist-schooled society for ritual, for the Church's "mysteries" — if not of its philosophical basis, that beauty is not truth and is not necessarily related to it — they are defined in a manner that is sociologically absurd. A relatively uneducated rural society at Manafon, deprived of the culture of Welsh-speaking districts which would have supplied the structural and technical knowledge of poetry if not that of painting, could not reasonably have been expected to answer such demands. Art forms require, for their development, not merely a continuous tradition but an education. Secondly, it may be that R.S. Thomas is driven so to express his dissatisfaction here by an attempt to avoid altogether any implication that beauty is an adjunct to a moralistic teaching. When, for instance, Sir Philip Sidney in *An Apology for Poetry* set out his manifesto —

> For if it be, as I affirm, that no learning is so good as that which
> teacheth and moveth to virtue, and that none can both teach and
> move thereto as much as Poetry, then is the conclusion manifest
> that ink and paper cannot be to a more profitable purpose
> employed,

— it was as plain as could be that he believed that the content, the ideal enshrined in poetry, did create virtue or conduce to it, that is elevate the morality of individuals beyond the level achieved by society's other means of teaching them. R.S. Thomas's avoidance of *content*, his concentration on the aesthetic or technical frame afforded by ritual or art, suggests that he wishes to posit beauty, as distinct from truth, as a teacher which his parishioners ignore. This impression is strengthened by one of the cruxes offered in and for 'The Minister'

> Protestantism — the adroit castrator
> Of art; the bitter negation
> Of song and dance and the heart's innocent joy —

The Protestant insistence on preaching, and preaching moralistically, he affirms, has proscribed and neglected the natural impulses of the people to fulfilment through their aesthetic nature. Whatever truth there is in this depends upon the kind of fulfilment envisaged, which, if not related to virtue, remains undefined in the context of R.S. Thomas's aims as a priest. Certainly there is an element of the ridiculous, in the context of the poem, in the idea of "innocent joy", that "song and dance" would have somehow diverted Job Davies from his fulfilment through *power* or from satisfying his lust with Buddug. The *permissiveness* of our present society, and its much greater aesthetic freedom, set all this in an odd light. R.S. Thomas provides his own contradiction in the same paragraph, perhaps inadvertently.

> Is there no passion in Wales? There is none
> Except in the racked hearts of men like Morgan.

The framing of that question in the negative — the "no passion" of it — implies that there *ought* to be passion, yet that passion by definition is the product of cramp and frustration. It was the source of his own invective that R.S. Thomas was searching for.

The failure, in any case, to draw a distinction between the kind of beauty that man might make, in artefact, in poem or song, or even in "innocent joy", and the beauty that Nature offers lays R.S. Thomas's argument open to serious objection. In the first place, if the word and the book are ineffective because they are part of the ordering of Man, why should the artefacts of Man, equally finite, succeed in leading him to God (if we may assume that this is what Man-made beauty is intended to do?). In the second, Nature's beauty is only one of the faces it turns to Man, as R.S. Thomas later acknowledges freely. Is there any reason why the farmer should learn from beauty and not from cruelty and the need for survival?

It is difficult to avoid the conclusion that much of R.S. Thomas's thinking on this subject is very confused. In 'Valediction', in any case, he *is* attempting to harness natural beauty to a moral cause.

> The two things
> That could redeem your ignorance, the beauty
> And grace that trees and flowers labour to teach,
> Were never yours, you shut your heart against them.

The reason for his complaint is his own hurt, his wounding by a

> spite or guile that is more sharp
> Than stinging hail and treacherous
> As white frost forming after a day
> Of smiling warmth . . .

It is not my wish here to deny philosophically any such connection between beauty and moral conduct. It may be enough to notice an ambivalence in the word "grace" (of which R.S. Thomas cannot be ignorant) which contributes to the confusion. The grace of flowers, of hills, of the village boy from whose poise, "Earth breeds and beckons to the stubborn plough", ('Farm Child') is a physical quality, of outline, of appearance, of movement, aesthetically satisfying the observer's eye. It has no necessary relationship to an inward grace (grace in the theological context), a spiritual quality necessary to turn the heart away from spite and guile. Indeed, it is difficult to avoid the conclusion that 'Valediction' and 'A Priest to his People' have strong personal and denominational overtones. It is noteworthy that in the latter poem he is apparently prepared to find his moral invective answered with a cold stare, believing it possible that his parishioners detect his ". . . true heart wandering in a wood of lies." Yet he cannot forgive them their rejection of beauty. And here the "ignorance of rhyme and sonnet" may be crucial. The failure of the "wantoners" to be more impressed with the poet than the preacher is a deep blow. "They ought to be, they ought to be", one hears him cry. The poet

knows so much more than the preacher and it is because he is a poet
that he can forgive them, seeing the beauty that they affect to despise
in "The artistry of [their] dwelling on the bare hill" and finding the
poetry they do not notice in that speech of theirs which in so many
other poems he bitterly castigates. This is the way in which he closes
the wound in 'A Priest to his People'. But it does not convince. Beauty
should have been a teacher. And we realise that what he is telling us is
something about himself. He really believes that it is the poet who
forgives, has the grace needed for it. And because this particular poet
has learned from natural beauty he can link the beauty of poetry with
that of nature, (flower and artefact together) without fear or
discrimination, believing that this is the source of the awareness of
God that others lack.

But all this is part of an argument that R.S. Thomas has almost
forgotten. His poems since 'The Minister' (which is confused most of
all because the old views and new are juxtaposed) say little about art as
a teacher and set the beauty of Nature in a more complicated
perspective.

Above all, he makes it clear that he knows that the earth releases
other powers than beauty. But this "brute earth" does not frighten
him. He still calls to account the people with "spick rooms'
discipline", who live in "houses on the main road / To God". The
farmer and the poet are better acquainted with the "old violence" of
grass raging under their floors. And as for Nature farther off

> Somewhere among
> Its green aisles you had watched like me
> The sharp tooth tearing its prey,
> While a bird sang from a tall tree.
> ('The Parish')

The word *aisles* recalls the "world for church", the arena of God. But
how, in the end, is this going to be *better* than Man's attempted
ordering of his rooms? What *is* it that Nature teaches?

The co-existence of beauty and cruelty cannot be ignored. The
green aisles are Ted Hughes country, in which "The fox" drags "its
wounded belly / Over the snow":

> . . . the crimson seeds
> Of blood burst with a mild explosion,

   Soft as excrement, bold as roses.
        ('January')

Theologically, however, R.S. Thomas provides no answer for this, except obliquely in his concept of time and the seasons and the lap of God. Time is that part of the concept that we best undestand. The country clergy preach their sermons unheeded, but

     God in his time
   Or out of time will correct this.
      ('The Country Clergy')

Moral preaching — practical preaching, that is — takes its place in this larger view. It is the worrying about its immediate impact (as in 'The Minister') that is futile:

     the road runs on
   With many turnings towards the tall
   Tree to which the believer is nailed.
      ('The Journey')

  That is one dimension. But the seasons do more than mark the passing of time. The earth, "where all is forgiven / All is requited", offers an ultimate unity, a final order, to the separations of beauty and cruelty, fear and hope. It is in this sense that God's blood darkens the evening sky. His sacrifice is an emblem of the reconciliation that His creation affords, most of all in death,

   In the calm circle of taking and giving.
      ('The Airy Tomb')

  Some of the elements in this position are present in very early poems, as the line just quoted makes plain. What has been abandoned is the nearer perspective, the more prescriptive teaching. R.S. Thomas has ceased to be deceived by "the old lie / Of green places". In 'No Through Road' he acknowledges that he has

    failed after many seasons
   To bring truth to birth,
   And nature's simple equations
   In the mind's precincts do not apply.

The possibilities of self-deception were always immense. 'The Conductor' listened to the small stars' orchestra

> trying to be sure
> That what he heard was at one
> With his own score . . . .

The night's overture, to which he listened with the day's breath, was an extension of his conscious will.

> It was this way he adored
> With a god's ignorance of sin
> The self he had composed.

R.S. Thomas recognises the presumption: he recognises that in his earlier argument he wrestled not with God but with himself. And his last position is equally self-generated. The forgiveness, the annihilation that Nature offers, can appear totally destructive of human ideals. It is "the mind's cession / Of its kingdom" ('The Moor'). Coleridge, says R.S. Thomas,

> . . . felt his theories break and go
> In small clouds about the sky,
> Whose nihilistic blue repelled
> The vain probing of his eye.
>   ('Coleridge')

Shelley's dream decayed no less. Love deceived him: your "broken vows", hypocrite lecteur, your despair, are an advance on such easy rationalisations.

> Winter rots you; who is there to blame?
> The new grass shall purge you in its flame.
>   ('Song at the Year's Turning')

If this appears negative, in a religious sense, it must be made plain that what it is doing is making room for faith. "And God said: How do you know?" — a question to which the observation of the learned (even the learned in birds and trees and flowers) affords no better answer than the blindness of the hill farmer. The poet goes out into the fields: nothing denies his faith, not even Man's broken heart. The cold landscape returns his stare, giving nothing away.

> There was no answer. Accept; accept.
> And under the green capitals,
> The molecules and the blood's virus.
> ('Amen')

Acceptance, then, is a matter of personal faith. It will not be distilled from the biological cruelties. And this is something which the poor castigated farmer has always known, whether he has faith or not:

> . . . no signals
> Cheer him; there is no applause
> For his long wrestling with the angel
> Of no name.
> ('The Face')

Familiarity with the earth brings with it no assurance.

But acceptance, "the mind's cession / Of its kingdom", the "still calm" imposed on that seething maelstrom, makes two triumphs possible. The first is the ability to praise a God who sees and judges not as we judge.

> Viruses invade the blood.
> On the smudged empires the dust
> Lies and in the libraries
> Of the poets. The flowers wither
> On love's grave. This is what
> Life is, and on it your eye
> Sets tearless, and the dark
> Is dear to you as the light.
> ('Because')

The second is the ability to bear the pains of priesthood. It is the "still calm" of the mind that frees the priest / poet to give his "heart to the racked world". Davies, ill in mind, "whose sickness . . . / Uncurls slowly its small tongues / Of fungus" is one sufferer to whom his heart goes out.

> . . . I watch you, and pray for you,
> And so increase my small store
> Of credit in the bank of God,

Who sees you suffer and me pray
And touches you with the sun's ray,
That heals not, yet blinds my eyes
And seals my lips as Job's were sealed
Imperiously in the old days.
                              ('Priest and Peasant')

The acceptance of suffering is not complete (the sun blinds his eyes): indeed, it depends in part on his office (which seals his lips). And there is self-castigation here — a brief satire on the pre-Reformation reliance on salvation by works, the thousand paternosters to reserve a place in the audience of heaven. But there is also the idea that the vicarious suffering of the priest is possible only if the "seething mind" is a "still calm", if the league with the stones of the field, in their harshness, their obduracy, their ultimate reddening with God's blood, has been made complete.

This view of the worth of the priest's function is not constant. Sometimes its "old ambivalence" casts a shadow on the farmer and their eyes meet with "brute glumness" ('Encounter'). In 'They' R.S. Thomas asks how he serves God, whom his parishioners have shut out, by indentifying himself with their suffering, which is too often

                    their worsting
By one whom they will fight.

His function is possible only by "calling their faults / Mine" and praying for the sins of Man *in toto*. Yet he senses the contradiction. Can one be Job and the children of Job at the same time? Even his last position, he knows (from his own feeling as much as from the attacks of others) can be assailed and taken:

            I know all the ropes
Of religion, how God is not there
To go to; how time is what you buy
With his absence, and how we look
Through the near end of the binocular at pain,
Evil, deformity. I have tried
Bandaging my sharp eyes
With humility, but still the hearing
Of the ear holds; from as far off as Tibet
The cries come.
                              ('After the Lecture')

What can prayer really achieve? God shows "the opposed emblems / Of hawk and dove". He is not human, reason cannot catch at him. Is he not that God who gave over Job, "one that feared God and eschewed evil", to the wiles of Satan so that he might be stripped of all but his life?

Whom the priest is in league with, whom the poet stands close to, he can neither interpret to his fellows nor himself approach. Like Icarus, his wings can melt, he can fall far. Has he dared too much or not enough?

Channels of Grace: A View of the Earlier Novels of Emyr Humphreys

Emyr Humphreys is not a novelist who happens by accident to be a Welshman but one whose qualities and intrinsic attitudes arise in the most direct fashion from his being one. His writing and its preoccupations are the result of Wales's heritage of the last three centuries: they begin in that Puritan seriousness about the purpose of living, about the need for tradition and the understanding of it, about the future of the community as well as the individual, that has almost no place in the writing of contemporary English novelists, however many wry soliloquies from the jazz of relationships they may from time to time throw out. Sadly, however, Emyr Humphreys stands alone as a writer, both in the context of his birth and in the choice he makes in celebrating the inheritance of his native land. Because of that, it is necessary briefly to try to "place" his work against the general development of the novel in the twentieth century.

In 1899 Henry James was of the opinion that the novel had already become self-conscious, that a split was taking place between its popular and its aesthetic development. What was disappearing then, it seemed, was the nineteenth century confidence in reality, in progressive sequence, in the relationship between the worth and interest of individuals and their moral and social progress. Accordingly, many young novelists were turning, and increasingly so, in an *inward* direction, concerning themselves with the complexities of creative consciousness, the angle of vision and the ambiguous connection between the inner and the outer life which the new psychology was beginning to stress. This new experimentation took the self-conscious novel — affected as it was at different times by the prowess of Dostoevsky, Mann, Joyce, Proust, Kafka, Faulkner and Virginia Woolf — as far as the Second World War, after which there was a revival of the liberal humanist/realist novel, conceived once again in terms of moral and social concern and having a sense of life as progress. It was just here that Emyr Humphreys began: *The Little Kingdom,* his first novel, was published in 1946. Plainly he was part of the new generation displaced by the War, affected by the enforced mobility (which brought him Italy as well as Wales), that perhaps compelled it to accept experience faster than its predecessors. Equally plainly he was by birth and upbringing outside the coterie values and the rather precious aestheticism of pre-War practitioners of the novel. Above all, he began with the impetus of a fresh start in the new peace.

But to leave him in the realist fold which, one cannot but be aware, he has never left, and to offer no further explanation is to suggest that his stance has become petrified. Nothing could be further from the truth. He is very certainly where he is as a matter of conviction. This point needs making because the realist novel has long since lost confidence. In the sixties those who wished to sustain it attempted to reinforce it by an insistence on reportage and documentary: those who were disinclined to sustain it thought in terms of the unreliability of text, of the corruptibility of history, of the difficulty of establishing solid character and identity as the sum of an individual's roles and appearances. These novelists, necessarily the more inventive, began to think in terms of inviting the reader into the novel in various ways, offering alternative endings (as John Fowles does), shuffling the chapters (as Bryan Johnson has done) to recreate, by technical contrivance, the cyclical effects of James Joyce, giving life a *fabulous* dimension or stressing art as forgery and the novel as a kind of life-game in which the reader plays his own hand and draws his own conclusions from the pack.

Now to Emyr Humphreys the concepts of art as forgery or as game are unacceptable, though he knows perfectly well what the limits of realism are and how far the picture can ever escape from the artist. The novel for him is essentially serious: "in our time", he wrote in 1953,[1] "the novelist's attitude is more crucial than his manner of expression". Not for him, then, "the quiet sport of technical experimentation". Unfashionable as it may be, he has not abandoned the idea of *progress*: his insistence on plot, on narrative development, is not a sop to the conservative reader, it is his announcement that he is interested in other people rather than in the self shedding its skins as the ego perambulates: the subject of the novel is Life. Experiment he does, technically, in the use of time by intercutting the narrative (and, less significantly, in the matter of punctuation) but it will appear from what follows that such shifts do not contradict in any way a true chronology or the idea of progress. And the area of uncertainty he leaves for the reader is not a matter of technical manoeuvre or the deliberate omission of several pieces of the puzzle: the uncertainty he leaves begins at the point where our serious ideas about life fall off the edge of the world we know. Where has our society been and where is it going? What is *good*? How is a good man or woman created? How can our ideas of good best be applied to our society, to other people, to ourselves, so that more good may result? Are good standards passed on by the establishment of just organisation, by the example of an individual's absolute integrity, or by such integrity conjoined with political or social wisdom? Emyr Humphreys does not claim to know: he inclines only, and not infrequently with different emphases. But he is certain that the quest for goodness (and it will be left to the reader to determine whether goodness is a matter of a just and loving morality, conceived in human terms, or whether it involves a mystery, a vision of the infinite, of God) is not merely so remarkably difficult that it exhausts human energy and wisdom but that it is also exciting, life-giving, creative. Emyr Humphreys is a committed Christian and he has for long set himself to write novels which make it plain that "personal responsibility is a Protestant principle."[2]

One has only to read a page or two of any of his books to realise that what is in hand is no stuffy or censored tract. Nothing that I have written so far must be understood in that way. There is no relationship between, let us say, *Hear and Forgive* and Canon Farrar's *Eric or Little by Little*. Emyr Humphreys's purpose is neither hortatory nor deliberately evangelical. Where the *Catholic* novel exists in Britain, as for example in the works of Graham Greene and Evelyn Waugh, it confines itself to affirming the existence of evil (*Brighton Rock* and much of Waugh) or exemplifying (as in *The Power and the Glory*) or disputing (as in *The Heart of the Matter*) points of Catholic doctrine. In other words, though rarely as referential in this respect as Francois Mauriac, these Catholic novels have recourse to a centre of doctrinal certainty, even where, in secular terms, they have difficulty in arguing it. What Emyr Humphreys means by "the Protestant novel" is something much less fixed than that. It draws attention to the principle of personal responsibility and the necessity of choice, not simply in the Existentialist sense that one makes one's own life by choosing (though that has its component of truth) but that choices have to be made with a responsibility both to the *status quo* (and everybody involved in it) and to the result hoped for, whether near at hand or distant. Where Existentialism is self-determining only, Protestantism is Christianly wedded to the City of God, to the ultimate community, to the salvation of all men. Choices therefore inevitably involve other people, and that is where the real responsibility comes in. The practice of *agape* or Christian love, at a time when, as Emyr Humphreys put it almost three decades ago, the human race was never harder to love[3], is infinitely difficult: such love often appears defeated, ineffectual, or successfully operative only over such periods of time or in such rarefied instances as scarcely to be worth bothering with. And yet there *is* progress — or our hearts think there is, however little we now believe in the claims of technology: our society, our world, moves on, perhaps immediately to violence and political extremism but also to honesty, compassion and continuing sacrifice. How does this happen? This is really Emyr Humphreys's terrain.

It should be plain from what has been said so far why amongst contemporary novelists he is virtually without companion. And yet in my recent reading I have encountered another writer — not a novelist but a poet and short-story writer — whose preoccupations were very similar. I refer to Alun Lewis, dead these thirty-five years but of a generation only just older than that of Emyr Humphreys. Alun Lewis was the product of a lapsed Unitarian household where the world's need for love, probably to be defined as a humanist version of *agape*, was a constant topic in a still-didactic family community. Indeed, this is the central theme of Lewis's poetry. The War, of course, was a tremendous shock to the notion of world-change within a single lifetime and experience of India revealed to Lewis that the only possible time-scale was so enormous as to paralyse the will to love. But I introduce this apparently digressive comparison for three reasons. First, that Alun Lewis was a Welshman still possessed in part of the Nonconformist heritage. That may help to suggest that there was something in the community of Wales (a point I hope to illustrate further from the work of Emyr Humphreys) in the past three centuries that made such seriousness about the salvation of the world or of the individual or both a *pre*occupation — an idea that one would never glean from twentieth-century caricatures of the Puritan community, whose chief characteristic was apparently hypocrisy. Second, that Alun Lewis, beaten out of his early hopes of changing the world, came to believe that the acts of kindness and love, small though they might be, that his place in the community might constrain or allow him to perform were the only acts, within an unknown time-scale, permitted to the individual in his pursuit of good for himself and others. This again is a point to bear in mind when the work of Emyr Humphreys is more fully looked at. And thirdly, that Alun Lewis, bereft in the end of the religious dimension, ceased to believe in the efficacy of love because he no longer believed in his own integrity. What is a stumbling-block to the humanist, however, does not deter the Christian, and it is implicit in Emyr Humphreys's work that love goes on despite sin and personal defeat and that its persistence and efficacy are not wholly examinable and testable against any law of probabilities that reason may evolve. This is neither to propose the visibly miraculous nor to assert the verity of the Apostolic Succession, as the end of *The Power and the Glory* does: it is to indicate the area of the unknown, to suggest some answers that do not work and one or two that on occasion do, and to approach God with the agnosticism of one who is well aware that all human answers fall short, even those of science. It is to look at life as a whole, murmuring repeatedly, "Lord, I believe: help Thou my unbelief".

Many readers of Emyr Humphreys may fail to recognise in this preamble any connection with their own recollection of his novels. There is in them such a wealth of incident, such a complexity of plot, such amusement and irony, so many characters and various, that the preoccupations I have outlined may seem restrictive and unreal. Any restriction that exists, however, is much more probably to be found in the reader's understanding of what Emyr Humphreys means by "the Protestant novel", a restriction that I can best illustrate from my own mistakes in this context. When I first read Emyr Humphreys's article in *The Listener* in 1953 I had just finished *Hear and Forgive*. Taking the point about conscience and personal responsibility, I could see that David Flint, novelist and teacher of Scripture in a London secondary school for boys, who had been living, in a curiously blank and frustrated fashion, with Lord Whiteway's comparatively wealthy niece, had, at the end of the book, come to the realisation that he *had* to return to his narrow-visioned, unintellectual wife in a provincial Shropshire town and to his spoiled and uncongenial son Stanley. Conscience required it, integrity required it, but there would be nothing pleasant or self-fulfilling about it. The last paragraph of the narrative is imprinted upon my mind:

It was seven o'clock in the evening when I walked down Warrington Avenue. It could not be far off Stanley's bedtime. I needed time to come to terms with Phyllis first before attempting anything with my son. I closed the garden gate as softly as I could, and walked round to the back door. I could see them through the window. The wireless was on. The boy was playing with a Meccano set on the table and listening to what sounded like Radio Luxembourg. His mother was darning socks, a pinafore over her black frock. Stanley was pretty obviously the master of the house. The puritanical Sunday of the old man's day would be something preferable to this.

    Suppressing the last flicker of impulse to turn back, resolutely I knocked; and opening the door myself, I walked in.

The idea of conscience in this conclusion persuaded me that what I was to look for in the Protestant novel was the character who was journeying through the wilderness of this world towards an ultimate and responsible choice and when I read *A Man's Estate*, Emyr Humphreys's next novel, I looked in vain for the same marking on the map and was entirely confused by the story's *dénouement*. I had made my choice, so to speak, of Ada Evans, the suborned but capable illegitimate daughter of the dead M.P. Elis Felix Elis, as the character who was freeing herself to make the necessary choice or to earn the right to make it, only to find that she did not figure at all in the book's conclusion, which was devoted to the survival and inheritance of the not-very-interesting Hannah Elis. What I was not realising, of course, was that Emyr Humphreys's list of considerations was much longer than my impressionist summary of them and that, if I had looked more carefully at *Hear and Forgive*, I should never have made such a summary at all. For one thing I had no notion of the importance of Phyllis, the deserted wife, and had no means then of recognising in her the part-prototype of Kate in *Outside the House of Baal* (of which much more presently). For another, closer observation would have made it plain that David Flint was not *journeying* at all: he was stuck, will-less, in his unsatisfactory predicament, and only the fact that his mistress Helen suddenly threw him over put him in the position to listen to his conscience. Even then he would not have listened to it but for his friendship with the headmaster, Edward Allenside, who nevertheless had addressed not one word to him on the subject. It was the fact of the emotional crisis and the existence in the mind's eye of an *example* that worked together to produce a new resolution in David

Flint. Not even years of teaching Scripture and expounding the Bible
had been able to create that moment for David on his own. The living,
journeying character was in reality Ailenside and the implications of
that were still hidden from me.

But it is time now to put away errors and to indicate broadly what
the various directions of Emyr Humphreys's novels are. I exclude
from this consideration *National Winner, Flesh and Blood* and *The Best
of Friends,* despite their undoubted relationship to *Outside the House of
Baal,* because they are the fourth, first and second, novels respectively
of a quartet as yet unfinished and it would be unwise to attempt too
closely to assess its direction while incomplete. Let me begin with
A Toy Epic (1958) which, in its original draft, was Emyr Humphreys's
first novelistic writing. As one might expect, this takes the writer's
experience to the limit of the then known and felt. It is the story of
three boys, Albie, Iorwerth and Michael, schoolfellows who grow
together and then separate again. Each of them has a social and a
spiritual comment to make, but the heart of the book, in my view, lies
in the relationship of Michael and Iorwerth. Michael was the rector's
son, whose first lesson, impressed upon him by an ambitious mother,
was that he was *different.* Privileged in school and in Sunday school, he
chose to emphasise his difference by refusing to acknowledge that he
could read Welsh:

> I would sit in a corner of the pew and eagerly await my turn to
> read when we read through the Psalms together, one verse after
> another, because we read them in English, and I could read
> English better than the others. If it was a long verse I was
> delighted and read as fast as I could to emphasise my
> superiority. For this the others disliked me and kept me out of
> their games and conversation. I looked back at them over my
> shoulder, delighted with my superiority, as I ran alone through
> the graves to the Rectory gate and they made their way down the
> broad path to the litch-gate. The advantage of having a path of
> one's own to come and go by! The advantage! The superiority![4]

For some years afterwards, during which Michael's academic
prowess was no more than moderate, lack of confidence made him
deliberately cultivate charm and choose popularity, especially when
it meant bad company. Realising at length the emptiness of such
acting, he worked harder, won an Open Scholarship to University
and recovered confidence: with all the points of the *persona* clicking

into place, he embraced the cause of Welsh Nationalism and became, in his own eyes, a man of destiny.

This sense of innate leadership is Emyr Humphreys's first target, then. What is its basis? Conscience? Belief? Or a psychological "mix" which goes back to early environmental factors? The fact that the cause Michael chooses is very near to Emyr Humphreys's heart makes his author's disquiet the more poignant. A just cause must be led by conscience, not charisma. For observe Michael in the penultimate scene of the book. He dreams himself a dream of dedication to Wales, of which his friend Iorwerth, "with all his naive innocence",[5] is the soul, the potent symbol. But he has just been seen by Iorwerth in the wood beginning to make a not-very-interested love to Dilys Maurice, the minister's daughter, whose prospective partner Iorwerth has until then imagined himself to be. In other words, Michael betrays that soul, that symbol, before he starts. What is leadership when the leader despises the values of the led, however limited they may be?

Again, how does Michael come to see himself as leader? In the beginning by choosing his mother rather than his father, a Welshman of modesty and scholarship. How, from his initially anglicised position, does he come to embrace the cause of Wales? By arguing with Watkin at a Summer School, Watkin with the "sticky eyes behind thick lens, a habit of sniffing, his lips always wet with excess saliva".[6] Why is this? The novelist offers no answer. His experience suggests that that is how influence and example work: there is a time for them, and an occasion too, that often defy rationality. This is a problem with which Emyr Humphreys is engaged in all his books.

Then there is Iorwerth, the Welsh-speaking, Calvinistic Methodist farmer's son, happy in his home and surrounded by love. He is devoted to the chapel and intends to enter the ministry, but partly because he is already in love with words, with the power of speaking. This is another danger to which Emyr Humphreys points. There can be no doubt of the Puritan mind at work here, even when it criticises an excess of the Puritan practice of preaching in a country once prostrated before it. In the end Iorwerth, successful academically but broken in purpose by the impending death of his much-loved father and by Michael's betrayal, goes home, with bitter questions on his lips. How is it that he, the heir of love and faith, loses everything? How is it that he, the innocent soul of Wales, no longer wishes either to lead or to be led? These are the questions with which Job challenged God and received no answer beyond the assurance that he was right to ask. It is difficult, moreover, to put away entirely the impression that Emyr Humphreys is hinting here at a Wales traduced by politicians, amongst whom move the shades of T.E. Ellis and David Lloyd George.

A Toy Epic is a book of questions without answers, which its limitation to the days of school makes possible. Beyond them lies a great continuum of silence in which the answers may lie. But before we leave the book, it would be well to note two limited girls, one the Dilys who tries to step outside her limitations by tagging Michael, the other the Ann who accepts hers cheerfully and would accept Albie's too, but gets from Albie, who has failed his examinations and turned Marxist, only the response of one who sees himself as already trapped.

Emyr Humphreys's first-published book, *The Little Kingdom,* which appeared in 1946, takes the Michael figure further, into a new career as Owen. Owen is the son of a minister but he has been to public school. Michael, it may be recollected, was a public schoolboy *manqué*: it was the one respect in which his father was successful in blocking maternal ambition. There was a significant occasion at school when Owen was bullied, as indeed there was for Michael (in *A Toy Epic*) when he and Iorwerth were at Llanrhos County School for the Scholarship exam (he regarded Iorwerth as having slipped out of the situation and deserted him). We should plainly add these ingredients to the already napoleonic confection.

Owen is older, post-university: he has also set himself a specific task, the prevention of the construction of an aerodrome on the land of his uncle Richard Bloyd and the damming of the anglicised tide that would certainly rise higher with the coming of new employment. There are echoes here, without a doubt, of the incident at Penyberth in Llŷn in 1936,[7] but *The Little Kingdom* is set in true Emyr Humphreys country, in the precarious Welshness of Flintshire, and the plot develops by Owen murdering his uncle, taking over his money, land and the local newpaper and finally getting himself shot in an attempt to burn the hutments of the aerodrome. The case against false leadership is being taken further, obviously, but there is a strain on its dramatic credibility. What may be sensed in this novel and in the one that follows, *The Voice of a Stranger* (1949), successful as they are (the second more so), is that Emyr Humphreys is trying to kill two birds with the same stone: he is seeking to provide a well-plotted narrative with a wealth of dramatic incident of the kind attractive to readers whose attention is usually given to a more popular kind of fiction while working in one or two of the problems in which he is himself interested. The effect of this dual intention, however, is that the writing is blurred in places. In *The Little Kingdom* Richard Bloyd is an enigmatic figure, clear enough in one light as Nonconformity lost in self-enlargement and in another as a father destroyed by his daughter's lingering death, but not seen adequately as Owen's stumbling-block and a traitor to the cause of Wales. Owen himself as a later Michael, his charisma obvious but charm diminishing, is indicted clearly enough: the insensitivity to other people (which causes his downfall) increases rapidly throughout and the care for the morality of means becomes a matter of memory only. But *The Little Kingdom* appears to raise fewer subsidiary questions than the books that follow: Rhiannon may easily be seen as no more than a girl who doesn't happen to love Geraint, who loves *her*, but is infatuated with Owen, who *doesn't* love *her* — or, indeed, anybody else: and Geraint who, shocked by his mother's behaviour when he was a child, needs to know what love is (*eros*, in this case) but finds that it means an agony which drives him to neglect and betray the cause to which he and Rhiannon and Owen are devoted. We may see here the beginning of Emyr Humphreys's indictment of *eros*, its limitations and its power to mislead, but the novel's *dénouement* is too easily read, in this context, as a version of the eternal triangle. As for the remaining characters, they can be lined up — on the one side Cornelius Evans, the sly, hypocritical deacon in cahoots with the outwardly rational but culturally insensitive schoolmaster James Pierce, and on the other Rhys, Rhiannon's crippled brother, and the farmers Gwilym Blethyn and Tom Seth, the sound, right-feeling people who become Owen's dupes. It is perhaps only in terms of the later books that the reader may sense here a lack of complexity and the presence of at least one stereotype in Cornelius Evans. On the other hand, it may simply be that at this point Emyr Humphreys has only one major question to put.

The Voice of a Stranger is that book of his (*The Gift* only excepted) which can most easily be read witout the smallest realisation that its author has particular preoccupations. Set in Italy, where the War took Emyr Humphreys as an official of the Red Cross, the novel is brilliantly plotted. It lacks nothing in the kind of growing tension and progressive readability that the general reader expects, and its backgrounds are authentic. What can be discerned in it is another illustration of the destruction of leadership — not, in this case, by the corruption of idealism but by the mistake of *eros,* by the apparently chance nature of romantic or physical love. The idealism here is unpoliticised Communism as felt by a wartime guerilla leader who has concentrated on the essentials of action. Guido Bordoni, the natural leader in the field, marries Marcella Vaspucci, the daughter of a liberal professor who is compelled to line up amongst his opponents in peace-time. Marriage "across the line", so to speak, is a theme explored again in *A Man's Estate.* Whether or not Guido's idealism *could* have been applied to the trickier conditions of the post-war sort-out without fading or dirtying, in fact it gets no chance: his influence is increasingly nullified by the more experienced Communist hardliner Riccardo Forli, who not only knows how to manage the party but treacherously seeks to seduce his friend's bride. Failing in this, he has to eliminate Guido himself to cover his tracks. The genuineness of the love between Guido and Marcella proves to be no defence: and Professor Vaspucci, who might have straddled the gap between the two political factions, has betrayed his own position by his liaison with the Spanish refugee Rosaura, which gives the corrupt ex-Fascisti a hold over him. There are portraits of two do-gooders, Red Cross officials — Morell, with red hair and short, sharp bursts of conscience, and the American Warner, whose Christian will to good is calmer and more persistent. But it is Warner who, like Guido, gets himself killed by Riccardo when he tries to help Marcella. *Eros* had begun to influence *agape* and the balance is lost. The issues are unmistakable if the pressure of the plot leaves the reader time to think.

Love between man and woman, then, solves nothing outside itself, brings together no other persons or views that are sundered. And it may affect, deleteriously, the action of the kind of love which might work powerfully towards a wider unity. The direction of Emyr Humphreys's first two published novels is, behind the surface brilliance, *downward,* the cul-de-sac notice set firmly in the face of brash optimism. It is the presence of a more clearly outlined and complex linguistic background for the characters in *A Toy Epic* which suggests, despite its originally conceived limitations, that it was fairly substantially revised before it appeared in 1958.[8]

A Change of Heart (1951), the third novel to be published, strikes one immediately, despite its sadnesses, as a warmer book. Emyr Humphreys begins in it to explore the positive. If there is truth, if there is honesty, if there is goodness, how is it transmitted? The backgound this time is that of a Welsh university and the chief characters are Howell Morris, Professor of English, who has made an ill-judged marriage with Lucy Davies, one of his students, and Frank Davies, her brother, himself a student and a poet but the product, like his sister, of a confined working-class home eastwards along the anglicised coast. The book opens with Lucy dead after many apparent unfaithfulnesses and Frank under the influence of Howell's enemy, Alcuin Phillips, who foments his conviction that Howell had given Lucy a terrible life. The burden of the book is essentially that of Frank's journey from darkness to light, through the tribulation of a love affair with the fickle and self-serving Gwen, through the rigours of work on a farm (to which his refusal of Howell's help and support had condemned him), to the final revelation, made by the Communist bus-driver Jimmy Hill, that Lucy died after the induced abortion of Alcuin's child. It is satisfactory enough, to be sure, to see the import of the narrative in the victory of one man's integrity over isolation and intrigue: but a survey of Emyr Humphreys's novels following must also make one aware that Howell Morris is the first of those who offer *example*. By whatever precise track influence passes, it must pass through a succession of such nodes of good.

> A soul cannot make progress *in vacuo*: many men are better for the existence of one good man, and one good man is the product of some kind of progress that was both individual and social.[9]

Thus Emyr Humphreys, making his own exposition. But has this progress come about through politics? Not in the novels under survey. Carrog Ellis (in *The Little Kingdom*) and Elis Felix Elis (in *A Man's Estate*) both stand revealed as eloquent sellers of what truth and virtue they once had for the dubious mite of power. Does it come about through education? Not if Alcuin Phillips and Ronnie Miles (in *Outside the House of Baal*) are the arbiters of moral health. And academic politicians, of course, are just politicians. How does it come about, then? By means of a succession of exemplars, whose connection with each other is not explicable rationally? Or not entirely explicable? The most obvious succession would be from parents to children, but in *A Change of Heart* there is the first demonstration that this does not work, at least not in any straightforward fashion. Lucy and Frank are brother and sister, children of conventional, limited and rather cowardly parents: what they have in common is academic ability, but Lucy plays faster and looser towards death and disaster (having a bravery of the wrong sort) while Frank is capable not merely of poetry but of recognising and choosing the good at the last (albeit to some personal advantage too). From this book onward Emyr Humphreys's novels become increasingly schematic and one plain reason for this is that he desires to examine the matter of inheritance (a term used here to cover the effects of birth *and* early environmental factors). Thus families appear, grandparents, parents, children: there are more and more generations of them. The move to the scale of *Outside the House of Baal* is significant, that to the quartet of books beginning with *Flesh and Blood* more significant still. Is the choice of the good predestined by the apparent accident of birth? Does the succession — the *real* succession — omit one or more generations? Or is the good man an existentialist from nowhere who chooses the good consistently because there is another kind of ordination which it is impossible to follow? Answers to such questions are hardly likely to emerge from the *schema* of the picaresque novel, where successive encounters and choices are likely to be meaningless except in terms of the passage of time. The unit of society under scrutiny must be tighter than that because Emyr Humphreys believes that inheritance is much the most likely as well as the most interesting bet, though his honesty compels him to show it working by such fits and starts, driving so often into cul-de-sacs, emerging again after an interval by roads that are not marked on the map. Free will and predestination, are they mutually exclusive? Perhaps not. The heart of the mystery for him lies somewhere there. And perhaps that is where God is. One does not know.

Before we leave *A Change of Heart*, let us examine Howell Morris, the prototype of the good man, rather more closely. He is not the most rewarding example, but he is the first. By no means ready in his own defence, uneloquent for all his learning, somewhat lacking in humour and often tense with the need to do justice in difficult circumstances, he also incurs the stigma of homosexuality by his persistence in trying to help Frank and his supposed inability to deal with Lucy. Something of a loner, unsupported by any close friends and secretly at odds with his mother, who thinks of him, disappointedly, in terms of his late father's position in the chapel, he resists the call to become a deacon though he does not absent himself entirely from worship. He tries to maintain a position of some detachment, a stance briefly described as follows:

> There were too many things in the suffocating institutionalism
> that his mother and Ewart and their like thrived upon that he
> resented and loathed. The astonishing thing was that through it
> all he had not lost his faith, if anything in a perverse way it had
> been strengthened. He believed in the cosmic Christ and the
> historical Christ; he respected the synagogue; a human
> institution was bound to have human failings; he looked to the
> Second Coming. He refreshed himself in the Scriptures and was
> able to endure the crushing load of his loneliness.[10]

Ewart the minister, he conceded in his juster moments, was "not a
bad old stick really".[11] But he was an oil-pourer, a paperer over cracks:
"he hated and feared the disruptive power of scandal so much that it
had seriously constricted his lively interest in human nature, his real
concern for his fellow-men". In other words, it was all he could do to
maintain the *status quo*. And here we must be aware of Emyr
Humphreys's attitude to change, especially in the context of the
Nonconformist heritage of Wales. Ewart fails because he cannot
muster enough conscience to move his society forward. Howell
Morris, on the other hand, could, intellectually speaking, have been a
leader. He has the virtue of abjuring all desire for power and more
particularly of abjuring revolution, but he fails in being a dry-as-dust
academic, unable sufficiently to involve his conscience in the
improvement of the would-be-good society. Comparison with
Hannah Elis in *A Man's Estate* and J.T. Miles in *Outside the House of
Baal* helps to make the novelist's view clear. Restlessness, the choice of
novelty for its own sake (as with Lydia, who becomes Miles's wife), a
light conviction that the eternal verities are superseded by rather than
added to by the discoveries of science, are all disbarments. Change is
needed but it must follow the light of conscience and only that.

    Howell Morris, then, is the first *example* of the good man, but he is
not good enough. His *agape* is directed too exclusively towards Frank,
which makes the popular talk about him understandable. His
reward, too, has something in common with that epilogue which
brought to Job all that he had had taken from him and very little with
the dialogue in which he put the unanswered question. It may have
appeared a neat irony that the Principal, pressed by Howell's mother
to extricate her son from his difficulties, should have nominated him
for the Abersant Readership in London, but it reads too much like an

evasion. What it does is to allow Howell to escape, his problems having resolved themselves, from the society, chapel and academic, that he has not succeeded in affecting for good, solely so that he may have Frank with him (a conclusion that that society is certain to misunderstand). It is, so to speak, Job in Sheol, a spectator of the continuing struggle, not the Job who seeks and questions to the end. *A Change of Heart* may be seen as the first novel of the *positive,* but it is not the searching book that the Protestant novel becomes in *Hear and Forgive* (1952).

I have already described the *dénouement* of *Hear and Forgive* and shall write the less about it now. But the character of Edward Allenside deserves a little examination. To begin with he is contrasted with his plausible rogue of a brother, Roger, and David Flint, in his capacity of novelist, works for some time on the sixteenth century Seymour brothers, Gay Tom and Protector Somerset, with Roger and Edward in the foreground as contemporary illustrations. Then we are shown the actual childhood of the two Allensides (at least from Edward's account of it): Roger in violent reaction against his pedantic, righteous but essentially well-meaning stepfather and Edward, the younger, accepting the *régime.* There are two points here, I believe: first, that revolt leads to no forward movement of the good (a view already noted): and second, that free will can nullify whatever benefits of inheritance there are as well as advance them. Edward grows up a Socialist and a man of conscience. He becomes headmaster of a large London boys' school and, unlike Howell Morris, he has *got to* make his human institution work in the way he feels is right. So successful in this is he (though not universally popular with staff — the assorted staff types are one of the especial joys of this book) that he is likely to be promoted to the directorship of an Educational Research Institute through the favour of Lord Whiteway: but, abhorring his patron's political stance and his habitual machinations, he deliberately chooses to disqualify himself. Two matters intervene: first, the discovery that Visot, one of the members of staff — another portrait of the Communist idealist — has used a sixth former to disseminate Communist literature: second and even more important, Allenside's determination to give a Special Responsibility Allowance to Brunt, a Communist loudmouth whom he does not even like. This finishes him with Lord Whiteway. There is, too, the possible error of judgment on Allenside's part in choosing Briarman as his Deputy. These choices would be much less important if they were not the product of a sincere, conscientious man — yes, a good man — making his way with others much less good. He does not choose in order to please other individuals or even himself: he is not particularly popular (the boys' dimension is missing from the narrative, which might have made a difference): he follows his conscience against his own interests. At home he has a go-getting, snobbish wife who is making a battered lump out of his not very bright son Howard, and has to suffer the dreadful experience of having his shady elder brother, Roger, try to steal the boy away to what seems to the poor youth a happier life. Besides the sorrow of the alienation, he can see the Roger pattern incipient in the next generation. We leave Edward Allenside, then, with none of his problems solved (as we leave Roger not quite in the hands of the police) and the good he stands for terminating with himself. But no, the spark crosses the void: his friend David Flint has at last learned from him and gone back to face his own responsibilities. That is perhaps, Emyr Humphreys is saying, one of the ways in which the good perpetuates itself.

I have already indicated that *A Man's Estate* (1955) puzzled me at first reading. That, it turns out, is because the inheritance theme is more complex and the real inheritor a much less forceful person than Edward Allenside. There is, too, a cross-theme of great, indeed, fundamental, importance. Let me take the cross-theme first. Idris "Flopper" Powell has come to Pennant as minister having renounced the love of his best friend's wife, believing that this has given him an impetus to love his not very lovable congregation. That impetus fades. This theme is devoted to demonstrating the folly of supposing that *eros* (even *eros* denied) leads into *agape*. For what does Idris do? He falls in love with Ada Cwm, who, though half-sister to Hannah Elis, the ultimate inheritor, is a girl from across the divide, so to speak, from the unrespectables, the anti-chapelites. The first point, therefore, is that *eros* often chooses unwisely (and we should keep Guido and Marcella in *The Voice of a Stranger* in mind). What follows is not miserable, erotically: even to the too-experienced Ada Idris, in his sincerity, has something to give. But of course the liaison is socially impossible and Ada knows that, even if Idris talks as though he believes he can ride out the storm. Moreover, Idris goes on to re-enter the dream world of impetus: in the strength of his love for Ada he can tackle the worship and the community life of the chapel afresh: he himself is livelier, more animated, more in touch with the young (or so he thinks) and all goes better for a while. Then it becomes plain to Hannah, who tries in vain to help him, that the young people are getting out of hand because of his foolish indulgence of them. The dancing ends with a brick through the window, the Ada affair becomes public knowledge and Idris is finished in Pennant.

The supposition that *eros* leads on to *agape* is mistaken, then, and the erratic choice that *eros* makes renders it even more unlikely. For all the time Hannah Elis is there, waiting and hoping that Idris will turn to her, playing the piano for him, warning him about his unwisdom. And Hannah is his natural ally, the inheritor of what he inherits, the one who can guide and channel his idealism towards the Christian love he needs to learn how to exercise. In her portion of the narrative she confides:

> I gave him all my sympathy and support. Uncle Vavasor believed me and listened to me when I said he was a young man of great promise, handicapped by a curious Christian innocence and inexperience. But he had nothing for me — I was only an undistinguished but sometimes useful female figure in the unimportant background. To be delighted with the reward of a quick smile.[12]

Another tragedy is revealed by this passage. Hannah is the one person who has the power to make the connection between young idealism and the dead world of Uncle Vavasor, who in this context represents the elderly chapel congregation he leads.

Uncle Vavasor is the key to the main theme of the book, which is no less tragic. I cannot assert with any authority that the farm of Y Glyn and the chapel at Pennant are Nonconformist Wales traduced by Lloyd George, but the more I think about it the more I believe it to be so. The old order has been cracked right across by the M.P. Elis Felix Elis, who has sold Wales short in London and exercised his libido in Pennant upon every female within reach. Vavasor Elis, the man of ideals, the just if sometimes narrow senior deacon of the chapel, has committed the irremediable sin, in his own view, by conniving at the M.P.'s death. But in the end it is Hannah, the Hannah who inherits Y Glyn after the renunciation of her long-lost, anglicised, scientist brother (who is introduced only as a catalyst: it is symptomatic of Emyr Humphreys's thinking that he could not possibly have inherited), the Hannah between whom and her mother there is something like hate, who is both the survivor and the carrier of the good. She disagrees with much in the hardline conservative attitude of her mother: she is even at a distance from the reserved figure of her step-father Vavasor, whom she calls uncle: but she is tight-lipped, reserved, willing herself to change what is but not willing to break the mould. This is how she describes the household:

> We are constant and unchanging: we are the Elises, the remaining fragment of a tapestry that for the last thirty years seems untouched by the moths of time. By the standards of our small community we are both wealthy and intelligent, but we live as quietly and as carefully as if the earth were fragile and the air about us inflammable if inhaled too rapidly or too roughly. We are unquestionably the busiest family in the district; but we are always busy in the same pursuits. Our routines fit so tightly upon our time that you might believe that the flux itself had been tamed and set to circulate automatically within the framework of some device that trapped part of the stream of time, using over and over again the same priceless seconds and successfully shutting out the great flood itself.[13]

A microcosm of the Nonconformist Wales that was. And yet, though Hannah does not know it when she so describes it, its ideals are already betrayed and only the form of the past remains. A society once devoted to the good has ceased to be its vehicle and what survives of that tradition must discover some other way forward. The change that Hannah is looking for is the return of her brother Philip, whom she has never seen because he has been brought up by a well-educated and snobbish cousin of her father, Elis Felix Elis. Depersonalised, it may appear that the inheritance is in need of an English education and an attitude more scientific and analytical. But Philip, unbeknownst to Hannah, has an identity crisis: he knows who he is, in the crude sense, but does not know his inheritance in Wales. And that, too, may be the author's comment on many who have thought to move Wales forward with such props and attitudes. Hannah, the book concludes, is the right inheritor because, whatever her father's failure (and her mother's too, for we must remember here the propensity of the good to jump a generation), she is the one who has stayed with and at the estate (important, this) and because too, she is conscientious, reserved and wise, desiring change and not revolution. At the same time (and no doubt this was one of the reasons for my initial difficulty over *A Man's Estate*) we have to be aware that the dimension of leadership is missing this time. The potential leaders have all taken wrong turnings — Elis Felix Elis, Vavasor Elis, even Idris Powell. Hannah is the supporter rather than the leader and it may be that we are to understand that in some generations good has a holder and keeper rather than an active promoter. It is not until the reader is acquainted with Kate in *Outside the House of Baal* that the part of Hannah is more clearly illuminated. The conclusion of *A Man's Estate* is really a muted statement of the positive with a silent question for epilogue. Hannah's two hopes have been mistaken and baffled, but the estate is still there, is hers, and there will be another day. It is the author, not Hannah, who, like Sion Cent, may be heard to mutter "My hope is on what is to come".[14]

The Italian Wife (1957) relates directly to *A Man's Estate* because it uses the latter's cross-theme in reverse. *Agape,* severely distressed, perceives its counterpart (or thinks it does) and is driven to express its yearning for communion in terms of *eros.* Paola, second wife of the rich ex-film-director and newspaper magnate Richard Miller, feels her passion growing for her stepson Christopher, ten years her junior. Christopher is a slow and careful developer, making his choices with deliberation, freeing himself from his tiresome mentor APB, taking time to consider whether to come in on his father's newspaper business, moving towards Anglicanism but cautiously and on his own terms. Richard his father, on the other hand, is a free-thinking wheeler-dealer who dreams of being the publisher-king of the Labour party: he has no firm beliefs or principles, lives for the minute, politely neglects his wife and children and, within the scope of the book, becomes slickly involved with Kay, a girl twenty years younger than himself but his counterpart in all else but the possession of money. Paola herself sees her passion for Christopher as a disease, and when Christopher hears and sees her attempt to express it he is shocked, reacting violently and with extreme distaste. Paola, rejoined at long last by a jilted and somewhat reduced Richard, has nothing to look to but her difficult future.

The background of this book is international — England, Austria, Italy — and it may at first appear that this is why *The Italian Wife* falls somewhat from the standard of Emyr Humphreys's most demanding and successful novels. But this is not really so. Italy, it is true, might as well not be Italy but for a thumb-nail sketch of Massimo, Paola's brother-in-law, known behind his back as Count Cheese. But in which of Emyr Humphreys's books has natural background — mountains, lakes, sea, air, sunset, morning, what you will —

constituted an aesthetic factor, even a mood factor, in the argument? The world is people and Mr. Humphreys retains the old Puritan distrust of beauty as anything more than a pretended influence on conduct. No, the trouble with this book is that there are real people in it but no community, no natural framework for their moral perceptions and no connection which they can exercise one with another except their stated one of marriage and inheritance. It is a world like the broken language and the fragmented circles of the end of *Outside the House of Baal*. Christopher, for example, moves largely in a void: a slow, athletic Christian who, we are told, achieves a pure and selfless love for the daughter of his father's one-time colleague, long become enemy (here we have a "crossing the line" theme again, but the quarrel between Richard and Tilson is a personal one, never evaluated clearly in moral, spiritual or even political terms). This love tells us very little more about Christopher and it appears to exist mainly to make inevitable his reaction of distaste to Paola's advances. Had he been a Joseph before Potiphar's wife it would, one cannot help feeling, have had a much more significant spiritual effect upon Paola. But this is to argue against the author's outline *schema* which reveals that Christopher's mother was much older than his father Richard and therefore hints at a precedent for the Paola- Christopher attraction. Presumably this precedent could have made its point if only we had known something about Christopher's mother. Without this knowledge Christopher's alleged good seems to come from nowhere at all and adds little to the equation. There is an impression from *The Italian Wife* that Emyr Humphreys is compelled, in the social medium he has chosen, to *state* rather than to illustrate and develop the significance of his theme.

One might go on to argue that Richard and Kay are far too long on the road to Munich airport just to demonstrate Richard's partial redemption. He re-discovers a feeling of identity in reaction to anti-semitism (he is a quarter-Jew) and the space given to this may seem to nullify what has been said already about the lack of a sufficient background community against which the principals may deploy their various moral states. But the truth is that it is only in this section that a recognisable community plays any significant part and it is from this that the sense of imbalance results. The real difficulty facing Emyr Humphreys, I am confident, is that the rich, the playboys, the jet-set, do not constitute the natural medium for the Protestant novel. It is in closer societies that the concept of duty can be most intelligibly

correlated with human conduct. Little dutiful Anton, the conscience
of the next generation, seems just a shade unnatural here.

The Gift (1963) is the one book that might have been written by
someone other than Emyr Humphreys. It followed *The Italian Wife*
after an interval of six years, during most of which its author had been
a drama producer with the B.B.C. This is not the place to begin any
kind of discussion of the odds on self-destruction facing any creative
artist who involves himself in day-by-day labour in television or radio.
Suffice it to say that Emyr Humphreys wrote little or nothing during
his five-year stint and when he realised, with the clarity necessary to
the decision to depart, that he would write no more novels unless he
freed himself, he decided that his first writing for some time must
make use of his recent experience. Perhaps he was no longer entirely
the man who had essayed the Protestant novel. And perhaps again he
was, but temporarily submerged in a new and superficially attractive
experience which must be made use of before the older preoccupations were resumed.

Intensely readable, the conversation always stimulating and often
pointed, the narrative development no more than partly predictable,
The Gift may well be the most popular and least Protestant of all Emyr
Humphreys's novels (and although these adjectives belong to
different categories their juxtaposition is not entirely meaningless).
Sam Halkin (Flintshire is never forgotten, though rather titular in this
book) is an actor approaching middle age, too often type-cast as a
villain and still waiting for the fortunate "lift" that will take him to the
top of his profession. He is living, in the most casual way possible, with
Polly Fleming and the main theme is concerned with Polly's
increasing indispensibility, the undermining of the actor's sense of
"freedom" and the threat of marriage (still off-stage at the end). It
could be argued, though not with much vehemence, that the book is
about Sam Halkin and the approach of responsibility. Another
marriage is looked at critically — that of the Danish producer Lars
Steensen and his wife René — and the fact that Lars's diary falls into
the hands of both Polly and Sam separately offers the opportunity for
an appraisal of "intelligence" and "success as an actor" through at
least three pairs of eyes. The background of plays, films and actors'
talk reads authentically, even excitingly at times, and there is the by-
now-ritual visit to Italy. Linsey Jones appears as the lead actor who is a
successful business man as well and Da Parigi as the film producer,
cultured and gentlemanly, who is nevertheless on the way out. As

entertainment *The Gift* is little to be faulted and the implied happy ending adds to its attraction for many readers. Sam is perhaps "over the hump" but Polly, whose beauty has brought her a film part, comes down from London to Cardiff to say that she prefers Sam and proposes not to take it.

But in the terms in which the other novels of Emyr Humphreys have been discussed here *The Gift* has little to say. Sam Halkin, despite his easy-going ways as a lover, is a decent sort of chap, unable to push himself as does Lindsey Jones or to crush the weak in passing. But suspect as we may that he is to prove that Polly's Uncle Alfred's New Rules about asking for less and giving more (as a norm of conduct) are to produce his happiness if not the betterment of society, all that Sam really does is to lose his supreme chance in films because his "friend" Linsey Jones won't let him have a part that is likely to steal the picture. He loses the shouting match that follows as well. Perhaps this, with his kindness to Lars, may suggest that he is the right match for Polly: but it has to be pointed out that he is a natural loser not a deliberate one.

Polly herself is, in any case, an even greater problem. The major architect of the happiness in the book, she is also every man's pre-liberation heroine, despite her odd beginnings as a teen-age misfit. But how it comes about that she is an actress yet essentially untouched by the ideas of individual freedom widespread amongst her kind is not explained. Neither she nor Sam is shown *becoming*, so to speak: they have juvenile points of reference in Southport and Flintshire respectively, and Polly reveals herself as now appreciating and caring for Uncle Alfred, whom she once detested. But what does Uncle Alfred amount to? Why is he taken off to prison towards the end of the narrative (except to clear the flat)? Polly's supposedly enduring passion is love for Sam and "the gift" is presumably hers to him (rather than his gift as an actor). This love crosses no social lines, however, as does that of Idris Powell in *A Man's Estate*. In the free-wheel of stage society what distinguishes Polly from other actresses is her closely domestic emphasis, something which safely ensures the romantic aura of the conclusion. The theme rests with an *eros* which is seen developing, optimistically, into the ground of an enduring partnership, but there appears to be no attempt on the author's part even to suggest an *agape* — which might, in any case, seem seriously unreal in the context of this novel. One might argue that the Protestant novel is as out of place here as with the jet-set, but it would be safer to regard *The Gift* as a popular and successful exploitation of particular and recent experience rather than any kind of development of the author's earlier philosphy of the novel.

With *Outside the House of Baal* (1965) Emyr Humphreys returns to his Protestant designs, which are enlarged schematically to cover four generations. It is the fullest and most elaborate of the drawings and inter-patternings to be considered in this essay and there will be space only to consider the themes that have been adduced thus far.[15]

The intercutting time-scheme of the novel (which works painstakingly through a very short period in the present and brings the past more rapidly up to it) has many functions: but one simplifying thing it does — it tells the reader that J.T. and Kate are the people to watch. J.T. Miles, the Calvinistic Methodist minister, is the spiritual idealist in full-length portrait, the open, selfless spirit moving on through changing times, often impractical but never eloquently empty. A pacifist in the First World War, a man sympathising so strongly with the unemployed in South Wales during his ministry there that he foregoes part of his salary to be in communion with them, he is also the man who comes to be hated and betrayed by his wife for his neglect of his own and his family's interests, who comes to seem to her no more than a "man of words" that are meaningless. He is the man, too, who, serving as a stretcher-bearer in that same First War, tries to rescue a wounded man against instructions and sees his comrade Cynwal killed in consequence. One of the developments of Emyr Humphreys's several themes here is plainly that Christian love, when practised, can bring its own share of sorrow and tragedy and can be seen as ineffectual, at least in the short term, against the heavy armour of power. Moreover, J.T. offers his wife Lydia *eros* within a life which is devoted to *agape* and still fails. *Eros* dies and *agape,* for many human beings in their unredeemed state, asks too great a sacrifice.

In a book which is rich in smaller patternings, there is one theme which I should like to draw out at some length, that of Argoed and Kate. Argoed is a name of great but not fully revealed significance. It survives in the Breton Ar Goat, the central region of Llydaw that was once forest, and derives its power in the Welsh context from T. Gwynn Jones's poem 'Argoed', published first in 1927. In this poem the ruthless, exterminatory tactics of the Romans in Gaul and Armorica fail, if by no great margin, to suppress the Celts of the western peninsula and are unable to penetrate to the secret places. "Argoed, Argoed, y manau dirgel"[16] is the phrase at the poem's heart and there is, perhaps, a fainter echo of it in "the ultimate stand / In the thick woods" of R.S. Thomas's 'Welsh History'.[17]

In the years when J.T. and Kate were young, the literary spirit of T. Gwynn Jones (if not the poem 'Argoed' itself) was strong and pervasive. Emyr Humphreys uses the name Argoed here for another secret fastness: he implies that the farm which was home to Kate and Lydia and Ned and Dan Llew and Griff and the rest of the family is the last bastion of Calvinistic Methodism, that faith and practice which of all those amongst the Dissenting denominations in Wales was the most Welsh, having drawn its sustenance from the circulating schools of Gruffydd Jones, the preaching of Daniel Rowland, the hymns of William Williams Pantycelyn and the sustaining organisation of Thomas Charles. *Yr Hen Gorff*[18] was the very symbol of that Wales from which the English language, together with the anglicised gentry and all their hangers-on, had been shut out, that Wales which had organised itself on egalitarian principles and amongst whose values the pursuit of wealth and social standing made scarcely a mark. In the Argoed of *Outside the House of Baal* all are equal and have their separate and distinctive jobs to do: they are all, too, under authority and are enveloped by the same view of salvation.

Hostile views of it are allowed to appear. To Griff, grown up, it is not only too close a society but totally misguided:

> What does religion do? Griff said [to J.T.]. Organize the world as though it were a damn great sheep farm, preparing everyone for the next world. You know what I think? I don't think there is a next world.[19]

But closeness and harmony are Argoed's strength. "Keep together in harmony. The only way to keep the storm out",[20] exhorts the visiting minister, the Rev. Benjamin Davies. The formal language of religion determines all procedures and sanctions all duties. It is the authority which is supposed to activate it that begins to show signs of shakiness: always narrower than it should have been — no Catholics, no laughing, for instance — it, as personified by Pa, at first punishes heavily, but is increasingly seen as absent during crises, usually at Presbytery meetings (a symbol of over-organisation and personal uncertainty?). Kate, as the eldest daughter, is intensely loyal to her father: she is the product of a patriarchal society, inevitably and at best a supporter: she is also the *moral* descendant of a declining *religious*

vision. Not truly spiritual and visionary as J.T. is, she is an immensely
hard worker: she keeps her promises rigorously, permitting no self-
deception: she tells the truth, moralises firmly and deprecates her
sister Lydia's shallow curiosities and essays into novelty for its own
sake. When Dan Llew, already embarked on his money-making
career (having partly opted out of farming proper) breaks his father's
rules in his absence, it is Kate who is angry. And, like her father, she
thinks it wrong for J.T. to laugh so loudly in the house when Griff
brings him in as a visitor. When she begins to differ from her father
about J.T.'s pacifism, whether from personal liking or not, she is so
circumspect (compare with Hannah Elis here) about sending him
food that Lydia, always changeable, beats her to it and, sensing
another novelty, gets J.T. to make love to her. Kate at this point suffers
an injury from a rose thorn and loses her eye. This incident is virtually
undescribed, but it symbolises both the wound of love and Kate's
subsequently impaired ability to see as J.T. sees. She is the upholder,
the aide who is there to be leaned on but J.T., misled as Idris Powell
was by *eros*, goes off on a wrong course. Kate's loyalty to J.T. survives
all vicissitudes but her understanding of him is necessarily
diminished by separation: when they come together again in the
book's present it is too late for both of them. J.T. has failed, or seems to
have failed, and Kate does not understand why he has done what he
has done.

The history of the younger Kate has its symbolic echoes too. After
her father's death and bereft of even his shaky authority, she shows
sadly impaired judgment in marrying Wynne Bannister, only to see
him squander all her money. At the last, still competent,
hardworking, gruff, denying the past (Argoed has been destroyed for
her) but fixed in it nevertheless by her sternly moralistic outlook, she
gives house-room to J.T., to whom, like everybody she has belonged
to, she offers her outspokenness and what loyalty she has left. To
Sheila, Ronnie's wife and J.T.'s son-in-law, she is an archaic old
Welshwoman whose views on drink make it desirable that she should
eat in the kitchen when they have guests. But she is still with J.T. at the
end (as Alun Richards finds her counterpart, perhaps to his surprise,
at the end of his *Home to an Empty House*) and when he is setting off on a
Mystery Tour of Anglesey to get to a specific spot (a marvellous touch,
this) to pick up his old friend Ifan Cole's watch, she, who has at first
refused to humour his quest, later decides to have him taken by car,
picking him up from Dan Llew's house (that he has long left to go on

his own), because *she* has the *address*. There's the metaphor, in the book's last sentence:

> Got to have the address or we won't know where to go.

Kate follows still, but less willingly and at a distance, seeking always to define, to pin down, to explain in human and moralistic terms J.T.'s aged but unimpedible vision.

But the question arises, writes itself large above the little semi-detached house at 8 Gorse Avenue: has not J.T. gone on too far and too fast, never caring sufficiently whether Kate and her like could follow? Did he indeed laugh too loudly in Argoed? And now Argoed is broken and gone, while J.T. sits, influenceless, across the road from the big new public house with the car-park for umpteen cars. Who listens to him now in his old age? Dan Llew calls his house Argoed because it means to him his lost youth but makes it plain that he recognises its language without understanding it. Out in North Dakota his brother Hugh has a ranch which is certainly not called Argoed (he was the one that married a Catholic) but Hugh's daughter Sally is very interested in all her relations. The old Wales has fallen apart and amongst the suburban villas of his anglicised seaside town J.T. is looking at the debris. He could not keep even his own wife faithful: two of his children have effectively stifled their consciences and the third, a reduced version of his father, is already deserted by *his* wife. What can he say he has achieved?

The question has a Welsh dimension and it has a general one too. In J.T. Miles Emyr Humphreys provides the kind of leader who cannot be faulted as Owen and Michael and the briefly-seen politicians are faulted. But he is human and *eros* separates him from the woman who would have stood by him. He moves forward by conscience, nevertheless, and seeks directly to influence the society of which he is part (as Howell Morris does not); but he sees, instead of a greater good, the godly community he loved broken into fragments and the worshippers flocking to the house of Baal. Behind it all lurks the enormous question of whether we know and understand what good is. And in front, nearer, are the impossibilities that brought Alun Lewis low. Is it meaningful to talk of *progress* within the span of a single life? Can we attempt to hasten *progress* by a positive leadership, even if it be of the most idealistic kind? May it not prove to be humanly mistaken and set *progress* back many years? Are there any actions we can take and views we can propound in society which are better and more effective for the advancement of the good than the simple reciprocities of love and kindness between members of the family, between neighbours and friends, between those to whom there comes a chance to show kindness and those who by chance receive it? In other words, is man stepping out of station in seeking to influence a society, a world, by means of politics, of education, even of what he sees as religious faith? May he not be usurping God's means?

Outside the House of Baal does not answer these questions. It leaves J.T. at a low point but still pursuing. We are not even certain whether he has been a carrier of good at all. He may be self-deluding. But he may also be Elijah whom God recognises even while he seems to desert him. There are no kings and priests whom he may appoint but a successor may have been provided nevertheless. Perhaps the little boy with the empty beer bottle in his hand who watches, speechless, while J.T. dries his toes on the beach — the little bugger who keeps crossing the road from the seafront hotel where his swearing mother rules — is the runner of the next distance, recognising the good in J.T., the son of an alcoholic father, just as J.T. did once in the uneloquent minister and the ecstatic, "uncalled" homosexual Price Parry.

It is an ending for which the reader must call upon his own faith. Kate cannot quite keep track of J.T. in human terms, even in his seeming defeat. So he may be supra-rational, an agent who does indeed carry God's quickening spirit. And he may not be. Is there a succession other than that argued in *The Power and the Glory?* How are Protestant apostles chosen? *A oes gobaith?* Is there hope? Is there?

NOTES

1.   A Protestant View of the Modern Novel: The Listener, 2 April 1953.
2.   *Ibid.*
3.   *Ibid.*
4.   *Op. cit.*, pp.18-19.
5.   *Ibid.*, p.151.
6.   *Ibid.*, p.121.
7.   For which Saunders Lewis, Lewis Valentine and D.J. Williams were committed.
8.   'Three Voices' by André Morgan in *Planet*, 39, August 1977 notes the difference between *A Toy Epic* and *Y Tri Llais*, the Welsh version published in the same year, but has no information about authorial revision of the original manuscript.
9.   *The Listener*, 2 April 1953.
10.   *Op. cit.*, p.99.
11.   *Ibid.*, p.109.
12.   *Op. cit.*, p.105.
13.   *Ibid.*, p.30.
14.   *Gabeithiaw a ddaw yold wyf* (Sion Cent, fl. 1400-30). c.f. Raymond Garlick's use of this sentence to open and close his poem, 'Anthem for Doomed Youth', in *A Sense of Time* (1972).
15.   Jeremy Hooker's article, 'A Seeing Belief' (in *Planet*, 39, August 1977) deals admirably with the time-construction of *Outside the House of Baal*, the author's filmic technique, the breakdown of Welsh Nonconformist society and belief (witness J.T.'s absurd idea, in Griff's eyes, that he could argue meaningfully *in Welsh* with the governmental orator of the First World War — the Lloyd George figure again), and a variety of other aspects of the novel not adequately referred to here.
16.   "Argoed, Argoed, the secret places".
17.   First published in *An Acre of Land* (1952).
18.   Literally, "The Old Body".
19.   *Op. cit.*, p.112.
20.   *Ibid.*, p.66.

II
SMALLER CLEARINGS

Address for the Henry Vaughan Service, 1977

I have been reading the Letters of Gerard Manley Hopkins recently and the agonies and difficulties hinted at and described in them on the subject of the poet himself, his place and true function in a God-directed world, and his attitude to fame and reputation, have prompted me to think more deeply about these topics myself — and, for this purpose today, to examine what Henry Vaughan has to say about any or all of them. Let me first, however, set the philosophical scene as briefly as I can. There is an extreme view, usually associated, though not entirely justly, with the Puritans, which sees Art as Religion's possible antagonist, as, indeed, a rival religion with its own set of votaries: this view would give the lie direct to Keats's identification of Truth with Beauty. The purist form of this attitude would probably snuff out the poet entirely, as it did the dramatist under Cromwell, but few of Art's antagonists would take so extreme a line: what they have to say — and I must interject here that they have had a very poor hearing in the twentieth century, as they did in the nineteenth, ever since Romanticism got fully under way — is most useful in a negative sense, in casting doubt upon the pretensions of the poet, upon his role as a man apart (whether in or out of an ivory tower), upon his claim to be outside society and social rules personally and at the same time to legislate for the freedom of that society and the world. Now we encounter the modified form of this anti-Romanticism in the Jesuit poet Hopkins and again in that great twentieth century Catholic poet David Jones. They ask the question, What is poetry for? and the answer is not, as so many Romantics assume, self-evident. And again, is the poet's gift intrinsically religious because he has it from God or is it a secular gift which has to be used with great care and under direction from the Church, always subordinate to the greater and more direct functions of the religious life? Can it be individualistic or should it speak always of an ultimate order? In this regard David Jones wrote:

> ....the workman must be dead to himself while engaged upon
> the work, otherwise we have that sort of 'self-expression' which is
> as undesirable in the painter or the writer as in the carpenter, the
> cantor, the half-back or the cook.

The dilemma of the would-be religious poet is perhaps best put in
modern times by Aldous Huxley in his novel *Time Must Have a Stop*.
He sees the attempt to be a poet as basically unreconcilable with the
need to serve God.

> He that is not getting better is getting worse, and he that is
> getting worse is in a position to know less and less about the
> nature of ultimate reality. Conversely, of course, if one gets
> better and knows more, one will be tempted to stop writing,
> because the all-absorbing labour of composition is an obstacle in
> the way of further knowledge. And that, maybe, is one of the
> reasons why most men of genius take such infinite pains not to
> become saints — out of mere self-preservation. So you get Dante
> writing angelic lines about the will of God and in the next breath
> giving vent to his rancours and vanities. You get Wordsworth
> worshipping God in nature and preaching admiration, hope
> and love, while all the time he cultivates an egotism that
> absolutely flabbergasts the people who know him.

To be a poet, in effect, one must retain a corner of selfishness, in
conduct as in purpose, in order to keep an individuality of
imagination and concept. If one says, I have given myself to God, as
Hopkins did, is that meaningful in terms of poetry? Must we then say
that God is writing through the poet? And how if he writes badly? Is it
sufficient answer to argue that the original gift of poetry to the
individual was a small one, for would not then the service possible in
other ways be so much more important that the poetic function would
be abandoned? And do not fame and reputation necessarily enlarge
the poetic ego and build it against God?

Let us hear what Hopkins had to say about reputation: writing to
Richard Watson Dixon, a Canon of the Church of England (who
assumed, rather easily, that any God-given gift could be blessed into
God's service), he said:

> When I spoke of fame I was not thinking of the harm it does to

men as artists: it may do them harm, as you say, but so, I think, may the want of it, if "Fame is the spur that the clear spirit doth raise To shun delights and live laborious days" — a spur very hard to find a substitute for or to do without. But I meant that it is a great danger in itself, as dangerous as wealth every bit, I should think, and as hard to enter the kingdom of heaven with. And even if it does not lead men to break the divine law, yet it gives them "itching ears" and makes them live on public breath ... What I do regret is the loss of recognition belonging to the work itself. For as to every moral act, being right or wrong, there belongs of the nature of things, reward or punishment . . . .

He goes on to write of the sadness caused by the fact that things go unwitnessed, unrecorded, but adds that since the wish for record comes within the human context, "it is a great error of judgment to have lived for what may fail us."

A few days later he added to his letter.

...fame whether won or lost is a thing which lies in the award of a random, reckless, incompetent, and unjust judge, the public, the multitude. The only just judge, the only just literary critic, is Christ, who prizes, is proud of, and admires, more than any man, more than the receiver himself can, the gifts of his own making. And the only real good which fame and another's praise does is to convey to us, by a channel not at all above suspicion but ... much less to be suspected than the channel of our own minds, some token of the judgment which a perfectly just, heedful and wise mind, namely Christ's, passes upon our doings. Now such a token may be conveyed as well by one as many.

This, I think you will agree, is a hard saying, and Hopkins wavered over it, as any mortal spirit might. Like the Order to which he belonged, he regarded the poetic gift as secular, ranking well below the gifts of preaching and ministering, and to be used only when the instruction came from God via his Superiors in the Order. That it came only once by these means was the basic agony of his poetic life.

Now you probably know that the result of Hopkins's prevarications about the publication of his work was the appearance of the body of his poems, prepared by his friend Robert Bridges, in 1918, thirty-one years after his death, so that the rhythmically revolutionary but socially staid Victorian became a twentieth century comet, violent in its effects on the poetic life of the thirties in particular and still reappearing, decade after decade, to influence and surprise. But what the poet Hopkins *accepted*, albeit sadly, was limbo. I have been some time coming to Henry Vaughan, but I can't help wondering what he accepted or expected in this matter. Because what he got was a much longer limbo than Hopkins's. I think the first time I realised this was when I read a poem by John Lloyd of Dinas about the river Usk, in which he mentioned other rivers made famous, like Shakespeare's Avon and the Towy seen from John Dyer's 'Grongar Hill', and appeared to be quite unaware that anybody had celebrated his own native river before him. This must have been as late as 1835 or thereabouts. Once I had realised this I searched the journals of the travellers of the late eighteenth and early nineteenth century, but in vain. They are not of equal value of thoroughness, of course, but when Samuel Heath Malkin said nothing I knew that nothing was known or remembered locally, or so little as to be literarily valueless. Possibly this may have been because the ordinary folk of the area spoke Welsh for so long and had no access to Vaughan's work, but then this only throws a greater responsibility on his English-speaking social successors.

My next recourse, naturally, was to Theophilus Jones, who wrote some five or six years after Malkin. Theophilus had done some research, as one might expect, but its results were mouselike. After some thirty-six lines on *Thomas* Vaughan, in which he quotes Wood's verdict on him as "a tolerable good English and Latin poet", there are nine or ten on Henry, most of them about his having been a doctor and his reaction to his brother's ideas. Here is most of the relevant passage:

> He seems, however, to have had no confidence in chemistry, and to have sought for gold in the usual way, by attention to his profession, neither did he profess any regard for magic or the muses; his brother indeed wished him to be thought partial to those ladies, and published two poems under the name of Henry Vaughan, Silurist, which are preserved in the Bodleian Library, and some private collections, but they are supposed to be the works of Eugenius Philalethes (Thomas Vaughan): one is entitled *'Olor Iscanus, or the Swan of Usk'*, in which there are some tolerably good lines, others are lame, and the poem concludes in such galloping titupping rhymes as almost compel the reader to forget the merits the author certainly possesses.

The following lines upon the river Usk would not perhaps be thought contemptible even at this day.

There follows twenty-two lines from 'To the River Isca' which omit the first and, to a modern eye, most significant part of the poem and cut out again twenty-two lines from the other end. Theophilus then continues:

> The other poem is called 'The Charnel House' and has so much merit that as the little pamphlet in which it is published (about the year 1650 to the best of my recollection) is very scarce, we trust an apology for its insertion here is not necessary.

The poem entire then follows, save for the first two lines, and for the last word of all Theophilus, obviously obsessed by the theme, renders *channel* as *charnell*.

Well, there it is. Theophilus Jones in unfamiliar guise as literary critic. And Henry Vaughan's *two poems* — two poems, mark you — assigned to his brother. Moreover, these two poems are part of his secular verse. Not a word of *Silex Scintillans*. What would Henry have thought of his vocation had he revisited Brecknock in 1809?

Before I pursue this, however, let me briefly record the gradual emergence of Henry's reputation. Thomas Rees's *Beauties of South Wales* (1815) gives seven and a half lines to Thomas Vaughan, three sentences to Henry and then quotes the twenty-two lines from 'To the River Isca' that Theophilus chose. There are, nevertheless, many pages on Theophilus Jones himself. Samuel Rees's *Topographical Dictionary of Wales* (1833), greatly daring, refers to *"Olor Iscanus* and *several* other poems" but quotes nothing and reduces Henry to one sentence. John Lloyd may well be forgiven, it would seem for *not knowing*. Henry Vaughan's rehabilitation is due, of course, to the enthusiasm of his first editor, Rev. Henry Francis Lyte, the hymn-writer, who in 1847 published a selection of Vaughan's sacred poetry from *Silex Scintillans*. His second editor — another clergyman, Alexander B. Grosart, Vicar of Blackburn — thought Lyte's selection "lovingly but most uncritically edited" and himself published four volumes containing all Vaughan's works, poetry, prose and translations, in 1871. Grosart was really the first to bring the Silurist to a wider public: it is significant that in 1879 Canon Dixon drew Hopkins's attention to Vaughan, and Hopkins, who had already read him, replied:

> Thomas Vaughan's poems were reprinted not so long ago. He
> was a follower of Herbert both in life and style: he was in fact
> converted from worldly courses by reading Herbert's poems on
> a sickbed and even his muse underwent a conversion (for he had
> written before). He has more glow and freedom than Herbert
> but less fragrant sweetness. Somewhere he speaks of some spot
> "primrosed and hung with shade" and one piece ends
>
> > And here in dust and dirt, O here
> > The lilies of his love appear.
>
> ...Still I do not think him Herbert's equal.

In view of the curious mistake about the Christian name, one is
bound to wonder how far back Hopkins's knowledge of what had
been said about Vaughan went: but the most obvious cause is that
Hopkins, as a Jesuit, was allowed to have no books of his own and so
often, indeed usually, had to *remember* his poets and their work from
youthful reading. The rest of the story of Vaughan's reputation is
well-known: there is the E.K. Chambers edition of 1896, the still-
standard Oxford edition of L.C. Martin of 1914, the many American
editions since then and finally the Alan Rudrum Penguin edition of
1976. And meanwhile, of course, the vast labours of Gwenllian
Morgan which emerged, for the most part, in Canon Hutchinson's
definitive book on Vaughan published in 1947. Do not imagine,
however, that we yet know all that we shall know of Henry Vaughan: I
think there is more to come, though the whole will still be
fragmentary.

What we can discover about Vaughan's view of the poet's role is
unsatisfactory and partial. He came, of course, at the end of a classical
tradition which was still Vergilian in its attitudes to landscape but
which, in human terms, had adopted a good deal of Renaissance
individualism and was classical only in the sense that it set high store
by wit, which was almost instinctively directed against persons rather
than against the shape of society. As one might expect, the Puritan
element was under-represented amongst poets, though in the
persons of Milton and Marvell (the former, in Hopkins's view without
peer among English poets — you see the connections and how curious
they are?) they had a significant contribution to make. Henry

Vaughan was plainly a conservative by nature, even to the extent of being, in some of his earlier poetry, conservatively violent, but because he belonged to the *old* order he accepted what his tradition gave him about the role of the poet and he questioned himself not at all, it would seem, in the manner which he might have done had he been a questioner by nature. It should be no part of our business, however, living as we do at the end of 150 years of questioning (I am thinking here of the impact of scientific thought), to belabour Vaughan with hindsight. The questions he did not ask he did not ask. I merely seek here to set out what he did say.

For whom did he write? Certainly not for "the populacy" whom he detested from the days of 1641 when he was in London about the time of Strafford's execution. He never wrote in Welsh, for instance, which he would surely have done had he meant to be read by ordinary people near at hand. Amongst his translations there is nothing from the Welsh, though Vicar Prichard's verse, subsequently to be collected in *Canwyll y Cymry*, was much circulated in Brecknock. But then Prichard was too Puritanical for his taste. When he published *The Mount of Olives* or *Solitary Devotions* in 1652, for whom was it intended? For whom was his poetry intended? He posits a Christian readership of *The Mount of Olives* — in England, obviously: he could hardly be bringing his Welsh neighbours to steady devotional habits. Gradually one realises that he was writing always for a kind of social cousinage — the Price household at The Priory, Brecon, his wife's relatives at Coleshill in the Midlands, his Oxford friends and a wider, more shadowy circle of royalist acquaintances and churchmen. That this was combined with a genuine love of his native terrain makes the situation all the more odd, but it was an oddness created partly by the predicament of any early Anglo-Welsh poet — that is, one who elects to write in English out of a firmly Welsh background — and partly by the rigid exclusiveness of his royalist and Church affiliations which severely limited both his sympathies and his possible audience. Need we be surprised that, much as he loved the Usk, Usk-dwellers did not remember him a hundred or so years after his death? His poems were in London, or in the Bodleian, where they existed: and moreover they were in another language.

All this came about quite naturally. Henry Vaughan was formed as a poet in Oxford and London, where he talked with the lady who came to be known as "the matchless Orinda" and wrote within the magnetic influence of Habington, Randolph, Cleveland, Cartwright and Davenant. When George Herbert became his master, it altered for good and all the essence of what he wrote but it did not change his initial assumptions as a poet. That he was a Welshman was still an accident: drawn into the classical English culture of the day, breaking up as it may have been, he did not know how to be either local or evangelical. If he praised his Wales, it was to prove to distant people that the cultured life, in their terms, was possible in what they thought of as wilderness. It was to prove that the true faith, religious and political, still flourished among the folk of a backward tongue.

His manner as a poet was so much within the classical tradition that he mentioned it only once (in the context I have in mind). In 'To the River Isca' he wrote:

> Poets (like *Angels*) where they once appear
> *Hallow* the *place*, and each succeeding year
> Adds rev'rence to't, such as at length doth give
> This aged faith, *That there their Genii live.*

This is confessedly traditional. He goes on, however, to what may seem an enlargement of his personal role:

> But *Isca,* whensoe'r those *shades* I see,
> And thy *lov'd Arbours* must no more *know* me,
> When I am laid to *rest* hard by thy *streams,*
> And my *Sun sets,* where first it *sprang* in beams,
> I'le leave behind me such a *large, kind light,*
> As shall *redeem* thee from *oblivious night,*
> And in these *vowes* which (living yet) I pay
> *Shed* such a *Previous* and *Enduring* Ray,
> As shall from age to age thy *fair name* lead
> 'Till *Rivers* leave to *run,* and *men* to *read.*

This is a moving personal statement, somewhat detracted from, as one reflects, by an apparent big-headedness. But one needs to reflect further. This more emotional statement depends upon the earlier one *That there their Genii live.* It is, admittedly, an enlargement of the classical *imperium,* but Rome had come so far centuries before and Vaughan was doing no more than Ovid or Vergil had done for their vine-dressed patrimonies. Wales was new territory for this long-lived classicism, for generations clothed in English.

What Henry Vaughan said more about the poet's role came about,

(as one would expect, as a result of his conversion. He was plainly in a)
difficulty then about his secular verse. It was one sign of this that *Olor
Iscanus* was postponed, as to publication, for three and a half years
after the dedication was signed and was entered at Stationer's Hall in
1651 by his friend Thomas Powell, vicar of Cantref. It was a way out of
a difficulty. He had been *persuaded* to publish. And this obviated the
need for a Preface. *Olor Iscanus* was published as 'Some Select Poems
and Translations *Formerly* written by Mr. Henry Vaughan Silurist'
graced only by his 1647-dated dedication to Lord Kildare Digby and a
Foreword from Humphrey Moseley, the Publisher.

The point was that Vaughan had committed himself fully in 1650
not merely by the poems of *Silex Scintillans* but by the language of his
Preface to it. And it is from this Preface that I should like to quote now.
He begins by castigating the many "ingenious persons" who "are
termed *Wits*" ... many of whom have "cast away all their fair portion of
time, in no better imployments, then a deliberate search, or
excogitation of *idle words*, and a most vain, insatiable desire to be
reputed *Poets*". This, he continues, will be a "soul-killing Issue": that
is the "Laureate *Crown*, which idle *Poems* will certainly bring to their
unrelenting Authors." But that is not the worst: if these "wilfully-
published vanities could defile no *spirits* but their own" the evil would
be limited. Unhappily, says he, "These Vipers survive their Parents":
their works defile whole generations to follow, "No otherwise" — to
use a translation from the Christian poet Prudentius — "then if with
Instruments / Of polish'd Ivory, some drudge should stir / A dirty
sink ..."

Vaughan here envisages clearly the egoism of the poet and the
totally secular tradition to which his works give rise. He does not
name Art as the votive goddess or reproach the egoism of the poet, her
assumed follower, as the real centre of and source of the denial of
Christ: his terms are strictly negative and he clearly envisages that the
poet's power can, by a moral and spiritual conversion, be turned,
without intrinsic contradiction, to Christian purposes. Indeed, his
complaint is most of all for the waste of talent and the power that
mental ability may give to such continuing aberrations. "... the more
acute the *Author is*, there is so much the more danger and death in the
work. Where the *Sun* is busie upon a *dung-hill*, the issue is always some
unclean *vermine*". One can almost hear at this point David Jones's
contention completed on the reverse: that the poet, a powerful sun,
must take himself out of the work. But Henry Vaughan's emphasis is

on the "lewd ware" sold by such poets.

> *If every idle word shall be accounted for,* and if *no corrupt communication should proceed out of our mouths,* how desperate (I beseech you) is their condition, who all their life time, and out of meer design, study *lascivious fictions:* then carefully record and publish them, that instead of *grace* and *life* they may minister *sin* and *death* unto their readers?

This is Anti-Christ in action, right enough, but it concentrates on the power of the poet as we might on the power of the media nowadays. It asks no questions about the nature and origin of the poet's power. All that is needed is the driving out of the moral sickness, as Henry Vaughan has done, having as he says "supprest *my greatest follies*", though they are, he feels, "as innoxious as most of that vein use to be". Nevertheless, he offers no excuse: his wish for his secular poems is that "none would read them".

There is some cake-eating-and-having about this, when we remember that neither *Olor Iscanus* nor *Thalia Rediviva* could have been published without his consent. But it is fair to say that nothing in the former collection would have deserved even a salacious glance, written as it was under the influence of the chaster love of Habington's *Castara,* and in the later *Thalia,* apparently published by John Williams, Prebendary of St. David's in 1678 (five years after the collection was ready), only 'Fida: or the Country Beauty' — plainly an early poem — might conceivably have made its ageing author blush. *Silex Scintillans,* of course, is the work of a single-minded creature of God and the only lines in it to our purpose contrast the seeming breadth of a former would-be cultured existence with the narrowness of the mind whose relationship with its Creator overbears everything else. In 'The Resolve' we find these lines:

> Loose, parcell'd heart wil freeze: The Sun
> > With scatter'd locks
> Scarce warms, but by contraction
> > Can heat rocks;

and in 'Distraction' the point is better personalised into a paradox:

> O knit me, that am crumbled dust! the heape
> > Is all dispers'd, and cheape;

```
.........................................
                                    But now
I find my selfe the lesse, the more I grow.
```

This latter poem ends with the poet mourning the continuance of the dust:

```
                    Oppressed I
Striving to save the whole, by parcells dye
```

he writes, but there is no real indication here or anywhere in *Silex Scintillans* that he sees himself as other than individual Man. He is not Man the Poet, the putter into memorable words of a deep religious experience. In fact, there is no self-consciousness of this kind at all and the mere fact that he could copy as much as he did from George Herbert is the best evidence of the near-extinction of the poetic ego in the immediate post-conversion years.

Thalia Rediviva, however, is a collection which contains more of the genuinely personal than any other of Vaughan's. Canon Hutchinson discusses whether the Silurist, who virtually gave up both writing poetry and translating by the time he was forty, may have fallen away from his first religious fervour but decides, chiefly on the evidence of his tombstone, that he did not. Equally, of course, a case might be made for the continuous erosion of his irreligious self, the poetic ego giving way entirely to the desire to serve others by means of his medical skills — the fate which Aldous Huxley said writers *had* to resist to preserve their creativity. We do not know. But that there is some relaxation of the direction of his poetry, as far as the discernibly later poems in *Thalia* are concerned, is clear enough. Not every poem had to be devotional. His elegy for his relative Charles Walbeoffe speaks of "the might / Of love" which

```
...from my sad retirements calls me forth
The Just Recorder of thy death and worth.
```

He sees now that even a poet encompassed by and devoted to his faith may have a duty, a historical duty, to record secular events justly, and in his marriage-poem to his cousin Morgan of the Wenallt there is a sad little reflection on the way in which poets have neither given nor taken justice in the past:

> When I am dead, and malice or neglect
> The worst they can upon my dust reflect,
> (For *poets* yet have left no names, but such
> As men have *envied,* or *despis'd* too much)...

That this has been the fault of the poets is clear: their vaulting egos have invited it. He aims to be the "Just Recorder", though even in that function there is a faint cry for the survival of his name where later in the poem he writes:

> Then late posterity (if chance, or some
> Weak *Eccho,* almost quite expir'd and dumb
> Shall tell them, who the *Poet* was, and how
> He liv'd and lov'd thee too; which thou do'st know). . .

It is a little human gesture which it is hard to condemn.

Again, that some significant change in Henry Vaughan had taken place is strongly suggested by the last and latest of his published poems, 'To the Editor of the Matchless Orinda', dated to 1667 or later. The Restoration of Charles II had brought a new perspective: there were follies and ribaldries at Court, placemen, trimmers and tricksters back in political life: to the grave and sober Vaughan, as to similar royalist stalwarts like Clarendon, much of it was a grief and a disappointment. He did not enjoy being nominally an Establishment man and could not help reflecting on how much better he had fought when those he had thought of as the Enemy oppressed him. And other poets too, secular ones: controversy and conflict had sharpened them too: their wit had had a cutting edge, knew what it believed in as well as what it struck at: whereas in the materialist 'Jack Pudding' times he now experienced there was nothing worth the arguing. Here is the first third of the poem:

> Long since great witts have left the Stage
> Unto the *Drollers* of the age,
> And noble numbers with good sense
> Are like good works, grown an offence.
> While much of verse (worse than old story)
> Speaks but *Jack-Pudding,* or *John-Dory.*
> Such trash-admirers made us poor,
> And *Pyes* turn'd *Poets* out of door.
> For the nice Spirit of rich verse

Which scorns absurd and low commerce,
Although a flame from heav'n, if shed
On *Rooks* or *Daws*: warms no such head.
Or else the Poet, like bad priest,
Is seldom good, but when opprest:
And wit, as well as piety
Doth thrive best in adversity;
For since the thunder left our air
Their *Laurels* look not half so fair.

A changed feeling, undoubtedly. Even those wits, so condemned in the Preface to *Silex Scintillans,* had their place in the same ambience which produced his devotion: perhaps all of them, having collectively "a flame from heav'n" — something never admitted by Henry Vaughan about poetry or poets before — throve on adversity, a point Christians often make in the present similar times. But the poet likened to bad priest? Now that's a new thought too, and one that we could well have heard developed. But Henry Vaughan wrote no more. For one reason or another, the "flame from heav'n" had been doused.

"Under the threatening train of steam-engines and schoolmasters": The Predicament of some Anglo-Welsh Poets in the Nineteenth Century.

> Rise, brothers, Deheubarth with Gwynedd, and render
>   True praise to our Mother loved dearly and long!
> Come Manhood intrepid, and Womanhood tender —
>   Come graces of Music and glories of Song!
> United, rejoicing, ask blessings upon her,
>   Who gave us for birthright so bounteous a part;
> Our pride and our pleasure — our trust and our honour —
>   The star of our memory — the hope of our heart!

So begins 'A Song for Wales'. The work of an Anglo-Welsh poet? No indeed, no Anglo-Welsh poet, until the very end of the nineteenth century, wrote anything so ostensibly confident of a Present and a Future for Wales. This is the work of Elvynydd, who declared in the Preface to his 1868 volume, *For Cambria*, that he was "not Welsh by birth, residence or connexions" — Elvynydd, otherwise James Kenward of Smethwick, Birmingham, Kenward the Cymrophile, Kenward the stirrer, Kenward the Gorsedd Member and friend of Ab Ithel[1]. It was precisely his role as an outsider that freed him from the fears and depressions to which mere Welshmen were subject. He could write to the Bishop of St. Asaph protesting about the non-preferment of Ab Ithel, an injustice which he judged to be a response to a patriotism unwelcome amongst the Church's hierarchy[2], and in his poem, 'What was Thought in Wales A.D. 1859', inveigh, in terms that few would call happily loyal, against the imposition of English bishops on the Welsh Church:

> O royal Lady of Earth's proudest throne,
>   Defender of the Faith, we hail thee still!

> So be thy mercy and thy justice shown
> To Cambria bowed 'neath one colossal ill
> Of English peer and bishop — they who fill
> Her Courts with grass, her people's hearts with gall —
> The pompous parasites who starve and chill
> The breast that feeds them like an idle thrall —
> Alien in blood and speech, what other could befall!

Elvynydd may have been unique in his daring, but his "hailing" style, as one may jocularly call it, is all too representative of the work of his genuinely Welsh contemporaries. Indeed, it is right and proper at this juncture to make it plain that, in this brief foray into the field of Welsh verse in English in the nineteenth century, there is little hope of discovering anything more than an occasional poem in which high literary quality may be detected. Now is the time to admit that, despite a pretty steady metrical competence and a general ability to develop an argument with commendable clarity, not one poet named in what is to follow, except perhaps Mrs. Hemans, an incomer, can command any consistent interest for quality of language, liveliness of imagery, tautness and economy of writing or novelty of poetic structure. Probably the greatest single reason for this is a natural one — lack of the necessary talent. But it should also be realised that the field to be travelled through is small, and that poetry in the English language from Wales bears few of the marks of confidence, either the confidence of an assured tradition or the creative confidence of the poet who is certain of his own beginning and the direction he intends to take. Many of those to be named look like individuals trapped in false positions by the accident of birth and language: much of their energy is taken up in reacting to their contemporary situation. The consideration that they best deserve is therefore not one of literary evaluation so much as social and historical exegesis. In other words, they have views and attitudes, even if they rarely express them memorably, and in discovering what they have to say it may be possible to throw light from a new direction on nineteenth century Wales, its institutions and national identity.

Let me begin with an admission. I have written and implied elsewhere that the tradition of Wales's *seniority* in the union with England, which derived its greatest impetus from the supposed historicity of Geoffrey of Monmouth's *Historia Regum Britanniae*[3] and was consummated, so to speak, by the accession of Henry Tudor to the English throne in 1485, dwindled and died in the middle of the seventeenth century, with James Howell[4] as its last significant protagonist. It is with some surprise, and a little mortification, that I discover it alive, if not exactly green and flourishing, in the mid-nineteenth century. Its outlines, diminished and plaintive as they are, nevertheless remain firm. Elvynydd presents one of its key phrases in 'Stanzas Read at the Llangollen Eisteddfod, 1858':

> O England! thou who art so great and free,
> As oft thy children vaunt, and foes confess;
> Think that thy might was not conceded thee
> To scorn thine elder Sister and oppress.

"Thine elder Sister"! There it is, the seniority principle. It can be seen again, ironically decorated, in 'The Hall of Nations' a poem by Goronva Camlann, whom I shall introduce in greater detail in the pages that follow. In this poem Britannia on her amber throne is supported by the dragon and the lion and at her side sit two daughters.

> The elder of the two and fairer far,
>   Was robed in melancholie beautie's charm.

The younger sister was

>   of ruder port,
> And somewhat fiercelie beamed her eye of pride;

> Her sons were large of limb, and void of grace,
>   With greedie eyes on gain and lucre bent;
> But dailie mingling with the elder race,
>   In nobler harmonie their features blent.

The union survives, then, with the help of wishful thinking. The reasons for the unflattering portrait of the younger sister I must delay a while, in order to note some of the other aspects of the Hall of Nations, through which Merlin acts as the poet's guide. In the international pantheon Arthur sits above the others and near him but below are Milton, "The blind old man renowned, of British blood", and Shakespeare, "The Bard who dwelt by Cimbric Avon's flood". Llywarch is there too, and Archbishop John Williams, Hugh

Middleton, Inigo Jones, John Gibson the sculptor, and Picton — except for the last an odd procession of North Walians — preceding and heralding "our second Arthur", no less a person than the Duke of Wellington. The curious reader here must not skip lightly over the obvious — the fact that the poet sees his *Britain*, the Britain of the Napoleonic War and its aftermath, as fully worthy of defence — in goggling a little at his much less likely view, that an Irishman, Arthur Wellesley by birth, is a contemporary fit to inherit the Arthurian mantle. A later and separate quatrain[5] begins:

> Great Britain's children we, on Belgic plain,
> With Arthur stemmed the iron-crested wave.

Wellesley was, it is true, an old Etonian and plainly from within the Pale (the relevance of this comment will be plainer presently[6]) but Goronva Camlann was the earliest Anglo-Welsh writer, in my observation, to possess a pan-Celticism pannish enough to include the Irish. Ever since the time of the Counter-Reformation the Popery of the people of Ireland had made them objects of deep suspicion even to the Welsh and Scots: the victory of the Parliamentary cause in Pembrokeshire in the First Civil War can be attributed, in part, directly to that suspicion. No matter that not all Irishmen were Catholics: no matter that many, like Wellesley, had fought bravely for an imperial Great Britain of which they felt part: the shape of an old prejudice changes very slowly and as Wales became more Nonconformist in spirit the Irish seemed even farther off. The first political collaboration between the Welsh and the Irish that I can trace belongs to November 1885, when Michael Davitt, the leader of the Irish Land League of peasant occupiers, spoke on the same platform at Ffestiniog with the youthful David Lloyd George and the ageing Nationalist Michael Daniel Jones[7]. And from that meeting most Nonconformist ministers kept angrily or discreetly away. In Anglo-Welsh writing the earliest pro-Irish stance of which I am aware — that is, a stance which unquestionably sees even Catholics as embraceable Celts — is to be found in *One of the Royal Celts* (1891), a novel by the sisters Gwenffrida and Mallt Williams[8]. In Goronva's Hall of Nations, forty years earlier, one may suspect that the lines are differently drawn: there may be no rejection of those outside "the Pale", but they are not consciously included. Perhaps, indeed, there are unspoken gradations: maybe the South Walian Picton, right-hand man of the Irish Arthur, was another of the "barbarians" needed to save the Empire. With whatever effort, Merlin is able to declare that

. . . our old Britannia is not dead.

Throughout 'The Hall of Nations' the adjective "British" is used to mean "Welsh", as it was before the union of England and Scotland in 1603, and the concept of Britain remains what it was after Bosworth, that of an island kingdom invaded by pagans who over-ran the ancient rulers but were themselves compelled to acknowledge the sovereignty of the rightful heirs when Henry Tudor ascended the throne. That for two hundred years and more there had been an inconvenient rent in this concept that the Pictons of Wales, not to mention the Wellesleys of Ireland, could scarcely fill is not acknowledged directly — a rent that in the twentieth century David Jones, the concept's inheritor, skilfully threaded round, in his *In Parenthesis,* by linking Welshmen and Cockneys in a battlefield, out-of-the-island setting and including little, either there or in *The Anathemata,* that could be dated later than the reign of Elizabeth the First.

Under severe strain in the nineteenth century the concept certainly was, as we shall see, but the outlines of it were still quite clear to patriotic Welshmen who had to make their way in English. The crimes of the English and the braveries of the Welsh could be fully explored and documented before and up to 1485, with a special preference, perhaps, for braveries against the Normans, whose tyrannies the English themselves had objected to: after that there was the heroism of silence. Thus John Lloyd of Dinas, Brecon, that old Etonian whose greatest hero was the Parliamentarian John Hampden, could mourn for the death of Llywelyn Olaf —

> Traitors of Bualth and of black Aberedw,
>   Oh! never shall time wear the foul stain away
> From those who could deed so detested and dread do[9]
>   As their country and king to a tyrant betray

— and, taking leave to differ from Goronva Camlann, object to the fact that the statue in Brecon's Bulwark is that of the Iron Duke[10] and not of Wales's Last Prince. Yet in another poem[11] he could remain content to claim for the Princess Victoria that

> . . . . within thy veins
> The blood of Tudor mantles still.

She is the "genuine issue of Britannia's kings". Indeed, amidst the "hailing" of this poem we may detect an "exulting Cambria" which remembers particularly the Princess's youthful visits to Cader Idris and Conwy and promises a fonder praise than that offered by any other part of Britain.

It is the privilege of old Etonians, however, to differ, for Goronva, another of them, reveals in his poem 'To the Prince of Wales'[12] the strain which the apparently easy solution supplied by the post-Bosworth loyalty convention placed upon him. "How can I", he asks,

> . . . . pay the homage of the heart,
> When thou art scarce of British race?
> How can I play the courtier's busie part,
> Or robe in smiles my eager face?
>
> Scarcelie a lingering drop of Tudor blood
> In all thy veins retains its force . . . .

In the end, however, facing the impossibility of further objection, he is reconciled by being present at the boy's baptism at Windsor and prays for a blessing on the rule "Of Her, our dearest dread and joy". Such queenly ambivalence, he perhaps felt, sufficiently masked his own.

Goronva's own poem on 'The Death of Llew-elyn', however, makes its way to an easier end. Although at one point he declaims

> What, are all the harp-strings broken?
> Have not Britannia's mightie perished?

he is able to approach the calmer conclusion that necessity commands:

> For, though, since Bosworth's righteous field,
> We bow to Tudor's royal child,
> And one fair hand the sceptres wield
> Of both our countries reconciled,
> Still are we free and firm as ever;

Still shall the ancient Cambrian river
Have honour in the mingling Ocean.

On the history of the farther past he could be less restrained. "Woe, woe the time" is the refrain he uses for the opening poem of his collection, a poem entitled 'The Banquet of Salisbury Plain' [13]. But this, after all, the convention allowed. There had to be more direct speaking than that if grievance was to raise its head. And so the Preface to *Lays from the Cimbric Lyre,* published in 1846 by William Pickering of London, Rees of Llandovery and Seacome and Prichard of Chester, becomes the most startling element in the book.

The moment has come when Goronva Camlann has to be introduced more fully, something which no more than a few months ago I could not have attempted. Goronva's identity was no secret by the time of his death — E.D. Jones referred to him by name in an article in *Barn* in 1966 and the (English) *Dictionary of National Biography* carries a substantial entry on him, inclusive of pseudonym, written in the seventies of the last century — but the entry for him in the *Bywgraffiadur,* curiously, makes no mention of his pseudonymous writings, perhaps because writing verse in English seemed an odd and unworthy addendum to his undoubtedly significant career. It is understandable, then, that in Wales, the most important context of all, Goronva was, in the present generation, all but unidentified. Rowland Williams, for that was his real name, was born at Halkyn, Flintshire, in 1819, the son of another Rowland Williams, an eminent cleric and scholar. He was brought up at Meifod, of which his father was then vicar, and educated at Eton, as already indicated, and King's College, Cambridge. After a short spell as an Eton master, he took holy orders and spent the eight years from 1842 as Classical Tutor at his old College. In 1850 he was appointed Vice-Principal and Professor of Hebrew at St. David's College, Lampeter, and spent some twelve years in a determined and partly successful attempt to reform the administration of the College and raise its academic standards. But, like his predecessor, he was in chronic conflict with the Principal and, unfortunately for his local reputation, his theological modernism became public after a sermon delivered when he was Select Preacher at Cambridge in 1854. When his contribution to *Essays and Reviews* was published in 1860, he was indicted before the Court of the Arches and found guilty of heresy — a sentence that was rescinded four years later by the Judicial Committee of the Privy

Council but *too late* to save him at Lampeter. During his last twenty-four months he sat isolated at High Table: "he dined by himself, generally reading a book, probably written by some German of Dr. Williams's beloved school of criticism" [14]. In 1862, after confronting the Principal over what he regarded as "the theft of a scholarship" [15] for the latter's son, he acknowledged defeat and removed himself to Broad Chalke, Wilts., the birthplace of John Aubrey, where he was incumbent until his death in 1870, at the early age of fifty-one. Acknowledged throughout Britain as a theologian of high rank (whose modernist pronouncements would now be regarded as conservative), he was a pioneer of the study of comparative religion, publishing *Christianity and Hinduism* in 1856. But just before he died he had prepared for the press *Owen Glendower, A Dramatic Biography.* It was theology that had purged him from the body of Wales, not history.

Lays from the Cimbric Lyre, however, came out when he was twenty-seven years old and still Classical Tutor at Cambridge. His Preface begins with some animadversions on the nature of poetry but soon gives up and admits that the impetus behind the book is grievance. Nothing in the pages following, he says, should be interpreted as anti-English, even though he might "hesitate, like most people who have studied mankind on a large scale, before [he] appropriated to John Bull all the peculiar virtues of which he claims somewhat too exclusive possession". His intention is only to rescue some of the heritage of Wales "from under the threatening train of steam-engines and schoolmasters". But then the mask of disinterestedness slips a little. There is no reason, he admits, for such an intention to become polemical, but he cannot help comparing the treatment afforded to the Welsh by the writers of the Elizabethan era, by Spenser, by Drayton, by Shakespeare, by Fletcher, by Massinger, and even by the later Milton, with the present "want of natural affection" shown by that "Anglo-Saxon race" who now see themselves as inheriting the earth.

> The great influence of the *Times* is constantly employed with mischievous ability in pandering to the self-love of those who, by a strange misconception of their own history, suppose themselves exclusively Anglo-Saxon. Even the *Daily News,* from whose general liberality of tone better things might be expected, was not able to refrain, in a recent number, from founding upon

a doubtful etymology a sneer against what it miscalls the Celtic race. In whichever of the three kingdoms a poor Celt may have been born, he can scarcely take up an English newspaper, but he finds himself and his birth and kin either disparaged, or, by implication, annihilated. A stranger to our history might infer from the tone of our periodical literature, that these same Saxons either found our island as desert as that of Robinson Crusoe, or exterminated all previous inhabitants; or at least that they possessed some qualities so brilliant as to render them alone in Great Britain thenceforward deserving of mention.

Resentment like this could, one feels at first reading, have been either temporary or the offspring of an individual bonnet-bee. But other writings, as we shall see, confirm its wider existence. When Goronva wrote

> . . . . slandered are the Cymry,
> And slandered are the Gael[16]

there were not a few in Wales to echo the first part of that allegation. This was, after all — to take its most superficial manifestation — the Railway Age. Isambard Kingdom Brunel had begun to build the Great Western Railway in 1823, and the Derby and Leeds (later the Midland) had been under construction since 1835. John Loudon Macadam had been re-making England's roads since 1815. The industrial entrepreneurs of the time were, for the most part, far ahead of their European counterparts. In foreign policy the London government had not yet reached the peaks of Palmerstonian gunboat diplomacy, but Britain was triumphantly industrial, imperial, interventionist and pleased with itself. No matter that Chartism was running down and the Corn Laws had not yet been repealed. This was not what got into the papers. The capital was complacent and full of the smell of money. As for Wales, it was peripheral in almost every sense and the new Klondyke at Merthyr was its only mark. Whatever it had of intrinsic and separate success, like the *Eisteddfodau* at Y Fenni — and North Walians like Goronva were not in touch with this (it was later said of him that he went to Lampeter in the same spirit in which Bishop Heber went to India [17]) — had always to survive against the odds. When the organisation at Y Fenni failed in 1854,

Courageous individuals like Lady Llanover were shunted off

into the sidings that the expanding railway culture of Victorian England provided for colourful eccentrics.[18]

The "threatening train of steam-engines" was real enough. And the "schoolmasters", as we shall see, also had their rails converging in a metropolitan distance. It is relevant to note that Lewis Morris, entering Jesus College, Oxford, in 1851, recalled, more than thirty years later, that "when a lad at the Welsh College at Oxford . . . we suffered much from a feeling of acknowledged inferiority to the young Englishmen at the adjacent colleges. It was considered . . . a somewhat audacious and presumptuous step on the part of a Welsh youth to enter into competition for honours with the undoubtedly better Englishmen".[19] But he and his friends did compete: Jesus College had up to that time managed no more on average than one first class honoursman in Classics every quarter century, but Morris himself became the first to alter that. By the eighties "the kind of hopelessness"[20] felt by Welsh youths had begun to disappear. What we are looking at here, of course, is the English university — that is, Oxford and Cambridge, with, low on the horizon and not widely regarded until 1858 or later, the new University of London, theological colleges at Durham and Lampeter, colleges of medicine at Leeds, Birmingham, Sheffield and Newcastle and an undenominational college at Manchester[21] — in which the bar on Nonconformists, at least in the humanities, was still general. Until 1872 three-quarters of Wales was shut out by that alone, irrespective of the absence of satisfactory schooling. The Anglicans who had any feeling for their country were undoubtedly few and lonely.

Before we leave the railway theme entirely, what Lewis Morris says about the writing of *The Epic of Hades,* published in 1875, may be of interest. Much of it was written amid

> the not inappropriate sounds and gloom *of the Underground Railway, at that time steam-powered.* I recall with distinct pleasure the battered note-book and the pencil, writing illegibly at express speed, as the lines rushed out headlong; and the nods and winks of the young City clerks who thought their fellow-traveller crazy, while he was in imagination basking happily in the sun of Hellenic skies, though really fathoms deep amid the grime and sulphurous fumes of our dear London.[22]

It could be argued here that steam, not to mention "dear London", had carried off another Welshman. But that Greece should live and Wales not was hardly the result either of so vaporous a mechanism or of so late a taste for metropolis. The causes lay much farther back.

A better match for Goronva Camlann and his bitter theme is to be found in Ivan Hues, whose *Heart to Heart: The Song of Two Nations* was published by Kegan Paul, Trench & Co. in 1889. Unfortunately no biographical information about Hues has so far emerged from my limited attempts at research [23]: the most that can be said is that the copy of his book that I was lent six years ago[24] was inscribed on the flyleaf "Ivan H. Hughes, Newport". Internal evidence, however — in particular the supposed residence of the central poetic figure at "Dynver Towers" — suggests that he was a Carmarthenshire man, certainly a Welsh-speaker but probably educated, like Goronva, at an English public school and either Oxford or Cambridge. The book-length poem which *Heart to Heart* is reads like that of a middle-aged man who has come less far than he hoped and feels the need to justify himself, but the most vital disadvantage under which we labour in considering it is that its central experience cannot be dated with any accuracy. Some of the aspects of the poem will be considered later, but this is the place, I think, to examine one part of its motivation and the resolution of the problem posed within the post-Bosworth loyalty convention.

Awen, the central figure introduced by the poet Aneirin (who then disappears), is the son of Syr Utar and at his birth Dynver's resident bard has prophesied that he will leave his native land. Just before the secret departure which fulfils this prophecy Awen's sister Gladysa finds him and hears his reasons for going. She, who has in some sort acted as his mentor until this point, had seen him as one who would "light and lead the Cambrian land"; but he, who has been out of Wales many times before and in his education has come to love the heritage of the English poets, is bitter that his native land is "a mark / For jest and jeer and jibe" and that his compatriots are "scoffed at, laughed at, and derided". Moreover, he says, what he loved no longer exists:

> Land of the Briton is no more
> The Isle of Britain, shore to shore.

Not even Wales is Wales. The scoffers

>   . . . so abound

> In all the teeming land around,
> For with our hills no more we boast
> Security against the host
> Of rude intruders. Here they come
> And make our Mountain Land their home,
> Though they affect sore to despise
> Both land and people.

All this a century before *Adfer!* But there is no historical time-slip here. Awen is serious: he is leaving Wales. And to convince Gladysa, he tells a clinching story. One day in "a world-famed city", probably in England, though its roofs uncharacteristically "shine / Under the burning sun", he came upon a crowd jeering at a "Cambrian Kelt", who presently caught hold of a Cit "whose gold-fringed lip was curled / With the last sneer that moment hurled", held him at arms' length, spoke a few fierce works in "the deep-fired vernacular" and threw him back into the midst of his fellows. The probable scuffle and confrontation were halted by the intervention of a more cosmopolitan Welshman who admonished the scoffers —

> ... who but mangle when you speak
> The mingled tongue you call your own

— and asked them why they derided another "nation's character or Pride". It was nothing but ignorance, he declared, and in the silence that followed the rebuke led his fellow-countryman away.

This alleged incident takes the charge beyond the sounding distance of Goronva's cry. It is not only journalists, not only railway capitalists, not only city speculators and office clerks who mock: it is the poor of the city too, or the chance crowd that gathers in the street. And Awen, at this stage, sees no cure for it in the maintenance of a Welsh patriotism. He must leave home and make his own way.

> No honour can be his, or fame
> And none will pay him deference,
> Who to the echo of a name
> Clings idly and in impotence.
> But he who bravely upward climbs,
> And leans on no proud ancestry,
> Will mark the music of the times
> And make his march in harmony.

The idea of *a country* must be given up and men from all nations must work together to raise the "human standard higher". Later in the narrative, when addressing the Archdruid and his followers, he repeats that it is the Present and the Future which are important: a particular history, its grievances and wrongs, must be put away. "Time", he says, will be "the arbiter" of the rightness of his words.

The rest of the poem, albeit with an occasional moderating argument, is a justification of this stance. From an armed encounter at a castle east of Offa's Dyke Awen is saved by the intervention of a maiden whom he later comes to know as Inglissa. She tells him that

> In the ocean the streamlet
>   Will vanish for ever

and that "hand in hand" they will go forward as one people

> To form an empire that shall be
> The grandest in Earth's history,
> Where no race shall itself esteem
> To be o'er all the rest supreme.

Not a hint of a contradiction in sight, apparently. Awen has only to seize his opportunity. The "sons of Britain" are those "Who her history compose" and the worthiest shall be

> Foremost in the glorious, grand
> Broadening nationality.

Awen, however, is not entirely easy about this: "Man cannot in his whole / Native character fail", he argues, adding that

> Even here . . . . in this fair Isle,
> Men will employ all wit and wile
> In limiting the liberties
> Of others, who in naught displease
> Save that they prize an ancient name
> And title in this land of fame

and will do their utmost to mock and degrade them. But Inglissa has her answer for this:

> Love of country in some breasts
> Only selfishness attests,

she says. All Welshmen are not blameless. Above all, those who have ambition must be open to change, accept the possibility of a "world-wide nationality":

> Antique forms they must amend
> Who'd be Britain's pioneers . . . . .
> Higher forms to comprehend.

At this point Inglissa disappears and Awen, now hopelessly in love, searches for her in vain. Presently, on "Craig Eirey", that "monarch mountain", he hears voices that are not mortal hailing him as "Morwyn's minstrel Childe" and urging him towards the shore

> Where Morwyn, goddess of the sea,
> And goddess, too, of poesie[25],

dispenses eternal glory and youth. Arrived there, he sees great poets of the past moving about in "gleaming robes of pleasing hues" but hears one voice that fills him with anxiety — not the voice of the poet he loved and sought for,[26] but one that completes the "scattered, fragmentary tones / That hovered long above the zones / Of his thought-world". It is the voice of Credwen,[27] who declares that it is she who inspires the poet's heart, she who first taught Awen, she who prophesies that "purer song / Will roll the Cymric hills along". Credwen leads Awen to the palace of Morwyn, where the goddess sits enthroned between Merlyn and King Arthur. Morwyn instructs him to take note of the pageant of the centuries which he will see: Merlyn adds that Inglissa and Awen are to be one.

Awen wakes at dawn, back in his own land, with Inglissa bending over him. He describes to her the scenes he saw, with Merlyn as commentator: the death of "Luarch the Noble and Wise, / Luarch the Learned",[28] the court of Arthur and Guinevere, with Merlyn singing in the background "Time to all things brings an end", the invasion of the Romans (a programme order thus far oddly in reverse of chronology), and finally the coming again of Arthur (presumably the identification that Henry Tudor, with his red dragon flag, would devoutly have wished) and a lasting peace (the post-Bosworth

convention idealised). The Spirit of the Mountains then declares that
there is no further need for a barrier between the hills and the eastern
plains and another voice is heard from Deva [29] urging the Welsh to go
forth and live:

> Ye were the first of Britain's sons,
>   First too of liberty

— the only mention here of the "seniority theme".

At this point the original narrator, Aneirin, comes back into focus,
Inglissa disappears, Awen is found dead on a high ledge, never to be
reunited with his father(s), and, in a section called 'Aftertones',
Morwyn and Merlyn are heard announcing that Awen and the fair
Inglissa shall be "joined in endless unity". The last voice heard is that
of Arthur, proclaiming that the union of Awen and the Rose of
England "Is a triumph, and no less / Than the doom of heathenness!"

Hues's Awen, charting a few doubts along the way, has thus
provided his own rationale of departure and covered himself against
charges of non-achievement both by his earlier acknowledgment to
Credwen that he had done nothing to deserve her praise and by being
found dead in the *dénouement*. The last word against his name when
living is Credwen's: "The bardic fire in you is pent", she declares. This
is neat, if not precisely in consort with the title and promise of
"Morwyn's minstrel Childe". It is all too easy, however, to look at
Hues's solution with an irony that belongs essentially to the 1980s and
to fail to realise what must have seemed its inevitability a hundred
years ago. The metaphor of the streamlet losing itself in the ocean is
one that recurs, as we have already seen, in the Anglo-Welsh verse of
the period between 1830 and 1880. Britain — or England, as
Goronva's hated publicists had it — had looked back militarily only
once since the phenomenal successes of the Seven Years' War: the
American colonials had severely dented the reputation of the British
army in the War of American Independence, but naval invincibility
and an outsider's victory on land against Napoleon had recovered
every stitch of glory: the British Empire was entering upon its headiest
days. First into the Industrial Revolution, too, Britain was far ahead of
its European competitors and, as Hues was publishing, only just
coming under threat from the coalmines and steelworks of the United
States. It was difficult for Anglo-Welsh poets, whatever their
reservations, to see themselves as refusing that part of this enormous

success they felt they were entitled to and opting instead for what must have seemed a dwindling if obstinate little tradition in which only the past tense had any force. Even Elvynydd, in calling for justice for Wales, was absolutely sure that in England was vested the greatest power and majesty of his day.[30] Ieuan Ddu, a representatively patriotic Welsh-speaking Welshman of the sixties — and one of whom we shall presently have a good deal more to say — saw no reason to refrain from extolling the battlefield exploits of his native Carmarthen's 'Gallant Twenty-Third', "St. Peter's Birds", as they called themselves: [31]

> While England's sway o'er earth extends,
>   Extend shall Cambria's too,
>   And the same glory
>   They'll share in story
>   Both in red coat and in blue.

Goronva again, bitter as he was against *England's* pretensions, identified himself fully with the prowess of the Britain of his own time, hedging only on the significance of and the precedence in its name. His response to a temporary hiccup in imperial progress, the 'Defeat and Captivity in Afghanistan',[32] is a sustained counter-threat to Britain's enemies:

> Even in their chains our children shall not sue;
> Even in their chains they shall have honour due;
> Better than hurt them, savage, haste and die;
>   We swear it by renowned Assaye[33],
>   And many a laurelled battle-daye,
> Our father's[34] spirit, and our own as high,
> They shall be safe and honoured in thy hand,
> Or else their funeral pile shall be thy land.

Only John Lloyd, in 'The Departure for Foreign Service', reveals underlying unease. On seeing "a soldier train / Approaching from the town" and hearing the cheering, he nods assent to the honour of dying in battle for one's country but as the marchers pass and clear the hill, he confesses:

> The day was bright as ever
> But I felt not as before.

It is an interesting re-allocation of accepted roles — schoolmaster unblinkingly patriotic, churchman fire-eating and squire reluctant.

In all this the parameters of the mid-nineteenth century Anglo-Welsh world have appeared clearly enough. There is the appeal to a glorious past and a regal continuity which, together, ought to justify a respected present but plainly do not; there is the ability to claim, on English terms, not much more than that Arthurian heritage which the English have already, by one of the oddest complexities of literary history, made their own; and there is the unwillingness, despite grievance, to relinquish that share in contemporary British success which even distant disciples of Geoffrey of Monmouth ought to enjoy. But where, amid the "hailings" and the silences of the post-Bosworth loyalty convention, does the Welsh language stand? Is its demise both logical and expected?

The Act of Union of 1536, of course, had envisaged just the sort of situation that Ivan Hues outlines when he speaks of "the glorious, grand / Broadening nationality" and its unmentioned correlative — that its language will be English. Its preamble declared that Welshmen should be and would be equal in citizenship with the English when they had abandoned their own tongue and become sufficiently proficient in the English language; twenty years, with the help of latimers (or interpreters), would be enough to make the change in the law courts; after that education, economic incentives, the law, all would combine to show the Welsh gentry where their best interests lay, and where the gentry led the *gwerin* would follow, if at their own, slower pace. That was not, for a variety of other reasons, how it had worked out: the gentry had mostly taken the bait but the rest had proved more obstinate. Did these nineteenth-century versifiers in English still accept the whole package that Henry VIII had left them? Did they see the bargain as valid still? They were, most of them, gentrified, if perhaps of late arrival at gentry status. Squire Lloyd of Dinas, not un-Welsh in his sympathies, sees the demise of the Welsh language as delayed but desirable: as a magistrate, he is aware of Welsh-speakers still at disadvantage in the courts and it is, understandably, beyond his imagination that the courts themselves should change. In 'One Language Desirable' he points the finger at the Ivorites[35] who would perpetuate the disadvantage and urges the smallness of the audience for future poets in Welsh. In comparison with the numbers who will listen in the language of Milton and Macaulay (note the Puritanism and the Whiggery of his choice)

> How few the thousands would that music cheer,
> The fame how partial would reward the lyre.

Ivan Hues presumably agrees, though his charge is more oblique and damaging. In *Heart to Heart* Awen claims that there is no Welsh bard whose work he has not read and, in an exchange of words which I shall look at again presently, tells the Archdruid and his followers, whom he encounters on his way eastward, that they live in a "superstitious haze" and should get out and about in the wider world. This may be no more than a put-down for the likes of Ab Ithel and Dr. William Price, but the poem's conclusion is explicit enough: Awen would not be leaving a tradition for which he believed there was a future.

Such a view, of course, had been rendered eminently respectable amongst many of those who claimed to have Wales's future welfare in mind. In 1866 Matthew Arnold, in delivering his four lectures from the Chair of Poetry at Oxford, had declared himself "overwhelmed" by the power and charm of ancient Celtic poetry, even though he knew it only in translation[36]. But he saw no purpose in the continuance and development of that poetic tradition into his day and, although as indignant as any native at the "swarms" issuing from the "Saxon hive" of Liverpool and invading north Wales, he nevertheless concluded, if under some pressure, that "the practical inconvenience of perpetuating the speaking of Welsh" was such that he felt bound to agree with his fellow-Saxons on the subject.[37]

Arnold's stance, however, was novel only in his outspoken approval of early Welsh poetry. In all else he had been beaten to it by a Welsh Self-Help movement. The pioneer of this was William Williams, the Cardiganshire-born businessman and M.P. for Coventry who, Churchman and Radical as he was, was ambitious that other Welshmen should put away the chains of language and succeed in an English world as he had done. Despite the sudden stop put to his movement by the hubbub that followed the publication in 1848 of the Blue Books — what came to be called by R.J. Derfel *Brad y Llyfrau Gleision*[38] — it was soon begun again, not least by Thomas Stephens, the Merthyr pharmacist, who, only one year later, published in English the essay with which he had won the prize at *Eisteddfod y Fenni*. In the Introduction to *The Literature of the Kymry* he wrote:

This is the way in which the Kymry can best serve their country,

as the preponderance of England is so great, that the only hope
of obtaining attention to the just claims of the Principality, is by
appealing to the convictions and sympathies of the reading part
of the English population.

It was apparently the right approach for the cool and scholarly:
Welshmen too could practise the academic method and puncture
with a few well-chosen words the madder dreams that came out of
that "superstitious haze". Stephens himself did just that at the
Llangollen Eisteddfod of 1858 when he thought he put down Madoc
from his seat. But this new, scholarly approach was all the more
persuasive for the accolade of an Englishman and it was Matthew
Arnold, affecting the same sympathetic approach, who provided it. It
was not yet a hundred years since Rice Jones of Y Blaenau had, in
introducing his anthology of Welsh poetry, *Gorchestion Beirdd Cymru*
(1773), prophesied a golden future for the Welsh language, declaring
that "Helicon is inexhaustible". But since that time England had
swollen like a giant; the glories of the Welsh literature of the past
might still, through the efforts of men like Arnold, be held in respect as
part of a less united past, but writing in Welsh could not, in the future,
expect the attention of any but antiquarians and the Welsh language
was not much more than an obstructive relic.

Very probably John Thomas (Ieuan Ddu) had not waited for
Arnold's particular view before expressing his own sense of "the
preponderance of England". His book of poems in English, *Cambria
upon Two Sticks*, was published at Pontypridd in 1867, the year
following the Oxford Lectures, and in his poem 'Harry Vaughan' this
Carmarthenshire man, describing his hero's classical education, says
of him that

> . . . . he was not thought the worst
> Of all the parrots whose incessant prating
> If it taught not what Greeks and Romans sung,
> Made them, at least, forget their mother tongue.
>
> And here that mother tongue, the English bounds,
> As its pale circle doth the watery moon;
> And ages have elapsed since those two sounds
> Have co-existed thus; but very soon
> Some prophets say, the English *blood* and *wounds*[39]
> Must so prevail, that not a knife or spoon

> Shall have been nam'd, but in old England's tongue.
> And for that reason, have I in it sung.

The issue of language was not easily separable, as is obvious enough, from that of education, and Ieuan, schoolmaster for many years in Merthyr and Pontypridd, had reached a position of balance in his views which his poems show some difficulty in explaining. Doughty champion of Welsh as he was, he too felt that in the tug-of-war that immigration and industrialisation had begun he was involuntarily giving ground. Much of his argument is devoted to the need for improving the teaching of English — or even for teaching the Classics through Welsh — so that the treasures of English and Classical literature might the more readily be available to the scholar aspirant in Wales. Like Raymond Garlick in recent decades, he sees no alternative to recognising both Welsh and English as *languages of Wales* and therefore fit to express the Welsh identity. That is, indeed, what I think his title of *Cambria upon Two Sticks* may be held to mean. He spends time, in his title-poem, in reading his Welsh roll of honour — the names of those who spoke to the *gwerin* in their own tongue: Vicar Prichard, on whom he spends many stanzas, Twm o'r Nant, Gruffydd Jones of Llanddowror and Thomas Charles of Bala, together with three men — Iolo, Idrison and Myfyr[40] — who seek "with modern lights, to make the ancient shine". And behind what has been made accessible there is the wealth of the more ancient Welsh classics:

> Ye learned Saxons who tell us ye find
> In Greek and Latin sips of every kind;
> If from dead languages such juice ye suck
> Must not a Cymro caper at his luck;
> When in this Cambria's classic verse he tastes
> From flower and stem and roots that which outlasts
> (For aught ye know) the scents Arabia wastes?

There is his plea for the Welsh heritage in literature, a plea which he hopes the English may understand the better if they recall their own history, think how once they had to fight the imposition of an official Norman-French in order to preserve

> . . . . for Milton, as for Holy Writ,
> The wedge-words that can gnarl'd hearts split.

Of more interest, perhaps, to the student of the history of education in Wales is the list of English authors he gives in his poem 'Harry Vaughan'. Ieuan's hero, like himself, is a Carmarthen man and in view of the extraordinary imbalance of the poem — a very lengthy introduction to Harry's education as a prelude to an unrelated frolic with a fair maiden and two bulls — it is not unreasonable to suppose that the literary input is autobiographical. Harry, he is at pains to tell us, is a gentleman by birth but kept at home by his mother's distrust of the society he might find at Oxford: his education proceeds, beyond adolescence, in Carmarthen itself. Perhaps Ieuan himself attended the Carmarthen Grammar School which Lewis Morris was later to adorn. However that may have been, he first, before coming to Harry Vaughan himself, orates upon the joys of reading Chaucer, Spenser, Milton, Goldsmith and, in smaller type, Shakespeare, with an amusing digression towards Edward Young of *Night Thoughts*[41]:

> Young too is great, so very great indeed,
>   That oft we wish he knew how to be less;
> Or, that his soul from big thoughts were so free'd
>   As not to make his song seem his distress:

Hero Harry, however, more closely observed, is seen practising his *amo. amas, amat,* poring over his Virgil, Horace and Homer and gradually, through the first-named, coming to appreciate that poetry has to do with "things we meet by every hill and grove". Not a word of his own native language or literature comes his way, but, having got two or three of Tully's Orations by heart, he goes on to appreciate the poetry of landscape in James Thomson and the more pedestrian Robert Bloomfield. Behind these, however, looms "the Great Bard of Twickenham", Alexander Pope, whose shortish figure is thrown up, large, on a critical screen, upon the corners of which appear, too, the heads of Dryden and Cowper. Conscious that he is going on a bit, the author interjects:

> Reader, I hear thee say, "What's that to me,
>   I want to know what Harry did or said;"
> Yet, courteous one, I may thus courteously
>   Reflect on works that furnish'd Harry's head;

But it is plain that he cannot make this excuse stick. After his first critical foray through Spenser, Milton and the others, his attempt to foist the remainder of his enthusiasms on Harry fails: what we are given is undoubtedly the substance of Ieuan's own reading, though much more probably that of a lifetime rather than of any early classroom in Carmarthen. If there is another curiosity to be noted in all this, it is the total absence of Wordsworth and the Romantics, who were surely by 1867 ancient enough, the first of them, to be admitted to Ieuan's study if not to a school curriculum.

Ivan Hues, in his pseudobiography, gives no such details. His Awen is a studious boy, who "soon discards / The tricks and toys of infancy / And takes to reading ponderous books". Claiming to know "each hill and wood and dell / From Severn to the farthest west" (probably literarily rather than literally), he has also travelled to "the level lands" eastwards.

> No bard had sung in Cymric Land
> Whose song to Awen was not known;

but, adds his author, he knew "song" in many tongues

> And in his brain sweet sounds had rung
> Which rose not west of winding Wye.

There was one voice, moreover, alien in accent and in tone, which he found loftier than the "homelier minstrelsy" of Wales, a voice which moved him to sing to his sister Gladysa a song which begins:

> All blooms beside the Queenly Rose
> With lessened lustre gleam.

Which poet it was who so affected him Awen's song does not confess, though Hues's own facile Romanticism makes it reasonably plain that his models were not those of Ieuan Ddu.

Hues's education, of course, cannot usefully become the subject of comment until he is identified personally. He may, like Lewis Morris, the third Carmarthenshire man in this *galère,* have been sent away to public school in England and subsequently to Oxford or Cambridge. His experience in "the level lands" sounds like that and the alleged extent of his reading makes it unlikely that he had freshly graduated.

As for Lewis Morris, although he was the great-grandson of his namesake, Llewelyn Ddu o Fôn, he had been brought up in

Carmarthen town with less even than a smattering of Welsh, so opulently upper-class was his family. And in the Grammar School, of course, he saw and heard none. The only recollection of his of his schooldays there to which I have access is of

> a certain number of students who were 20 to 22 years of age and were perpetually reading elaborate treatises on Civil Law by Grotius and Puffendorf.[42]

The young Lewis himself, at the age of twelve or thirteen, was remembered as a clever, assiduous boy who every morning brought to his teacher some sixty lines of Latin composition which scarcely needed correction. At the age of fourteen, however, he was despatched to Cowbridge Grammar School where, in due course, he won a prize for his Latin poem on Pompeii. After three years there, however, he followed his headmaster, as did some other pupils, to Sherborne School. In his one school year remaining he was awarded the prize for a poem in English on 'A Legend of Thermopylae' and read right through (though some of this may have been at Cowbridge) Aeschylus's 'Agamemnon' and 'Prometheus Vinctus', Sophocles's 'Antigone', and the whole of the Iliad and the Odyssey[43]. He was equipped for Jesus College, right enough, and for his first in Classics. But his poetry, when it came, had a similar inevitability about it: his *Epic of Hades* (1877), the pattern for which was provided by the *Idylls of the King* of Tennyson, with whom he became more than an acquaintance, was an educational tour, in worn and easy language, round a number of those classical characters whose acquaintance with Hell appeared to be close or more than temporary. The fact that he saw himself as a popular educator in and through verse and therefore did little to reinvigorate the language and imagery in which he described his classical figures is more relevant to his ultimate failure as a poet, for all the immensity of his sales at the time, than it is to my concern here. What we see is that he could fight his way to Greece on the steam underground, but never back to Wales. And so the odds must be cast for anyone whose education has been so drained of every tradition and particularity native to his country. Although Lewis Morris came back to Wales in later years and played a valuable part in the financial stabilisation of University College, Aberystwyth, his poetic zest was largely gone: I have found only two poems of his which are both amongst his best and carry a genuinely

Welsh "charge" — 'David Gwyn', a piece in rougher metrics than he normally used, about a Welsh prisoner in a Spanish galleon who roused his fellow-slaves at the oars and seized the ship,[44] and 'In Pembrokeshire, 1886', a strangely calm and resigned recollection of his failure as a candidate in the Parliamentary election there. Of his other poems on Wales, most, including the lengthy 'Physicians of Myddfai', seem mere routine.

Obviously the Welshness drains very easily out of a man so educated, especially when there is no family background in the Welsh language. What Rowland Williams and John Lloyd learned at Eton must similarly have distanced them from Wales, but the latter, though he spoke no Welsh, was always resident in Wales thereafter and his view of empire, even at the height of Britain's imperial success, was unenthusiastic, perhaps because of what his father had told him of the East India Company[45]. Lloyd's values, for whatever reason, had less to do with Bosworth than with the Civil War: of the Five Members[46] he writes:

> ..... we are free,
> For to thy glorious temple, Liberty,
> These men were pioneers .....

and nothing since then had been worthy the death of good men. Lloyd of Dinas was, in several respects, an unusual squire. Rowland Williams, with his thoroughly Welsh background, is the one whom we can more clearly see reacting *against* his education and all that was implicit in it. In his guise of Goronva Camlann, he claims to see better from his window in "the level lands" than men can in Wales the folly of the education to which Welsh children are subject. In his poem 'Education in Wales' the penultimate stanza runs:

> *I pray you, deign to follow Nature's guiding;*
> *Teach men their own tongue first; not there abiding,*
> *But stretching thence your hands for more:*
> Who drinks the well of knowledge, thirsts again;
> Who understand a little, not in vain
> Will come to learn your newer lore.

This is explained further in a very cogently argued appendix. "What", he writes

. . . . . is the greatest error in the existing schools in our rural
parishes? the true though paradoxical answer would be, not that
it is the want of English teaching, as the member for Coventry
supposes, but *the neglect of teaching Welsh.*

Even if Welsh should be expendable in the longer run, he goes on, it
makes sense to educate children to read and write and *think* in the
language they already know, so that, better equipped, they can then
tackle English. But that is only a first supposition. "What if by our
neglect of Welsh we are throwing away a great gift of Providence?"
There are many parts of Europe where even the peasants speak two
languages. "Almost the only argument against the retention of the
Welsh language is, that by rendering more difficult the task of the
clergy, it ministers to dissent". With this backhander at the hierarchy,
which, if they ever read it, must have delighted those who have been
called "Yr Hen Bersoniaid Llengar"[46], he leaves the matter, making it
plain that he fears the disappearance of Welsh but feels it utterly
repugnant to yield ground willingly or by direct policy to an
increasing Englishness of language, manners or customs.

The position of the Welsh language was not made the safer by the
way in which the Eisteddfod evolved during the first eight decades of
the century. Here, too, poets writing in English afford a little
additional information. At first, in the days of Bishop Burgess and Ifor
Ceri and particularly from the moment in July 1819 in the garden of
the Ivy Bush in Carmarthen when Iolo Morganwg made the Bishop a
member of that Gorsedd which he had just succeeded in attaching to
the Eisteddfod, there seemed a strong chance that the allegiance of
writers in English would be added to the new national apparatus.
Felicia Hemans (née Browne), who had lived in Wales since she was
seven and had been resident at Bronwylfa, St. Asaph, since 1809,
probably had some knowledge of Welsh. If the translations of Welsh
poems she included in her volume *Welsh Melodies* (1822) were very
free, and her lyrics on Welsh historical subjects heavily dependent on
The Cambrian Biography and Owen's *Elegies of Llywarch Hen*[49], they
were at least attuned to the spirit of the time; brief, romantic glosses as
the latter are, one or two of them — like 'The Sea-Song of Gavran', a
fifth century chief who allegedly went in search of the Green Islands —
have some memor-ability. Perhaps prompted by John Humffreys
Parry, a key figure in the London Eisteddfod of 1822, she wrote for it
'The Meeting of the Bards', which Parry read for her. At the concert

later in the day Edward Jones, the King's Harper, played three songs — one of them 'Owain Glyndwr's War Song' — written by Mrs. Hemans. But she had not many more years in Wales and does not seem to have been involved with *eisteddfodau* again.

Thomas Jeffery Llywelyn Prichard was another writer influenced by John Humffreys Parry. Having already contributed to *The Cambro-Briton*, of which Parry was editor, he was inspired by the mood of the time to be more ambitious. He dedicated his volume *Welsh Minstrelsy* (1824) to Bishop Burgess, not, as he explains, because of his services to the Church in general, but because of

> . . . . . the strong feelings of nationality, so peculiar to a Welshman, towards a prelate warmly endeared to my countrymen, for the protection yielded to their dearest, and most valued rights — the cultivation of their native language, and enforcing its usage in the Church service . . . . .

Prichard himself spoke little or no Welsh, but he was one of the first to express his patriotism in a concern for his country's native tongue. The main offering in this volume, however, a long poem called 'The Land Beneath the Sea', is both fatally facile in style and remarkably oblique and digressive in content: Tennyson burst out laughing when he read it at Aberystwyth in 1839[50]. But there is better work in the rest of the book. Prichard, although a Churchman, was an expatriate with a background in the theatre and only periodic residence in Wales: he drops out of our consideration at this point because he responds not so much to his country's contemporary problems and disadvantages as to the romances of its history. His verse is useful, though not in this context, for two things in particular: his digressions into and animadversions upon the customs of the common people, and the emphasis upon a local patriotism — for Breconshire and the Wye Valley — most notable in 'The Sevi-Lan-Gwy', where he adds a new paradox to the theme of *Bradwyr Aberedw*[51]. But Prichard, some years after he had written *The Adventures of Twm Shon Catti* (1826), was snubbed by Lady Llanover — or thought he was — and lost contact thereafter with such other patriots as he had worked with.

John Lloyd of Dinas, otherwise not much in touch with Welshness of language or institution, acknowledges in the Preface to his *Poems* (1847) that it was the theme of the prize poem at the Cardiff Eisteddfod of 1834 — 'Ode to the Princess Victoria' — and his winning of that prize that set him upon his course as a poet. Whether so Britishly loyal a theme caused fewer problems to the Old Etonian than to the Eisteddfod organisers it is impossible now to say. Lloyd seems not to have been in touch with what would have been, for him, the much more local *Eisteddfod Y Fenni*, which began during his period of writing.

Goronva Camlann, at a distance in Cambridge in his earlier years, had no part in *eisteddfodau*, though one of the poems he wrote before 1846 has a line — "Song, the abject bribe disdaining" — which, if it is not a generality about the Welsh tendency to toady in verse, may indicate that some rumblings of competitive malpractice had reached him. Ivan Hues, too, though considerably later, was never a Iolo man. His Awen, encountering the Archdruid Vyvyan and his party at the Rocking Stone on the day of the Summer Solstice, hears the "sculptured patriarch"

> . . . . . in the Eye of Light proclaim
> This island's oldest creed and fame,

declaring that men had gathered at that spot traditionally to be taught by Menw, "son of Tergwith of the Rays", so that they could disseminate everywhere the "glories of the Mystic Trwn".[52] Awen challenges this backward-looking stance, arguing that grievances should be put away, history and mythology diminished in importance:

> The Present only may we seize
> Our country's greatness to increase.

The response is acrimonious. Vyvyan answers that he, too, has travelled the world but, not being fooled by it, does not propose to abandon his country's tradition:

> . . . . . dear we'll hold our ancient laws,
> Nor brook restraint, nor seek applause.

Heart rules head, declares Awen finally: Time alone will show who is right.

It is when we come to Ieuan Ddu that the most valuable evidence of and about the Eisteddfod appears. Some eighty-five pages are devoted to his title-poem, 'Cambria upon Two Sticks' and most of them concern the Eisteddfod, its shape and practice. Ieuan, as critical as George Orwell of the *milieu* with which he is familiar, has in his Prologue a few words that he has turned and turned on his night-pillow:

> It is undeniable that at our Eisteddvodau there often seems to be a greater desire in those who promote them as well as those for whose sake they are promoted to secure praise than to deserve it; and there can be no doubt that indiscriminate praise has too often made fools of adjudicators and competitors. As to the latter, it has on many occasions, to my knowledge, determined them to have, if possible, only judges of their own choice: while the donors of prizes have, on their part, as often taken upon them to hint, and at times even to dictate as to whom they would have to win. With equal disregard for justice have committees too made favourites, and done their best for them, to the cruel injury of their superiors in merit.

The year of this Prologue, let us not forget, is 1867, nine years after the *débacle* at Llangollen and the apparent moral victory of Thomas Stephens. In 1860 Thomas Gee and the Calvinists had begun their control of the Eisteddfod. But an increase of population was beginning to make itself felt: there were more Welsh-speaking Welsh than there had been in 1800 and the trickle of incoming English was darkening to a stream. If a wider spread of patronage had been achieved, the hope of higher standards had been largely nullified by a proliferation of *eisteddfodau,* in which new men and pettier ambitions had come to the fore. Things had not really changed.

There is too little space here to allow us to follow Ieuan's ironic contemplation of the Eisteddfod in all its parts, but Canto VII, entitled 'The Discussion', which devotes itself to the obviously live issue of an all-Welsh Eisteddfod, not long previously mooted at Neath, may well be worth our attention. In this Gethin, for the continuation of the bilingual Eisteddfod, and Moelmud, for the change to the all-Welsh, are the disputants. Gethin opens with the time-honoured vaunt that he is just as good a Welshman for all his English speech and argues that he and his like are not going to pay for an Eisteddfod of which they can understand little. Moelmud replies that the projected Eisteddfod is for Welsh-speakers, for the defence and improvement of the Welsh language, not for any and every

Welshman. He quotes what it has already achieved, even in its bilingual form:

> Some fifty years ago, none made a speech
> In Welsh, save he, who in it meant to preach.

Even in a club-room, he recalls, there used to be no confidence at all in speaking publicly in Welsh. Gethin is not impressed. If you exclude us, he says, we'll establish our own eisteddfod weeks and concentrate on prizes for English in schools: you'll exclude a whole caste of Welsh people and before long find yourselves unable to pay for the kind of pavilion[53] you had at Neath. You are behaving like a brook challenging the ocean (by this time evidently a proven imperial simile), putting Welshmen at a permanent disadvantage. Echoing John Lloyd, he questions:

> Who's that poor lout that aye in Courts of Law
> Stands, statue-like, as one seized with lock'd jaw?
> Stands but to say what blockheads, in his stead,
> Translate that they may walk o'er Cymro's head.

But this is too much for his opponent.

> Now pause, says Moelmud, what you said of courts
> Makes me impatient — scan me the reports
> Of our assizes, and when that you've done,
> Prove what we have by English converse won.
> Ah! how they strove who filled the famed Blue Books
> On us to turn John Bull's astonished looks:
> How England's Journalists with jibe on jibe
> Each in his turn showed up the godless tribe,
> And still, in spite of facts and figures they
> Hold out our crimes all England's do outweigh:
> And hope to make us, in the end, confess
> That nought but English teaching made them less.

All that you have done by your enthusiasm for teaching English, he concludes, is to separate the children from their parents. And what good is all this book-learning, this vast new world of education which you claim comes by English?

The conclusion of the Canto is less than tidy as argument:

Moelmud continues to descant upon the disrespect for the Welsh language which spills over into disrespect for parents: Gethin is prepared to agree that there must be respect for both languages and points to the success of the bilingual policy in previous *Eisteddfodau*.

> . . . . where'er we wish their uses, we
> Where'er there's need, can make two tongues agree.
> If we cannot, no remedy see I,
> But let this suicide say, when 'twill die.

This forecast of the not-too-distant death of the Welsh language is a pretty fair reflection of the views of a large majority amongst Welsh-speakers in the sixties and seventies of the last century. Opposed vehemently only by Michael D. Jones, Emrys ap Iwan and a tiny group of Nationalists, it was a position of reluctant acceptance still some way from the terminal abandonment advocated by Ivan Hues. But that it was the position of Ieuan Ddu need not be doubted: the Canto ends as quoted and Ieuan's hopes for the continuance of Welsh depend largely on the survival of the Eisteddfod in its existing bilingual form.

What poets writing in English contributed to the Eisteddfod, whether before the time of Ieuan Ddu or after, can hardly be described as an enticement to abandon Wales's first tongue. Most of their work is dull stuff, a fair match for the imagination of those who set the subjects. The path from Mrs. Hemans leads down rather than up. At the Brecon Eisteddfod of 1889 S.C. Gamwell of Swansea took the prize for a poem on 'Brecknock Castle', a subject which allowed the victorious poet a safe run amongst the unlikable Normans, even to the extent of having the Princess Nest, whose ubiquity one need not doubt, marry Bernard de Newmarch and henpeck him to his distraction and the ruin of his line.[54] There is a glimpse again of the eisteddfod production line in the pedestrian *Songs of Siluria* (1916) by W.J. Williams, who won the Chair at many local *eisteddfodau* as well as the National. Almost the only verse I have encountered which attempts to be contemporary — and even that comically in a strictly local situation — is that of Rhys Davies, secretary of the Brecon Eisteddfod of 1889, who was a Welsh-speaker from Llywel and whose *Sketches in Wales* (no date, but possibly 1884), filling more pages with Welsh than English, are addressed to the tap-room rather than any literary *pabell*. But it is too easy to be hard on this eisteddfod poetry.

Charles Wilkins's *Red Dragon*[55] had nothing better in its pages than an occasional poem by Elfed[56]. There was precious little talent about.

One subject remains on which poets in English have something to say: the Church. There were, of course, a number of poets like D. Pughe Morgan, curate of Llandrinio, Oswestry, when he published his *Gethsemane and Other Poems* (1869), who wrote exclusively on religious themes. Morgan's verse, he tells us, is by way of compensation for the amount of leisure time he has as a curate, something which any reader of Kilvert's *Diary* will readily understand. There was, too, the occasional journalist like Richard Richards, a Llanymynech man writing for the *North Wales Chronicle* in Bangor, whose lyric verse is correct and unmemorable but whose real punch was reserved for his prose 'Letters to an Old Mountaineer', a regular needling of Dissenters which is plainly a response to Gwilym Hiraethog's *Llythyrau 'Rhen Ffarmwr* in his paper *Yr Amserau*. And there was Thomas Marsden, the son of a Newcastle Emlyn miner, who, as rector of Llanfrothen, had ambitions to become the *bardd gwlad* of his Anglican contemporaries and who, at his most inept, has some small claim to be the M'Gonagall of Wales. My purpose here is not to pursue Marsden to his residual awfulness, though his ability to include rack-renting landlords in his Christian community might call for comment in a fuller context. But in the pages of his volume entitled *The Poet's Orchard* (1848) there survives that "Brittish Church" which George Herbert and Henry Vaughan had treasured from its reconception by Bishop Richard Davies. In Marsden it appears as part of a violent anti-Catholicism. In the course of the long poem with which he opens, 'The Church under the Christian Dispensation', he postulates that in the time of the mythical King Constantine[57]

> Strong was the light that shone on Britain's land,
> No Druid darkness could before it stand:
> The British Church thus flourish'd for a space
> In love to God, and ev'ry Christian grace,
> Till the soul-damning heresy of Rome,
> Corrupted truth, and filled the Isle with gloom! —
> Till Austin with his Popish Priests came o'er,
> In *guise* to teach — in *fact* to darken more!
> The British Bishops to the truth adher'd
> And neither Rome nor other power fear'd;
> The Pope's demands they manfully withstood,
> And seal'd the truth, as martyrs, with their blood.

How far this account accords with an ascertainable historical truth is not in point here: attitude is all that needs to be demonstrated. But Marsden could let go in fashion much more ridiculous. His 'Epistle To the Rev. Dr. Newman, the Apostate, formerly of Oxford' is so generally laughable that I cannot resist digressing to quote a sample stanza:

> I understand you've ta'en your scope,
> And left Christ's Church and join'd the Pope,
> And now in darkest errors grope,
>   Without least light;
> And without faintest glimm'ring hope
>   Of heaven's sight!

This Evangelical or Low Church view, however ignorantly held, makes an interesting contrast with the much better known or publicised Tractarianism of the largely absentee Isaac Williams[58], especially since it is reinforced, in more learned fashion, by Goronva Camlann, whom we already know for his Modernist tendencies. In 'A Cathedral Service on Sunday Afternoon' Goronva questions the relevance of the fretted roof, the stained glass windows and "The organ's peal made eloquent by art". Are not the congregation "Spectators merely of some well-played part?" He decides he would be happier in a mountain church which lets the rain in. And in a poem called 'Misochlos' he appears to address the Church as a whole, declaring that when it weans men from their better selves, "from food the heart / Requires to live on" and offers it "Unmeaning words . . . . painted forms and feigning art", he disdains it and determines to stand apart. Goronva and Marsden and, no doubt, many others, saw themselves as the inheritors of that "Brittish Church" of which Herbert and Vaughan had been proud and preserved, too, those Puritanical tendencies which were essentially pre-Methodist, proudly parochial and perhaps related to that inter- denominational evangelical feeling which made it possible for Stephen Hughes to publish Vicar Prichard's *Canwyll y Cymry*[59].

Like Arthur James Johnes of Garthmyl[60], Thomas Marsden and a good many others, Goronva strongly opposed the move to abolish the see of St. Asaph and amalgamate it with that of Bangor[61] in order to use some of its revenues for the creation of a new diocese of Manchester. Some of his most outspoken poems (and one of these at least, he tells us, has been censored by his own caution) attack this proposal. 'A Comparison of the Massacre at Bangor in Maelor', a title which in itself demonstrates the outrage and violence of his opposition[62], asks rhetorically:

> What curse is on us? What unhallowed deed
> Has stained our soil, that now we must behold
> Our ancient sees abolished, and their gold
> Torn from our mountain povertie to feed
> Some citie swollen high with wealth untold?
> . . . . .
> Or how can men, impenetrate by shame,
> Look coldlie on, consigning to decay
> The godlike tongue of Britain, and the lay
> Of sacred bards? or how can we betray
> Our primal church? . . . .

Other poems — there are some five or six in all — refer to "the heartless stranger" and call upon the "sons of Cambria" to scare "the Saxon vulture from our land". His pseudonymous cover was obviously necessary for outspokenness of this sort and he could scarcely have been appointed to the Vice-Principalship at Lampeter had it been broken before 1850.

John Lloyd of Dinas, meanwhile, had his own reasons for disliking the hierarchy of the Church. In his poem 'Llansaintfread' [sic] he commends "holy Freda" for choosing for prayer and worship so congenial a spot as that on which her church rises by the banks of Usk and concludes:

> To yon grey porch if now but few repair
>   Meek-hearted maiden hers' the fault was not:
> Strange to her gentle thoughts alike they were
>   Schism and prelatic pride, our age's twofold blot.

The reference to "schism" may be interpreted in either of two ways — historically, as a comment on the contrast between post-Reformation times and those of the saint or as a regretful glance, like that of Arthur James Johnes, at the ever-growing ranks of the Dissenters. But the particular instance of "prelatic pride" he had in mind was almost certainly that of the Bishop of St. David's who had diverted the foundational revenues of Christ College, Brecon, into the diocesan accounts and reduced the College's usable premises to one schoolroom (with piles of dung and rubbish outside the door), in which one master taught a handful of boys. It was this local scandal that provoked a violent pamphlet from Lord Llanover ('Big Ben'), the first important industrialist in Wales to remove his support from the Church Established.

The preponderance of Churchmen amongst writers in English in the nineteenth century has been shown to be the likely result of the sort of higher education then available. Not before the eighties and nineties do representatives of Nonconformity appear with English as their language of preference and not even then, with William Parry and John Hughes as the poets who come to mind, is there significant change in the quality of the work. Parry's *The Old Welsh Evangelist* (1893) does indeed break new ground by celebrating homelier persons: he is conscious of Islwyn and Wil Hopcyn as well as C.H. Spurgeon and Christmas Evans, but he devotes to them no more than a modest talent. Hughes, who also wrote in Welsh, made his *Tristiora: or Songs in the Night* (1896) a carefully metrical exercise in devotional writing. He is a better craftsman than D. Pughe Morgan but even more repetitive. Not until the turn of the century, when Ernest Rhys published his *Welsh Ballads*[63], was there a genuinely new initiative and then it was the project of a man who, not unlike Thomas Jeffery Llewelyn Prichard, had been away from Wales for all but his first few years. Patriotism, for him, could identify its literary objectives more clearly.

There are, of course, other poets whom I have not mentioned — Richard Llwyd, "the Bard of Snowdon", who in the century's early years provided in English the kind of writing offered by the less distinguished amongst *Welsh* bards long before, rarely voicing a thought inappropriate to the realm of his increasingly lofty patronage; Thomas Jenkins, reputedly very close to Rebecca[64], whose verse is well-turned but almost devoid of the social content hoped for; James Motley, the Leeds engineer, afterwards beheaded in a Borneo uprising, who swallowed Edmund Jones[65] whole in order to write his *Tales of the Cymry* (1848); and Richard Hall, the Brecon pharmacist, whose Cambria was unrivalled anywhere for rural sport and comradeship and over which no shadow fell but that of separation and death[66]. There are, too, the *Ystradffin* (1839) of the expatriate Mrs. Bowen, the *Rhaiadr Gwy* (1840) of the Herefordshire schoolmaster Daniel Carter, and the ultimately unrewarding verse exercises of D. Rice Jones, Aberhonddu[67]. Last may be mentioned the expansive and patriotic *Llewelyn; A Tale of Cambria* (1838), a volume whose author is unknown and which was published, in circumstances that will surely invite investigation, by the Military Orphan Press of Calcutta[68]. But for my purpose these are all disparate, patternless.

Even amongst those poets whose work I have chosen to display at greater length the most notable quality is that of isolation. They are all, or almost all, men and women "of affairs" — that is, they occupied some position in the ecclesiastical or secular hierarchy which pressed them to a declaration or a decision relevant to their contemporary Wales. The isolation they felt was that of a minority within a slightly larger but still gravely outnumbered minority — English-writers and Churchmen who were members of a group not noted for its patriotism. The pity of it is that the stresses they felt were powerless to lift even one of them to notable poetry. But then, the nineteenth was not a great century even for poetry in Welsh. The native literary tradition would hardly choose to stand or fall solely by Islwyn and Ceiriog.

NOTES

1.   John Williams (1811-62), rector of Llan-ym-Mawddwy, a fiery Nationalist, founder of *Archaeologia Cambrensis* and its editor till 1853, when he founded *The Cambrian Journal,* which he edited until his death. Ab Ithel was also responsible for 'The Great Llangollen Eisteddfod' of 1858.

2.   The letter was written in 1859. In 1862, broken in health, Ab Ithel was transferred to Llanenddwyn and Llanddwywe in Ardudwy.

3.   'The History of the Kings of Britain', which first appeared in 1136. It is in this dynamic mixture of history and fiction that the author outlines the descent of the British kings from Brutus the Trojan through Lear, Cymbeline and Arthur to the Norman rulers of his own day. Attacked in the sixteenth century by Polydore Vergil, this tradition was vigorously defended by Sir John Price and many others, secure in its completion by the return of a Welsh king to the throne of Britain.

4.   1593-1666. Best known for his *Familiar Letters (Epistolae Ho- Elianae)*, 1645. I have in mind here particularly his *Parly of Beasts* (1660).

5.   'For Waterloo'

6.   Vide page 253.
7.   Kenneth O. Morgan, *Wales in British Politics* (1963), p.70.
8.   The Williams sisters used the pseudonym 'Y Dau Wynne' and under it published another and notably more Nationalist novel, *A Maid of Cymru* (1901).
9.   It is only fair to John Lloyd to state that a tongue-twister like this line occurs very rarely, if at all, elsewhere in his work.
10.   The sculptor was the Brecon-born John Evan Thomas, who had studied under Chantrey and practised in London. See Edwin Poole, *The Illustrated History and Biography of Brecknockshire* (1886). It is said that though Wellington sat for this likeness he afterwards refused the statue as a gift and Thomas then presented it to his native town. One of the bronze panels on the pedestal has a bas-relief of Picton charging the French cavalry at Waterloo and on the back of the column, perhaps as an after-thought, the name of Picton is inscribed.
11.   'Ode to the Princess Victoria' (1834).
12.   Albert Edward, who succeeded to the throne fifty-nine years later as Edward VII, was born on 9th November, 1841 and baptised at Windsor on 25th January following.
13.   *Brad y Cyllyll Hirion* (The Treachery of the Long Knives).
14.   Quoted in D.T.W. Price, *A History of Saint David's University College, Lampeter*, (1977), p.101.
15.   *Ibid.*, p.100
16.   'St. David's Street, Edinburgh'.
17.   D.T.W. Price, *op. cit.*, p.47.
18.   Emyr Humphreys, *The Taliesin Tradition* (1983), p.136.
19.   From an address to the Liverpool Welsh National Society in 1885, quoted in Douglas Phillips, *Sir Lewis Morris* (The Writers of Wales Series) (1981), p.15.
20.   *Ibid.*, p.16.
21.   Founded by John Owens in 1851. The date 1858 has been mentioned above because, although it refers only to the two colleges of London University, it was in that year that examinations were thrown open to all men who applied to sit them. *Vide* E.L. Woodward, *The Age of Reform 1815-1870* (1938), pp.472-74. I have discovered only one Welsh Nonconformist writer — Lewis Edwards (1809-87) — who took early advantage of the new facilities of London University (afterwards University College, London), opened in 1828. But Edwards wrote exclusively in Welsh.
22.   From his autobiographical essay, 'In the Confessional', which prefaced *Songs of Two Worlds*, Third Series (1875), in which *The Epic of Hades* first appeared *in toto*. Quoted in Douglas Phillips, *op. cit.*, p.28.
23.   The National Library at Aberystwyth has a copy of the book but no other information.
24.   By Mrs. I. Lee of Newport, Gwent.
25.   Welsh tradition makes no mention of a goddess called Morwyn. The name means "maiden" and was much favoured in the Welsh verse of the nineteenth century. Hues, apparently feeling that there *ought* to be a goddess of poetry in Welsh literature and legend, as in Classical, invents one, using the first syllable, *mor-*, to make a sea connection as well.
26.   *Vide* p.31.
27.   Ceridwen, the source of inspiration. She does not always appear, however,

as the neat, dark-haired woman who becomes Awen's guide. In the story of Taliesin, for example, she is the witch-woman who sets Gwion Bach to stir her cauldron brew and afterwards pursues him through a number of body-mutations until she swallows him.

28.   Llywarch Hen of Powys or, as John Morris would have it, of the Shropshire Cornovii. His dates are certainly post-Arthurian.

29.   The Roman name for Chester, the station of Legio XX (Valeria Victrix).

30.   Particularly in 'What was Thought in Wales A.D. 1859'.

31.   *Cambria upon Two Sticks* (1867). The poem is entitled 'The Gallant Twenty-Third'.

32.   This refers to the central episode of the First Afghan War when, in January 1842, Elphinstone's force, retreating from Kabul, first offered hostages (the women and children, some of the officers and the commander) and then was annihilated in the pass of Jagdallak. One survivor got back to Jallalabad.

33.   I have been unable so far to identify this battle.

34.   *sic.*

35.   The only contemporary Friendly Society which made a point of using and upholding the Welsh language.

36.   These lectures were published in *The Cornhill Magazine* in the same year and in book form in 1867. Arnold had read Macpherson's Ossian poems (1760), Villemarqué's *Barzaz Breiz* (1839), Lady Charlotte Guest's *Mabinogion* (1849), Thomas Stephens's *Literature of the Kymry* (1849) and Eugene O'Curry's *Manuscript Materials of Ancient Irish History* (1861).

37.   It is only fair to record that, despite this, Arnold was keenly concerned that the English should show respect and sympathy to the cultural traditions of the Celts, for all their likely disappearance in the near future.

38.   The Treachery of the Blue Books.

39.   Presumably two of the oaths still current in Ieuan's day, as they were in Shakespeare's.

40.   *Iolo Morganwg* (Edward Williams 1747-1826), John Jones (1804-87), whose bardic title correctly was *Idrisyn,* and Owen Jones (1741-1814), better known as *Owain Myfyr.* A prominent London Welshman, the last was chiefly known for the two large volumes published in 1801 entitled *The Myvyrian Archaiology of Wales* in which the work of the *Cynfeirdd* (early bards) and *Gogynfeirdd* (bards of the period of the independent Welsh princes) appeared.

41.   Edward Young (1683-1765) was rector of Welwyn, Herts. His chief work was *The Complaint, or Night Thoughts on Life, Death and Immortality* (1742-45).

42.   Quoted in Douglas Phillips, *op. cit.,* p.11.

43.   *Ibid.,* pp.12-13.

44.   The eponymous hero did exist historically, though his exploits during the attack by the Armada on Britain are probably apochryphal. The only known copy of his *Certaine English Verses* (1588), three poems in praise of Queen Elizabeth, is to be found in the Huntington Library in California.

45.   John Lloyd *père* (1748-1818), born at Dinas near Llanwrtyd, was an East India Company official and fought against Tipu Sahib. With the fortune he made in India he bought the estate at Abercynrig near Brecon where his son was to build a second Dinas.

46.   "The old literary clerics", a title first given to such as Ab Ithel,

W.J. Rees of Cascob, Gwallter Mechain, Carnhuanawc and Ifor Ceri (for the last of whom see below) by R.T. Jenkins in his *Hanes Cymru yn y Bedwaredd Ganrif ar Bymtheg* (1933).

47.   Thomas Burgess, Bishop of St. David's from 1803 to 1825, though an Englishman, was one of the few episcopal exceptions of the century in not only being resident within his see but actively interested in the welfare of Welsh-speaking society. He founded St. David's College, Lampeter, in 1822.

48.   John Jenkins (1770-1829), a Cardiganshire man who had served as a naval chaplain, was vicar of Kerry in Montgomeryshire when he and Bishop Burgess decided in August 1818 to arrange *eisteddfodau* in the different provinces of Wales. That of Carmarthen in 1819 proved to be the first. *Ifor Ceri* directed it and those that followed until the Denbigh Eisteddfod of 1829, when he objected that English influence was creeping in and that the proceedings were becoming an "Anglo-Italian farce".

49.   See the notes to the selection of 'Welsh Melodies' included in *Poetical Remains of the late Mrs. Hemans* (1836). There are indications also that she was a reader of *The Cambro-Briton*. The eisteddfodic information presented in this brief account of Mrs. Hemans is taken from Peter W. Trinder's *Mrs. Hemans* (Writers of Wales Series) (1984).

50.   Herbert G. Wright, 'Tennyson and Wales', in *Essays and Studies* by Members of the English Association, collected by H.W. Garrod, vol. XIV (1929), p.71.

51.   "The Traitors of Aberedw", a phrase of opprobrium directed at the inhabitants of the district (expecially the smith Madoc Min Mawr) who, in the traditional story, informed his pursuers of the direction taken by Llywelyn Olaf on the day before his death near Cilmeri in 1282.

52.   Menw mab Teirgwaedd appears as a character in the tale of Cilhwch and Olwen: it is he who both returns with force the spear thrown by Ysbaddaden Bencawr and, at Esgeir Oerfel in Ireland, transforms himself into a bird to try to snatch the jewels from behind the ears of Twrch Trwyth. Also called in one of the Triads one of the three chief enchanters of Britain, Menw (not Teirgwaedd) figures in an allegorical tale about the discovery of the bardic alphabet, published by Taliesin Williams, Iolo's son, in 1840, in which he saw three rods, like three rays of light, growing out of the mouth of Einigan Gawr. On these every kind of knowledge and science was written, except the name of God.

53.   Gethin's word here is "temple".

54.   Bernard de Newmarch was the victor in the battle outside Brecon in 1093 at which his opponent, Rhys ap Tewdwr, King of Deheubarth, was killed by treachery. Bernard did indeed control the area of the former Brycheiniog thereafter and his wife was named Nest; but her attributes in this poem are those of her much more famous namesake, mistress of King Henry I of England and wife of Gerald de Windsor, Castellan of Pembroke — the much married (and raped) daughter of the dead Rhys who was seized from Cilgerran Castle by her cousin Owain ap Cadwgan.

55.   1882-87. From 1885 it was edited by James Harris. For further details see 'A Glance at Anglo-Welsh Magazines' in this volume.

56.   Howell Elvet Lewis (1860-1953), for many years minister at the Congregational *Tabernacl*, King's Cross, London, who is chiefly remembered

in English as the author of a number of regularly used hymns like 'Lamb of God, unblemished' and 'Whom oceans part, O Lord unite'. He was Archdruid from 1923 to 1927.

57.   Constantius, a Roman general, recovered Britain for the Empire in 296 A.D. by defeating Allectus, the successor of the original rebel Carausius, commander of the Roman Fleet in the Channel. A Yugoslav (as he would be called now), he became Emperor in 305 but died at York after a triumphant campaign against the Picts. His son Constantine was immediately proclaimed Emperor by the Army in Britain and some years later became the first Christian Emperor, ruling both at Rome and Constantinople. His role as a British king owes something to the aura of Christianity, which had probably reached Britain from Gaul before his reign, and something to the confusion of his wife Helena with Elen Luyddog. Augustine, of course, arrived in Kent nearly three centuries later.

58.   Williams (1802-65), despite his Cardiganshire roots, was brought up largely in London. Curate to John Henry Newman at St. Mary's, Oxford, as well as Fellow of Trinity College, he was prominent in the Oxford Movement and earned particular praise (and animosity) as the author of *Tracts for the Times* No.80. In 1841, after John Keble's retirement, he stood for the Chair of Poetry at Oxford and was expected to obtain it, but after bitter wrangling withdrew his name.

59.   Stephen Hughes (1622-88), a Nonconformist, was the first to publish the moralistic verse of Rhys Prichard (1579?-1644) and it was he who, in his 1681 edition, gave it the title *Canwyll y Cymry* (The Welshman's Candle).

60.   Johnes (1809-71), a county court judge, is best remembered for his essay on 'The Causes which in Wales have produced Dissent from the Established Church'.

61.   About 1838.

62.   The title recalls the Angle massacre of the monks of the monastery of Bangor-is-y-Coed in 613 by Aethelfrith of Bernicia.

63.   The date ascribed to this is 1898, but my copy is undated.

64.   Jenkins, whose only volume, *Miscellaneous Poems,* was published posthumously in 1845, was clerk to the solicitor Hugh Williams, now commonly believed to have orchestrated the Rebecca Riots.

65.   Known as Edmund Jones the Transh (Pontypool) and *'Yr Hen Broffwyd'* (The Old Prophet), he published in 1780 *A Relation of Apparitions in Wales.*

66.   His only volume, *A Tale of the Past and Other Poems,* was published in 1850.

67.   The author of *Isolda and Other Poems* (1851).

68.   I owe my knowledge of this book to a copy lent me by Mr. Meic Stephens, one of only two copies at present known.

The Lonely Editor:
A Glance at
Anglo-Welsh Magazines

I am not here to startle a tear or two from naturally unsentimental eyes. The editor whom I shall depict is lonely in a number of ways, none of them worthy of your even momentary grief. In the first place, he is lonely because, unlike the Belshazzars who sit in glass-panelled offices guarded by janissaries and mamelukes and intruded upon only by especially delectable houris with shorthand pads, he sits at home, in his makeshift study, guarded only by a wife who is not entirely sure why and for what he sits so long. The editor of a literary journal is, very possibly, a one-man band. If he has assistance, it is probably at a distance, where another devoted soul sits in an equally makeshift study sorting out and organising books for review. Communication between them is infrequent. Thus it is that that horrible thump that the post makes of a morning as it hits the hall floor is for your editor alone. Only he can conjecture from the sound just how many would-be poets have trusted him that day with substantial portions of their *oeuvre*. Let me hasten to add, lest I be accused of an outdated male chauvinism, that role-reversal is entirely in order these days. It may well be a husband who polishes the spoons in the kitchen and underestimates the travail of the figure at the desk. In the end it does not matter. Your editor is probably so reduced by incessant reading and correspondence that his or her sex is of no greater importance than the granular quotient of Lot's wife as she solidifies.

The world of the Little Magazine is therefore tied to life by the merest thread. And in the literary division, to which belong the Anglo-Welsh magazines of our consideration, that world often seems to bob about at less than arm's length. Or perhaps that is just how your editor feels. For his contributors are very close to him, not exactly past the sentinel wife and knocking on the study door, but likely to be encountered in mountainous person at some literary or academic function before many months, nay weeks, are out. The smallness of Wales brings great benefits, or can: it also brings terror to the choicemaker compelled to fraternise with those who want his blood. The editor realises then, if he did not before, not merely that his part is a lonely one but that he cannot hope to be given his deserts, much less to be popular — a deprivation which a genial soul who imagines he can pull the levers of his organisational and critical machine with a natural cheerfulness may well find hard. For those would-be contributors whose work he does not choose to print in the next, or indeed any, issue are, not a few of them, convinced of their own genius and ready and willing to assert that only Establishmentarianism, cliquishness, corruption or downright idiocy could have failed to discover the high quality of the manuscripts submitted, while those he does choose to print have a habit of assuming that such inclusion is no more than their due and that no editor who was even going through the motions could have kept them out. It is not every editor, I grant, who has received, as I have, a bundle of mss. accompanied by a letter explaining that the sender has been persuaded to direct his work to Journal X because a friend has told him that the editor of X "is rather less corrupt than most of the members of the literary Establishment", only to have the work demanded back a fortnight later because another friend has judged the same editor a knave outright. Nor is it every editor who has been shaken by the lapels after a BBC programme or had consigned to him a parcel of stinking fish — though here it has to be acknowledged that an obscure editorial address is perhaps the best sentinel of all, the malodorous parcel being delivered to and, under suspicion, opened by the impervious janissaries of the Welsh Arts Council! No, the editor is lonely, right enough. His chances of being loved do not rate very high. The timider members of the editorial species may well be tempted to edit from hiding.

Why, then, does anyone become an editor? That, in a way, is what we want to discover today. If he is a writer himself, it cannot possibly be to his advantage to let so much of his time be engrossed with reading other writers' typescripts, with correspondence, administration and considerations of literary policy. Such work saps creative energy as well as taking the time from creative writing. Yet the great majority of editors whom we shall look at in the Anglo-Welsh field have been and are writers, some of them writers of quality. Can it be that becoming an editor is some sort of means to wealth? No, it cannot. Nowadays, when literary magazines in Wales are subsidised, an editor rarely gets more than his expenses, very occasionally a small honorarium, and in the days before subsidy there were only two alternatives for an editor — either to find a sufficient patronage to make his journal financially viable and to meet his own expenses, or to hope that subscriptions received would meet production and printing bills. No imagination is needed to understand just how financially disastrous the latter situation commonly was and it is no secret that the editor after whom and in whose honour this lecture is named was one who had to abandon publication because his pocket could no longer stand the cost.

Becoming an editor, then, is not the first step to wealth. What, we may ask, is left? Why does anybody seek to edit a literary magazine? It is possible to suppose a man or woman so desirous of becoming an arbiter of taste, so ambitious for literary power, that loneliness, likely unpopularity, engrossment of time and absence of financial reward might fail to dissuade him or her from the task. But in the Anglo-Welsh context this is next to impossible. We have not yet thrown up a Julian Hodge with a consuming passion for literature. No, we have to accept that in an editor's mind, in Wales, there must exist some concept of service — either, narrowly, service to his fellow-writers (and I have often thought, and said, that if the majority of writers were not so selfishly wrapped up in their own writing and their own success, they could do much to create their own platform and ensure the financial viability of any magazine edited with their interests at heart), or, more widely, service to the literary history of his people, to their education and culture, even, perhaps, to literary definition and a sense of national identity. It is, perhaps, matter for amazement that there are, from time to time, individuals — even writers who have ambitions as writers — who are prepared to put themselves at disadvantage for reasons of this sort, but so it must be. If it were not for this concept of service, the number of those who have been pushed into, rather than themselves clambered into, editorial chairs would be negligible.

My endeavour will be, in what follows, to take a brief look at the journals, from the beginning of the nineteenth century until now, which belong to the Anglo-Welsh literary context and to discover, if I can, what their editors believed they were doing, what their stated policy was, and how far they were successful in carrying it out. I must, however, make a disclaimer of some force: I have looked at only such magazines as in my rural fastness I could lay hands on — which means that many (the great majority of the early ones) are omitted from consideration. Moreover, what I shall say can scarcely be designated by the name of research, unless a rapid turning over of pages can be so called. I tell you, in effect, what I have been able to find out in cursory fashion. And what I have not found out, or have managed to misemphasise, even to misunderstand, will doubtless be sufficient study for several doctoral theses in the years to come.

Let us take a stand, then, in the year 1819, and discover what John Humffreys Parry has to say in his first of June Prospectus for *The Cambro-Briton*. Parry was born at Mold in 1786, the son of a vicar. He was called to the Bar in London in 1811 but neglected his practice, fell into debt and took to journalism. He was a member of the Gwyneddigion Society and in 1822 became the first Secretary of the revived Cymmrodorion Society and editor of its *Transactions*. Obviously he was a patriot in the contemporary mould, if his personal reputation lacked the highest acclaim.

In his Prospectus Parry claims the initial idea of *The Cambro-Briton* for himself, though he acknowledges that there existed, or had existed, a previous journal — perhaps the very first Anglo-Welsh literary magazine — called *The Cambrian Register,* which had appeared intermittently, at four or five-year intervals. He comments on "the favourable spirit by which our country appears at length to be animated" and declares that his "chief aim" is to "diffuse amongst strangers a knowledge of the history, the manners, the genius of Wales, and to extend beyond her mountain-barriers the fame of those literary treasures which are now, as it were, covetously hoarded within them". In a word, the emphasis is to be on translation from the Welsh, though "the English muse will also be a welcome guest, whenever she may devote her lays to the cause which the *Cambro-Briton* has undertaken to espouse". Was it not odd, one may think, at a time when there was no journal of a literary nature in Welsh, that Parry and his supporters in the Gwyneddigion should think in terms of presenting Wales to the English in their own language? Yes, but this was part of the defensive antiquarianism of the London Welsh of the time. No more was heard of Wales as the senior partner in the Union instead, the Welsh of the metropolis were anxious to be seen as true Britons (in the English use of that term), loyal to the House of Hanover and "demonstrating a due reverence for our Established Church" (of the hierarchy of which many of them had cause to be afraid). Whether the "favourable spirit" mentioned corresponded at all with that of Methodist and increasingly Dissenting Wales is another matter. But John Humffreys Parry is not abashed. He defends his use of English by declaring that "Our venerable language (meaning Welsh) stands in no very urgent need" of cultivation and preservation: "consecrated . . . by the ennobling genius of the Bards . . . it may be securely left to its own energies".

In practice, *The Cambro-Briton*, when it appeared in September 1819 and every month thereafter till June 1822, consisted of translations of The Triads and the Wisdom of Catwg, genealogies of the Saints, observations on the Welsh language and on Welsh music, critiques of recent translations into Welsh like William Owen Pughe's *Coll Gwynfa* (a version of Milton's *Paradise Lost*) — English interest in this was surely minimal — , memoirs of important Welshmen of recent years, news of Wales (usually in the form of reports of Societies like the Gwyneddigion and of *Eisteddfodau*), death notices and desultory, if individually important, letters in English from significant Welshmen of the past like Edward Lhwyd. Of poetry in English little was seen, apart from a few poems by Jeffery Llywelyn (later more fully described as Thomas Jeffery Llywelyn Prichard, the author of *Twm Shon Catti*, but then an actor or theatre administrator in London) and even fewer from Richard Llwyd, the Bard of Snowdon, who had been one of the founding patrons.

When *The Cambro-Briton* ceased publication John Humffreys Parry sent a letter, dated 27 August 1822, to *The Carmarthen Journal* (so directed because he had had, allegedly, high hopes of the new Cambrian Society in Dyfed, founded in 1819) in which he referred bitterly to his "too easy credulity" and "causeless enthusiasm". The indifference with which the Welsh regarded the cause of their national literature had, in his opinion, "its root in those peculiar propensities to which Wales has, for a long period of years, been proverbially subject". A taste for *literae humaniores* was "too often obscured by the gloom of fanaticism, or lost in the baneful vortex of theological controversy". This hit at Dissenters, whether just or not, does little to explain why it was a service to Welsh literature in Welsh-speaking Wales to publish a journal about it in English when no Welsh equivalent existed. Parry was not the last amongst our editors seeking to provide what, apparently, no sufficient proportion of the literate public desired.

Thus, anyway, our first editor, whom I allow to speak at some length so that the quality and context of his "loneliness" may be fully understood. Parry, however, went on to excel any successor in unpopularity. Calling once too often at The Prince of Wales tavern in North Street, Pentonville, to enquire after the health of the landlady, he was followed, on leaving, by an agent of the landlord, who knocked him down and beat him so severely that he died shortly afterwards. There is a lesson there, I am sure, but perhaps not for editors in particular.

The London of the Gwyneddigion — even with William Owen Pughe and John Parry at hand and Welsh outriders in Gwallter Mechain, rector of Manafon and W.J. Rees, rector of Cascob — plainly did not represent a Wales which, if it regarded the matter at all, suspected what was predominantly "North Wales and Church". The *Transactions* of the revived Cymmrodorion Society, however, provided, at least till 1828, a continuation of the *Cambro-Briton* mixture, with plenty of Hu Gadarn and even less poetry in English. What is quite clear is that English, if the language of culture and information, was not a language in which Welshmen were expected, or even encouraged, to be creative.

Our next sighting, *The Cambrian Journal*, first published in 1853, was distinctively historical in emphasis. The quarterly organ of the London Cambrian Institute, its editor, up to 1862, was the Reverend John Williams ab Ithel, rector of Llanymawddwy, who had been co-founder of *Archaeologia Cambrensis* and its first editor until 1853. In the 1863 volume of *The Cambrian Journal* he was posthumously celebrated in a sequence of three articles. But his editorial career had not been plain sailing. In his Preface to the volume for 1860 he alleged that he had "encountered much opposition at the hands of some persons, who, whilst they bear the name of Cymry . . . are notorious for their anti-national prejudices". Ab Ithel was an enthusiast but an unsatisfactory scholar: he may even have been referring to the repercussions from his "Grand Llangollen Eisteddfod" of 1858 at which Thomas Stephens, a member of the *Cambrian Journal's* Historical Committee, had been refused the prize for his essay on Madoc. Ab Ithel, moreover, had received no preferment at the hands of the Bishop of St. Asaph, who presumably objected to his patriotic activities, and even a letter of 1859 from that devoted Celtophile James

Kenward of Birmingham moved the prelate not at all. Another editor, then, who, if he did not bite the dust unnaturally, certainly tasted it. The 1863 volume, however, which is the latest I have, makes it plain that Ab Ithel's successor, whoever he was, was much more open to the possibilities of verse in English: besides Elvynydd's topographical poem, ' A Song of the Dee', he printed 'Glyndwr' by John Vaughan Lloyd of Jesus College, which had been awarded a prize by the Cymmrodorion Society in 1826 but which, unlike the winner in Welsh, had not been published in the *Transactions*.

My next jump is to the year 1882 and to *The Red Dragon*, which called itself 'The National Magazine of Wales' and claimed to be the only one of its time in English. Its founding editor was Charles Wilkins, who described himself as "a literary pupil and a personal friend" of Thomas Stephens, though in an article he published on the *Gododdin* the friendship was not particularly noticeable. Wilkins was born at Stonehouse in Gloucestershire but came to Merthyr Tydfil as a boy, his father setting up first as a bookseller in the town and then, in 1831, becoming Postmaster. Charles was Librarian of Merthyr Subscription Library from 1846 to 1866 and served as Postmaster himself from 1871 to 1898. A man of tremendous energy and a prolific writer, his establishment of *The Red Dragon* was an indication that he had outgrown a merely local patriotism and was ready to try to create a reading public for the diffusion of a more national sentiment.

The Red Dragon was overwhelmingly a *South* Wales monthly and, since the English-speakers of Wales had multiplied by four or five times since the days of *The Cambro-Briton*, its editor intended greatly to diminish the latter's concentration on literature in Welsh and offer instead a framework whose regular stanchions were a romantic novel in serial (only occasionally with Welsh content), a short biography of a memorable Welshman of the hundred years previous, a sketch of an old Welsh "character", a short story or two, 'Gossip from the Welsh Colleges', an account of Welsh affairs at Westminster, attenuated book notices and 'Literature and Art Notes for the Month'. It is true that 'The Triads of Catwg the Wise' did turn up in the first number or two and that there was regularly a translation from Welsh poetry, into which field Wilkins was fortunate in attracting both Lord Aberdare and A.J. Johnes. One or two early issues seem almost to be the work of the editor *solus*, but *The Red Dragon* acquired momentum and it was a mark of confidence (as well as a symbolic moment) when the October 1883 number included the heading 'Original Poetry' (meaning by

that poetry in English). Not that that heading altered much the nature
of the verse published, often over pseudonyms, which continued,
with models exclusively English, to be either heroic on Welsh and
continental subjects or romantically topographical. One must,
however, recognise the difficulties of modestly-endowed poets from
Cardiff and Swansea who had not realised the need for a personal
philosophy, close and critical observation and wide reading. The only
names amongst them that might be recorded in a history of Anglo-
Welsh poetry or remembered elsewhere are those of Howell Elvet
Lewis, then writing in from Buckley, William Parry of Pontypridd
and Arthur Mee of Llanelly.

At the end of 1885 Charles Wilkins, who never wrote editorials,
gave way as editor to James Harris of Cardiff, presumably because,
having finished and published his *History of the Literature of Wales*
(1884), he had embarked heavily upon his *History of the Coal Trade of
South Wales.* The light content and the delicate balance of the *The Red
Dragon's* first four years had clearly been a calculated attempt to reach
out to a new public literate in English but unschooled in a knowledge
of Wales. Under James Harris, seen previously only as an informed
contributor, the balance began to change — and to change back to an
older model. The *Notes and Queries* section, which Wilkins had
allowed in towards the end of his time, grew enormously, engrossed
the pages. The articles became more academic. The whole emphasis
of the magazine moved back towards the antiquarian. I do not know
why *The Red Dragon* ceased publication in 1887 because I lack the
copies for that year. But some few of the contributors had appeared to
be having a marvellous time with a foot and a query in each issue, and
it may be that the six noble subscribers of whom the publishers had
boasted earlier, not to mention more ordinary readers, had not found
the magazine latterly quite such fun.

Towards the turn of the century there was a proliferation of
magazines in English, with varying emphases — *Young Wales* (1895-
1905), *The Celtic Review* (1904-16), *The Nationalist* (1907-12) (there was
even one called *Y Dyn: The Man* and described as a duoglot magazine)
— but, having of necessity to be selective, I move forward to *The Welsh
Outlook,* which evidently took the place of J. Hugh Edwards's defunct
Wales. The Welsh Outlook, whose first number appeared in January
1914, described itself as 'A Monthly Journal of National Social
Progress'. Sponsored and subsidised by Lord Davies of Llandinam,
the coal and railways magnate, it had for editor none other than

Thomas Jones of Rhymney, back in Cardiff from Belfast as Secretary of the Welsh National Memorial Association, the anti-tuberculosis campaign, but soon to be whisked away by Lloyd George to become his Secretary to the Cabinet. In manner and appearance *The Welsh Outlook* was a very different animal from any of its predecessors. It was not simply that it was a large magazine, set in double columns: it had numerous illustrations in black and white (art reproductions as well as photographs of Welsh housing): it dealt extensively with industry, with education, with town planning as well as with drama, art, music and literature: and it had a seemingly comprehensive list of book reviews. In his Foreword to the first number the editor writes of a divided Wales attacked by outside economic forces and penetrated by English newspapers: his central concern is to preserve a Welsh identity:

> We hold that the assertion and maintenance of our nationality is justified; that our moral and political and social traditions are a precious inheritance the loss of which would impoverish humanity; and that local patriotism is not incompatible with imperial loyalty. Holding this faith we wish in these pages to witness to the unity of our national life and to deepen and enrich it. This we would do not by refusing what other nations offer but by taking of their best, making it our own, and returning it with interest. We believe we can make some contribution, however small, to the common treasury of the nations, if we have the courage to be ourselves, and to put our trust in knowledge and discipline rather than in rhetoric and intrigue.

This combined rebuke for parochialism and plea for confidence was to be repeated, if in very different words, by a subsequent editor in another journal.

But here, one might think, was an editor who was *not* lonely. He had a sponsor, he had a substantial budget, he had early contributors like T. Gwynn Jones (surprisingly, writing in English as well as Welsh), R.G. Berry, Abel J. Jones, E. Roland Williams, Professor Gilbert Norwood, T.H. Parry-Williams and Eifion Wyn. He envisaged a better Wales in which he and his readers would "make explicit the Christian ideals we vaguely hold...and bring them into some sort of relation to the realities" which surrounded them. There was, it might appear, a consensus. But such safety it is that fits one for higher and more imperial things. By 1916 Thomas Jones had departed. Under his successors, Edgar Chappell and R. Silyn Roberts, *The Welsh Outlook* drifted slowly away from the emphasis on industry and social progress and back to the Charles Wilkins formula, if always with greater resources and more significant names. Under Thomas Jones there had been poems but no short stories: instead of Wilkins's English romances there had been long extracts from *The Life and Opinions of Robert Roberts, y Sgolor Mawr*. As the years went on towards 1927 the literary content steadily increased: anecdotes and short stories appeared ever more frequently: with the series 'The Old Cobbler of Llansionyn' we are back again with Wilkins's 'Welsh Character Sketches'. Nevertheless, throughout the years 1914-27 there was a genuine and sustained attempt to provide a comprehensive survey of the Arts scene in Wales, even if the "European" infusions of T.J. were rarely repeated. Book reviews, for example, covered Edward Thomas's *The Happy-Go-Lucky Morgans,* J.O. Francis's three-act play *Change* and the stories of Caradoc Evans, even if these last were given short shrift: there was an article by Geraint Goodwin on Edward Thomas and one by E.A. Reid on A.G. Prys-Jones: there was even one in 1926, by Lewis Davies, on 'The Anglo-Cymric School of Poets'.

But none of these virtues could save *The Welsh Outlook* when Lord Davies withdrew his subsidy in 1927. Insufficient advertising revenue, too few subscribers (not many more than 800 towards the end), not enough money to cut a dash — all circumstances very familiar since — rendered the tenure of the last editor, E.H. Jones, author of that neglected classic, *The Road to Endor,* very precarious, despite some help from the Misses Davies of Llandinam. In 1933 the journal ceased publication.

What every Anglo-Welsh magazine so far considered had lacked was the confidence — the daring, if you like — which genuinely creative writing conveys. Controversy, too, no doubt — what Lord Davies had called for in one tone of voice and forbidden in another. Keidrych Rhys's *Wales,* which first appeared in the summer of 1937, had both. Its first number, a mere 32-page offering, published from Penybont Farm, Llangadog, made no pretence of consensus or breadth of subject matter. It was defiantly literary. It began without Editorial and the first words were those of Dylan Thomas's 'Prologue to an Adventure':

As I walked through the wilderness of this world, as I walked through the wilderness, as I walked through the city with the loud electric faces and the crowded petrols of the wind dazzling and drowning me that winter night before the West died, I remembered the winds of the high, white world that bore me and the faces of a noiseless million in the busyhood of heaven staring on the afterbirth.

Derivative in part, no doubt, but not caring. Confident, ear-catching and barely comprehensible. To follow, there were poems by Glyn Jones, Nigel Heseltine, Ken Etheridge, Wyn Griffith, Idris Davies, Vernon Watkins (that 'Griefs of the Sea' that Dylan altered without the author's permission) and the editor. No.2, however, described as an Eisteddfod number and dated August 1937, set the editorial style. It was fierce, colloquial and as difficult to understand as Dylan. *Wales* was not the organ of a literary clique: "once more we stress" (when previously, we may interpolate?) "that we are with the People". A new age had dawned: it was no time now for "such Newbolt-Fascist piffle" as A.G. Prys-Jones had collected in his *Welsh Poems* of 1917: younger writers would get the opportunity denied them "in the English Literary Map of log-rolling, cocktail parties, book clubs, knighthoods, O.M.s and superannuated effeminacy in Bloomsbury editorial chairs". Caradoc Evans wrote in to congratulate *Wales* on not having a *Parch* amongst its contributors. The scene, it might seem, was set. But the editorship alternated: Nigel Heseltine was in charge after war broke out, and when *Wales* reappeared again in January 1944 Keidrych Rhys, his head cleared by Army service, explained himself all over again. He welcomed the new spirit of realism in the country: he did not propose to ignore practical politics any longer, though the magazine would be non-party. His greatest complaint seemed to be that Welsh representatives in London were so mealy-mouthed and evasive, "out of touch with the feeling of the people generally . . . . Yet we are not a nation of toads".

The sentences were longer now, the editorial style less a series of short, sharp barks. But it was still a no-holds-barred approach: his country must measure up to metropolitan standards, compete in the English arena, shed its parochialism, its inhibitions and some of its more antiquated absurdities. Later numbers of *Wales* were frequently virulent and rude, especially in the reviews and correspondence columns. Like most of those to whom he was closest, Keidrych felt that the Welsh heritage, while in general conservable, was splendidly strange material with which to assault metropolitan readers and mark a Welsh place on the map.

That such a policy approximated, in the end, to one of maiming the goose that laid the golden egg was not then foreseen. It is only in retrospect that we can see that such daring would not long have much to be daring about and that the Welsh way of life, already weakening, was not helped by Anglo-Welsh ridicule. Most of the writers involved did indeed change tack within a decade of the launching of *Wales*. But there is a curious paradox about it all. When the post-war magazine settled down more quietly to provide a few of the elements of *The Welsh Outlook* and *The Red Dragon*, in addition to its poems and stories, its correspondence columns remained full but "the people" — the realist *people* for whom it claimed to speak — never supported it in sufficient numbers to make it financially viable. In its last manifestation in 1958/59 Keidrych Rhys had to abandon publication because he could not maintain the minimum of a thousand subscribers the publishers demanded.

We must return now to February 1939. In that month there appeared another journal devoted to Anglo-Welsh writing, *The Welsh Review*, edited by Gwyn Jones, then Senior Lecturer in English at University College, Cardiff. Inevitably cooler and more magisterial in style, it was to be a platform for the best writing that Wales and Welsh writers could produce: the first editorial declares that it stood for "tolerance, progress, knowledge, freedom of thought and expression, and a firm belief in the dignity of mankind and the unqualified wickedness of all that outrages it". Curiously, it makes no mention whatsoever of Keidrych Rhys's *Wales*. "For more than ten years", the editorial announces, "there has been talk in Wales of a journal for English-speaking Welshmen, and now, suddenly, here it is".

The very format of the magazine, initially, with its page size 9 ½ inches by 7 inches, single-columned, was a symbol of the breadth it aimed at, and the contents of the first number, with stories by Glyn Jones and Jack Griffith, poems by W.H. Davies and Huw Menai, a scraper-board sketch by Myfanwy Haycock, an article on the Swansea Little Theatre by Thomas Taig, other articles on drama, the BBC and public health, reported comment by A.W. Wade-Evans and others and substantial book reviews, suggested the *The Welsh Review* was aiming at a continuity which the vaguely radical outbursts of *Wales* had disregarded. In some respects, however, the first number was deceptive. The editor, while emphasising the basic need for a journal in English in Wales — "Can any work be more useful to Wales, as things are, than to keep the English-speaking Welshmen bound to their homeland?", he asks — began in subsequent numbers to attack with a controlled ferocity specific issues like air-raid precautions, the threatened development of Pontcanna, and the problems involved in despatching English slum evacuees to Welsh-speaking Wales. These issues, however, were confined to editorials. The body of the magazine displayed an increasing literary wealth — Welsh stories in translation like Tegla Davies's 'Samuel Jones's Harvest Thanksgiving' and A. Edward Richards's 'Worthy is the Lamb', articles by Llewelyn Powys and R.M. Lockley, wood engravings by Reynolds Stone, Brenda Chamberlain and John Petts, and, best of all, stories by Kate Roberts and Geraint Goodwin, especially the latter's 'Ap Towyn' and 'The Lost Land'.

When *The Welsh Review* re-appeared towards the end of the war (it had been compelled to cease publication in November 1939), it was edited, in a more modest format, from Aberystwyth, but Gwyn Jones was able, in the March 1944 number, to claim that in its first manifestation only six significantly creative Welsh writers in English had not been published in its pages, and that three of those were under promise at the time of the magazine's suspension. One of the three remaining, Caradoc Evans, was published in that very issue, a sign that the attitudes of *The Welsh Outlook* had been despatched for ever. Alun Lewis also made his only Welsh appearance in these pages, though Dylan Thomas, I fancy, never quite made the grade. Later, the editor entertained the work of Margiad Evans and that teenage Welshman lost to America, Idwal Jones — both little known in the Welsh context — and amongst poets the work of Henry Treece, Norman Nicholson, John Ormond and — who would have thought it? — Roland Mathias.

Despite these very particular virtues, there was less and less support from the public. By the summer of 1948 Gwyn Jones found himself unable to continue. Keidrych Rhys's *Wales* went down, penultimately, about the same time.

It was in these dolorous circumstances — and the period 1948-65 still strikes me, in retrospect, as especially dolorous — that in the far south-western corner of the Principality there appeared another magazine, *Dock Leaves*. Its first editor, Raymond Garlick, an Englishman and a confirmed Welsh Nationalist, was aware that his new journal was, initially, a rather derisory inheritor of the good work that had gone before but was of the opinion, and rightly, that English-speaking Wales could not do without *some* platform for its writers. Noting the "appalling publishing situation" in his first editorial, Raymond Garlick described *Dock Leaves* as "Pembrokeshire speaking to Wales" but with the strict corollary that there would be no Little England beyond Wales nonsense: it would be, in essence. "Wales speaking to Wales". Discussing the question of nationalism and nationality raised by Wyn Griffith's book *The Welsh,* a Pelican published that year (1950), he dismissed emotion as the key motive for self-identification. "Ultimately", he writes (very much to his own condition), "a man is of a certain nationality because he wills it to be so: he wills to associate himself with a certain people, land, culture or language, and express its characteristics and values". But the main direction in which he was taking *Dock Leaves* emerges more clearly in the editorial to the Michaelmas 1951 number. Satirising the declaration of an M.P. who had opined that "the soul of Wales" was "finding expression in the writings of the Anglo-Welsh school of poets and authors", he points out that the literary mainspring of Welsh life was the Welsh language, some sort of contact with which was still essential to the Anglo-Welsh writer. When in 1954 he moved north to Blaenau Ffestiniog, he was able to begin in earnest the main task he had in mind — the healing of the breach with Welsh writers caused by what he saw as the serious disservice to Welsh culture caused by many Anglo-Welsh writers from Caradoc Evans onwards. In 1957 he changed the magazine's title from *Dock Leaves* to *The Anglo-Welsh Review* in response to its Wales-wide, if thin, support, but the times continued sad and unpropitious and in 1960, feeling as "lonely" as any editor we have mentioned yet, he gave up the chair and took a post in Holland.

The financial infra-structure of the magazine, which was very much local and unliterary, became largely inoperable when I left Pembroke Dock for Derbyshire in 1958, and the survival of *The Anglo-Welsh Review* for the next ten years owed something to the techniques of Houdini. When I became its editor in December 1960 I had to write at least two early editorials announcing the magazine's demise, but deficiency grants from the Welsh Committee of the Arts Council (of which Professor Gwyn Jones was Chairman) arrived just in time to prevent it. It was not really until 1968, when the first regular grant from the new Welsh Arts Council was received, that any editorial intention could be expansive, but, not having the necessary contacts and editing now from England, I had long had to abandon Raymond Garlick's emphasis on liaison with Welsh writers and had begun to create a sort of spectrum of the Arts in Wales, including regular articles on painting and music as well as literature. Later still, while turning out editorial after editorial urging greater understanding between the English-speakers and Welsh-speakers of Wales, I sought to create another kind of unity, by making *The Anglo-Welsh Review* a vehicle for a greater part of the authorial output of Wales by having reviewed books in and from other disciplines which seemed not incompatible with a central interest in the Arts. Reviews of books, thereupon, occupied at least half the magazine, which was often accused of being too bulky and fuller of material than even the enthusiastic reader wanted. Perhaps this phase is best summed up in a joking comment made by my successor, Gillian Clarke: she alleged that she took over just in time to prevent me from having reviewed a book on snails because it was written by a Welshman. That was in 1976. Gillian Clarke is still the editor: she has brought the poetry out front, subdued the manic urge to review and put a photograph on the cover. And *The Anglo-Welsh Review,* thirty-three years old last Christmas, is now the second-longest-running literary periodical in Britain. Only *Outposts* is older.

Meanwhile, in 1965, the Dolorous Time had been despatched by the first number of another magazine cradled in Merthyr. *Poetry Wales,* edited by Meic Stephens, with the hortatory support of Harri Webb and Gerald Morgan, was deeply dissatisfied with an English-speaking Wales which appeared spiritless and unenterprising. In an account he gave of his motives in founding *Poetry Wales,* written after his first relinquishment of the editorial chair, Meic Stephens says that of the dozen or so Anglo-Welsh poets he knew "only three had volumes to their name and the only magazines that published their work were *The London Welshman* and *The Anglo-Welsh Review,* both of which had other responsibilities and were based in England". As he was correcting the proofs of his first number, he read the report of an address given by Professor Gwyn Jones at the London Welsh St. David's Day celebrations in which he had said: "That there is no new or better *Wales* or *Welsh Review* appearing in Wales today is inexcusable. That there is no little magazine which would allow us to see and sift the poets is shocking". Fortified by this in his resolve, Meic Stephens got *Poetry Wales* off to a bouncing and highly successful start. Eschewing an editorial until the third number, he describes the sell-

out of the first two as very heartening, a showing much to be
contrasted with that of *The Anglo-Welsh Review,* "sporadic and heavily
subsidised". "We are not crowing", he continues. "But lifting our
daicaps to the memorable example set by *Wales* and *The Welsh
Review,* we match our hope with firm intention to do our blue best.
Our shutters are open and the door is on the latch". There was a duty
to the country too, and to the Welsh language, for which, he avers,
there was more sympathy than twenty years before.

As I look back I can see that my own editorial residence outside
Wales fuelled a good deal of the feeling of neglect that had existed. I
plead guilty to not having known that the buds of a new enthusiasm
were about to break. But *Poetry Wales* No.4 carried a long letter from
Raymond Garlick in Holland wishing the new magazine well but
warning it to beware of *hubris.* "Heavily subsidised", he wrote, was a
sadly inaccurate description of *The Anglo-Welsh Review,* especially
from a magazine subsidised from the beginning. Which of them had
borne the heat and burden of the day? Thereafter he launched into his
argument about the continuity of Anglo-Welsh writing from the
fifteenth century, a view which in the next number brought a response
at length from Harri Webb, postulating a much more recent paternity
from Welsh writing. In no time the correspondence columns of *Poetry
Wales* were humming and the volumes of new poetry published made
the reviews in early numbers rewarding reading.

Meic Stephens, however, ceased to be editor late in 1967 when he
was appointed the new Welsh Arts Council's Literature Director. But
early in 1969 his successor, Gerald Morgan, became the headmaster
of a comprehensive school and could no longer manage the
considerable extra work of editing. The Spring number of 1969
announced the return of Meic Stephens — on licence, so to speak,
until another editor could be found — anxious to print poetry in
Welsh as well as English. He remained in office until more than 21
numbers had been published and his ultimate successor, with the
Summer number of 1973, was Sam Adams, who had been reviews
editor for some time previous. Early in 1975 Sam Adams, too, was
translated — in his case to H.M. Inspectorate — and was succeeded
by J.P. Ward, an English poet on the staff of University College,
Swansea. Ward, noting in his first editorial that *Poetry Wales* had
become very steady and up-market ("miles from the crazily
exuberant but most sadly defunct *Second Aeon*", as he puts it), began
consolidating that position with a more academically critical

approach and the regular interpolation of special numbers — on Henry Vaughan, on Vernon Watkins, on Poetry and Education, on Translation, on Welsh Traditional Forms and the like. Cary Archard, who took over wholly with the Autumn 1980 number, launched *Poetry Wales* into the publication of books — before, that is, the Poetry Wales Press was granted a subsidy to do so by the Welsh Arts Council. The journal itself, notwithstanding, is very much alive and has reached Volume 18 No.3.

I shall complete this hop, skip and a jump with the advent of the first number of *Planet* in August 1970. Its editor and prime mover was Ned Thomas of University College, Aberystwyth, and it was immediately apparent that he intended the magazine to deal with those political, economic and social aspects of life in Wales which the literary journals already dealt with largely ignored. Those missing aspects, moreover, would be dealt with from a sharply radical and nationalist viewpoint. The editor's opening article (he did not deal in editorials as such) was entitled 'The George Thomas Era'. Here are a few key sentences from it:

> What the last years have shown is that the old idea of having a good Welshman working for you inside the governing party is breaking down; it just does not work and it encourages a kind of irresponsibility in everybody else . . . . The important thing for the language is a properly codified policy, which, if we had, could equally well be administered by a non-Welsh speaker.

In the same number a reviewer of John Wain's *A Winter in the Hills* comments on "the Welshman's grotesque cowardice and his deeply-embedded death-wish", phrases that echo the early Keidrych Rhys years before. *Planet,* however, was the opposite of introvert: it was European in interest, concerned with the fate and experience of all small nations, and some of its satire on what passes for Welshness (particularly an early pull-out of a *Western Wail,* with its Wastegate column) must surely have been laughed at even by adversaries. Meanwhile literature, though confined as to space, was not neglected: with John Tripp as literary editor, poems, stories and book reviews kept the more expansive literary journals on their toes. *Planet's* broad, glossy format and very professional appearance were always pleasing and it was, in many ways, a sad day when Ned Thomas announced in January 1980 that he proposed to cease publication because he could no longer give the time to it and because he believed its job in changing attitudes was done. It would need a Kenneth Morgan at this lectern to document this belief in any detail and to sum up the changes of the decade, but it might not be too much to say that the arrival of S Pedwar Ec was made possible in part by the early spadework of *Planet.*

One last comment on the journals of the seventies may be appropriate. When *The Anglo-Welsh Review* (mainly articles and book reviews, with some poetry), *Poetry Wales* (mainly poetry and book reviews, with a few articles), *Planet* (politics, economics, social questions, with European comparisons, plus a small literary content), Peter Finch's *Second Aeon* (avant-garde and transatlantic poetry) and *Rebecca* (left-wing investigative journalism — when it appeared) were all in existence together with a minimum of overlap, the Welsh scene was as well served with national and cultural material, enquiry and comment as it could well have been, granted the minimal readership behind it all. When *Second Aeon* disappeared, however, and then *Planet,* the question-mark against that total readership darkened and the decision to attempt a generally cultural, multi-party-political magazine resulted in the arrival of *Arcade.* I shall not comment on *Arcade's* short existence except in two respects: first, that despite the efforts of editor after editor for some eight generations the hard-core readership of a general arts and information magazine proved not to have risen significantly above that achieved by *The Welsh Outlook* when it first started in 1914 — a desperately slow development and not at all comparable with, for example, the sales of quality newspapers in Britain as a whole (query, is Wales below average in this context?). I remember how, despite all the personal contact possible, the readership of *The Anglo-Welsh Review* never topped 800, more than half of that number outside Wales. Second, that *Arcade's* editor, John Osmond, put his whole fortune where his pen was, in a manner not comparable in the last five decades, by resigning his post on *The Western Mail* in order to take the editorial chair. It was infinitely sad for him that the venture lasted so short a time.

Editors, then, so far from pulling hard on the bridle when too far in front of their handful of cavalry as they charge the guns of apathy (as was alleged of Sergius in Shaw's *Arms and the Man*) have too often found themselves *lonely* in no-man's land, on foot and searching for a platoon lost in a shell-hole somewhere, unsure in which direction they first set out. There is, I repeat, no need to be overly sorry for them:

not a few, as you have seen, have been recognised as so important that they have been taken out of the line altogether and re-jigged as brass-hats: others, who pleaded they were pushed to the front by unseen arms, must have been standing within the fated circle already: all of them, stayers as well as non-stayers, have been devoted to Wales and to its continuance as a national entity. They have found their satisfaction in stepping outside the egotism of the writer and in *doing* something for their people, successfully or unsuccessfully, in their time. What they hope for most, in the larger field, is that the succession will not fail, that there will always be someone for whom loneliness is not too high a price.

Acknowledgements

'David Jones: Towards the "Holy Diversities"' was given as an address to the Cymmrodorion Society in London, 20 May 1981.

'Grief and the Circus Horse: A Study of the Mythic and Christian Themes in the Early Poetry of Vernon Watkins' was first published in *Triskel One*, edited by Sam Adams and Gwilym Rees Hughes, 1971.

'Lord Cutglass, Twenty Years After' was first published as 'A Niche for Dylan Thomas' in *Poetry Wales* vol.9 no.2 (Autumn 1973, Dylan Thomas Special Issue). It was republished in *Poetry Dimension 2*, ed. Dannie Abse (1974).

'The Caseg Letters: A Commentary' was first published in *Poetry Wales* vol.10 no.3 (Winter 1974, Alun Lewis Special Issue).

'"The Black Spot in the Focus": A Study of the Poetry of Alun Lewis' was delivered as a paper to the annual conference of the English language section of Yr Academi Gymreig at Coleg Harlech, 1 September 1979. It was first published in *The Anglo-Welsh Review*, no.67, 1980.

'Philosophy and Religion in the Poetry of R.S. Thomas' was first published in *Poetry Wales* vol.7 no.4 (Spring 1972, R.S. Thomas Special Issue).

'Channels of Grace: A View of the Earlier Novels of Emyr Humphreys' was delivered as a paper at the annual conference of the English language section of Yr Academi Gymreig at the College of Librarianship, Aberystwyth, 2 September 1977. It was afterwards published in revised form in *The Anglo-Welsh Review*, no.70, 1982.

'Address for the Henry Vaughan Service' given at the Annual Henry Vaughan Service at Llansantffraid Church on 22 April 1977. It was afterwards published in *Madog* vol.1 no.2 (Summer 1978).

'The Lonely Editor: A Glance at Anglo-Welsh Magazines' was delivered as the annual Gwyn Jones Lecture at the University College, Cardiff, in April 1983.

Acknowledgements for the cover photographs are due to Mrs Gweno Lewis for Alun Lewis and to the Welsh Arts Council.

Index